The author, Dr Philip Robinson, is Head of the Collections Division at the Ulster Folk and Transport Museum, and Chairman of the Historic Buildings Council for Northern Ireland. His academic training was as a geographer and cultural historian, and he has retained a particular interest in settlement and landscape history. This study of the Ulster Plantation is an expansion of his doctoral thesis on the Plantation in County Tyrone. As a specialist in urban history, he represents Northern Ireland on the RIA committee for the Irish Historic Towns Atlas, and at the Folk Museum at Cultra he is responsible for the development of the open-air Folk Park of re-erected vernacular buildings.

THE PLANTATION *of* ULSTER

British Settlement in an Irish Landscape 1600–1670

PHILIP S. ROBINSON

ULSTER
HISTORICAL FOUNDATION

First published 1984 by
Gill and Macmillan Ltd

First published in the United States of America in 1984
by St. Martin's Press, Inc.,

This edition published 1994 and republished 2000
by The Ulster Historical Foundation
12 College Square East,
Belfast BT1 6DD
Email: enquiry@uhf.org.uk
Website: www.ancestryireland.com

Robinson, Philip
The Plantation of Ulster.
Includes index.
1. Land settlement–Ulster (Northern Ireland and Ireland)–History–17th century. 2. Ulster (Northern Ireland and Ireland)–Emigration and immigration–History–17th century. 3. Plantations–Ulster (Northern Ireland and Ireland)–17th century. 4. Ulster (Northern Ireland and Ireland)–History. 1. Title. HD620.5.Z8U477 1984
333.76'09416 83-13895

ISBN 1-903688-00-0

Printed by ColourBooks Ltd

Cover and Design by Dunbar Design

For Helen and Amy

Contents

Maps

Figures

Tables

Appendices

Glossary

ballybetagh An Irish land division which was supposed to contain 960 acres. In fact it usually contained sixteen townlands (see **ballyboe, tate** and **poll**) of an estimated fifty or sixty acres each, but the actual extent of the townlands varied greatly (see **plantation acre**).

ballyboe A small Irish land division which, before the plantation, represented the territory within which several families worked the land. Although the real area of the ballyboe varied greatly with the quality of the land, it was assumed by the plantation surveyors to contain sixty acres of profitable land in most areas of north-west Ulster. Many modern townlands have evolved from these ballyboes.

barony An administrative division of an Irish county, rarely resulting from the domain of a baron. Some of the Ulster counties were not subdivided into baronies until the first decade of the seventeenth century, when, for the purpose of the plantation, they were known as **precincts.**

clan A descent group of pre-plantation Irish (Ir. *clann*: descendants; children) which functioned politically over a distinct territory. Many Irish scholars avoid the term, believing it to imply that all the people in its territory had common ancestry. Here the term is used to identify groups claiming common ancestry and with a definite organisational hierarchy, controlling a greater area than the local **septs.** Its use does not imply that all 'followers', 'tenants' and other occupants of the clan's territories were of unilineal descent.

creaghting The seasonal movement (transhumance) of cattle and their keepers to and from summer pastures.

erenaghs Hereditary tenants of ecclesiastical land in pre-plantation Ulster.

escheated lands All the land in Ulster which was forfeited to, confiscated by, or surrendered to the crown on the eve of the plantation.

English In the broad differentiation between English and Scots for the general purpose of this book, British settlers with Welsh surnames are classified as English. 'Old English', or the descendants of the Anglo-Norman Irish where they can be identified as such, are classified as Irish.

gavelkind An early English (Kentish) system of land inheritance which gave all sons equal shares. The Gaelic custom of periodically redistributing **sept** lands among all members of the sept was often referred to as being in the 'manner of gavelkind'.

Irish Society When first formed, this corporate body of London companies was known as 'The Society of the Governor and Assistants, London, of the New Plantation in Ulster'. Its function was to oversee the Londoners' role in the plantation, and it was known in Ireland as the 'London Society'. The later, shorter and better-known title 'Irish Society' is used for convenience throughout this book.

plantation acre Unit of areal measurement adopted for plantation purposes in the granting of land, in subsequent plantation surveys, and in the Civil Survey of 1654-56. The basis of the plantation acre was an assumption that the **ballyboe** contained sixty acres of profitable land. Although the actual areas of ballyboes varied greatly, and were on average about six times larger when measured in statute acres, plantation acres were a useful comparative assessment of land potential.

poll An Irish land division of County Cavan, similar in nature but rather smaller in size than the **ballyboe.** Estimated by the plantation surveyors to contain only fifty **plantation acres.**

precinct The name sometimes given to a division of the county, usually equivalent to a **barony,** for the purpose of designating land for use in the official plantation.

proportion The name sometimes given to the plantation estates of **undertakers** and **servitors.**

quarter An Irish land division (Ir. *ceathrú*; angl. *carrow* or *kerry*) which was found in most counties, being a quarter of a **ballybetagh.** In County Donegal, however, many townlands appear to have evolved from quarters rather than smaller subdivisions.

Scottish Roman Catholic highland Scots resident in pre-plantation Ulster were often regarded as 'Irish'. Unless otherwise stated, only lowland 'planter' Scots in Ulster are classified as Scottish.

sept Distinctive territorial group of pre-plantation Irish under the local control of a petty chieftain, sometimes regarded as a division of a **clan.**

servitors A class of plantation grantee composed of English administrative and military officials who were mostly resident crown servants in Ireland.

tate An Irish land division of Counties Fermanagh and Monaghan. Similar in nature to the **ballyboe** and the forerunner of most townlands in those counties.

termon Pre-plantation church land which enjoyed special privileges of sanctuary and protection.

uirríthe Irish sub-chiefs, generally controlling those areas or 'countries' within Ulster counties which became plantation **precincts** or **baronies.**

undertakers A class of plantation grantee composed of influential English and Scots who were to 'undertake' the plantation of British settlers on the estates they obtained.

Note on Measurement

To avoid confusion with measurements obtained from documentary sources there is no metrication in this book.

Unless acres are specifically referred to in the text as statute acres, they should be assumed to be 'plantation' acres (see Glossary).

Preface

The seeds of many present-day cultural divisions in Ulster were sown during the seventeenth century when a massive influx of English and Scottish Protestants occurred. During the reign of James I an official scheme was drawn up for the 'plantation' of designated areas in Ulster west of the River Bann. However, the actual area settled by the new colonists was much more extensive, and they continued to arrive in increasing numbers well after the time had elapsed wherein the scheme was to have been completed. Environmental factors were to prove more important than governmental controls in shaping the new settlement pattern.

This book is not a history of the Ulster plantation, but a geographer's view of change and continuity in the Ulster landscape as it was affected by these broad movements of population. In addition to the emerging settlement pattern, the processes and phases of colonisation are examined, along with the extent of territorial segregation involved between settlers and the indigenous population. The emphasis throughout is on landscape rather than legislation, on economy rather than events, and on undertenants, their buildings and their culture, rather than undertakers, their castles and estates. With the colonists came innovation: a radical transformation of the lowland landscape had begun, even if influenced by pre-plantation precedent. Spread of a market-based rural economy resulted in a quite spectacular growth in urbanisation. Permanent dwellings of a more sophisticated construction became commonplace, and around the towns new field patterns emerged. The spread of hedged enclosure heralded innovations in agricultural methods, tools, livestock and systems of land tenure. In a less tangible form, the settlers also brought with them a new language, new surnames, new religion and, of course, a change in politico-historical allegiance.

Previous studies of the plantation have been published, most with a mainly historical perspective. The earliest and best known is the Rev. George Hill's *An Historical Account of the Plantation in Ulster at the Commencement of the Seventeenth Century, 1608-1620* (Belfast 1877). This is an account of the development and implementation of the plantation scheme up to the granting of the plantation estates. It appeared shortly after publication of the relevant calendars of state papers and Irish patent rolls in the 1860s and 1870s. Indeed, Hill describes his work as a 'connected narrative' of the events to which these sources refer, although for more than a century this 'narrative' with its carefully researched footnotes has remained the definitive account of the early plantation period in Ulster. The first comprehensive historical investigation of the Ulster plantation for an individual county was T. W. Moody's *The Londonderry Plantation, 1609-41* (Belfast 1939). Professor Moody provides a detailed account of the progress of the plantation in County Londonderry. He traces the changing relationship between the London companies and the crown in the early seventeenth century (with the consequences of these changes for plantation settlement). The comparison between developing governmental thinking and legislation on the one hand, and the progress of the plantation in Londonderry on the other, represents the most significant advance in plantation studies this century.

The Londoners' plantation, however, was not necessarily representative of the whole plantation; and much of the settlement in the remaining counties, and particularly in Antrim and Down, has been researched and published in a more recent study. M. Perceval-Maxwell's *The Scottish Migration to Ulster in the Reign of James I* (London 1973) is again historical in character, but with a high socio-economic content. Stress is laid upon the role of landowners and governmental legislation, but this is compensated for by an account of economic conditions in Scotland during the early seventeenth century and a description of the trading system between the areas of Scottish settlement in Ulster and the Scottish mainland. Perceval-Maxwell also provides a useful estimate of the total number of Scots in Ulster *circa* 1622 and identifies a period of colonial stagnation from 1619 to 1625 which is related to decline of the corn trade with Scotland. Of course, his study is restricted to Scottish settlement, and it deals comprehensively with Antrim and Down, where Scottish settlement was strongest even though the official plantation scheme did not apply there. Perceval-Maxwell undoubtedly interprets the Scottish settlement involved in the official plantation in west Ulster as being related to the Scottish settlement in Counties Antrim and Down. In turn this raises the question of the extent to which the plantation in the west of the province was only part of a more widespread colonisation of Ulster by English and Scots during the seventeenth century. Most of the documentary material relating to the plantation was concerned with (or prepared by) the government and the principal landowners, so it is understandable that histories of the Ulster plantation should stress the role of those responsible for decisions concerning the plantation. This approach, however, minimises the importance of the environment and the economy and presents the Ulster plantation as a somewhat artificial, but nevertheless successful, scheme superimposed on the landscape.

The view that the plantation developed in response to political decisions taken in the early seventeenth century is difficult to reconcile with the observed pattern of British settlement. Indeed, the actual settlement pattern is sometimes better explained by theoretical concepts of colonisation and migration, such as those proposed in Sweden by Bylund, Morrill, Olsson and Hägerstrand. Morrill suggests that migration depends on such environmental variables as distance, economic differential between source and destination, and previous population movement. Similarly, Bylund's theories of colonisation are deterministic, involving expansion either radially from individual 'mother' settlements or in waves from linear fronts of mother settlements. Although the Swedish theories of colonial processes are essentially deterministic and do not accurately reflect reality, they do stress the importance of environmental factors such as distance, economic forces, population pressure and land values in colonial population movements. One aim of this book is to study the role of environmental variables in the development of the plantation settlement pattern. My approach is environmental, and the tools of the historical geographer are used where the limitations of the source material permit. Even when the data of the best-known documentary sources are mapped, revealing evidence of the controlling factors of plantation settlement emerges. The colonisation on the ground was not as dominantly influenced by governmental legislation or by individual land-owning undertakers as is sometimes assumed.

Acknowledgments

Many scholars have freely given me a great deal of their time to discuss various aspects of plantation, settlement and landscape history. Some have helped me in the past, particularly during the early 1970s when I was preparing some of this material for a doctoral thesis on the plantation in County Tyrone. Many others have helped me more recently during the preparation of this book. To them all I give my thanks, but I must make special mention of R. Glasscock, R. A. Gailey, R. Gillespie, W. H. Crawford, W. Macafee and the late G. B. Adams. Indeed, I am doubly indebted to Dr Gailey for undertaking the tedious task of reading my script. Other scholars whose work has greatly influenced me include A. T. Lucas, R. J. Hunter, M. Perceval-Maxwell and Professors T. W. Moody and E. E. Evans. To them I offer my thanks, and my apologies for any misinterpretation of their work.

I am most grateful to the following institutions and their staff for their help and for allowing me to consult and, where appropriate, cite from their documents: the British Library; the National Library of Ireland; the Public Record Office of Northern Ireland; the Public Record Office, London; the Diocesan Library, Armagh; the Chester Record Office; the Devon Record Office; the Hampshire Record Office; the London County Record Office; the Northamptonshire Record Office; the Staffordshire Record Office and William Salt Library; Goldsmiths' Hall; Mercers' Hall; Skinners' Hall; and the Guildhall Library, London. For permission to cite various documents I am particularly grateful to the Clerk of the Worshipful Company of Drapers and to the archivist at Drapers' Hall, Mr A. K. Sierz, whose enthusiastic help I found very heartening. To the Clerk of The Honourable the Irish

Society, Mr Bernard Manning, I also offer my thanks for his friendly interest and assistance.

I acknowledge with deep appreciation the practical help in preparing this book I have received from the Trustees, Director and my colleagues at the Ulster Folk and Transport Museum.

Introduction

Despite the short distances involved, the Ulster plantation has proved to be one of the most politically significant mass migrations to have taken place in western Europe since medieval times. The use of the term 'plantation' emerged in the sixteenth century to describe a changing concept of colonial expansion. The old idea had been one of military conquest followed by the installation of war-lords and the absorbtion of the colony, along with its native population, into the domestic kingdom. Although in Ulster all these features were present, 'plantation' was felt to infer something more: it was an adventure officially sponsored by the nation-state and involved the transfer of an entire package of personnel, laws and materials into a new territory. In its purest form this territory should ideally be 'virgin' or almost devoid of significant native population. The plantation settlement of Virginia in County Cavan in this respect was not as aptly named as its American counterpart (even if both were actually named in honour of Elizabeth I). Indeed, a more difficult colonial situation in Ireland was inferred by James's Lord Deputy, Sir Arthur Chichester, when he declared: 'I had rather labour with my hands in the plantation of Ulster, than dance or play in that of Virginia.'[1]

The migration of English and Scottish Protestants to Ulster in the seventeenth century was contemporaneous with English colonial settlement along the east coast of North America. It is tempting therefore to equate the personal motivations of colonists destined for Ulster with those taking the longer journey. Certainly the British crown did not regard these two adventures as completely divorced, but the American colonies were seen basically as an opening for commercial expansion and an outlet for surplus population. The Ulster plantation may have been viewed in a similar light by the colonists themselves, but the factors motivating the government were closely linked to a desire to extend English political influence and stability into the most troublesome parts of Ireland. It was hoped that this in turn would reduce the costly military presence which had been necessary throughout the Elizabethan period. Of course, the religious motivation itself was an important factor for the government. While the Reformation was being firmly and permanently established in England and lowland Scotland during the sixteenth century, there were few signs that Protestantism was making any significant headway in Ireland. It was also clear that in the event of a European conflict either Spain or France could use Ireland as a weak link in the British defences were she alone to remain Catholic. For most of the colonists, however, it was free land rather than religious freedom that provided the incentive. English interest in colonisation as a means of increasing the power of the state and correcting social ailments had risen dramatically throughout the Elizabethan era. The conditions giving rise to this expansion were complex. England was considered to be overpopulated with increasing numbers of idle poor.[2] Colonial schemes would therefore not only relieve this social problem, but eventually provide profit in the form of new outlets for the export trade and an exploitation of resources such as the fisheries off the American coast. After a series of trial runs in Ireland during the sixteenth century, there was an unprecedented colonial expansion in the early seventeenth century. Not only was Ulster successfully planted under James I, but thriving colonies were also founded in Virginia, New England and the West Indies. Indeed, even the earlier Irish plantations, which were faltering or had failed by the end of Elizabeth's reign, were to receive a fresh transfusion of planters during the reign of James I.

The story of English colonial expansion in Ireland begins with the Anglo-Norman invasion of south-east Ireland in 1169. This vanguard of conquest was quickly followed by the immigration of many English and Welsh colonists, particularly into Wexford and east Leinster. The nucleus of the Norman colony was the area known as the Pale, which had contracted by the late fifteenth century to the four counties of Dublin, Kildare, Meath and Louth. The boundaries of the Pale were not fixed, but fluctuated according to the relative strength and influence of the colonists on the one hand and the Gaelic lords on the other. Within the Pale, English traditions of language and clothing became established, and in particular the English legal system was enforced and administered from Dublin. However, the extent of Norman conquest and subsequent influence in Ireland was much greater than this. Beyond the Pale the Norman armies had penetrated most of Munster, Leinster, and into many parts of east Ulster and Connaught. While never in fact controlling the whole island, Anglo-Norman lords occupied a broad area of south-east Ireland. In this middle ground fortified settlements became manorial villages, and English building, tenurial and agricultural practices were adopted. The contraction and general decline of the Anglo-Irish colony was a slow process accelerated by the expansion of the Gaelic lords in the fourteenth and fifteenth centuries. Many of the Norman lords became hibernicised through intermarriage with the native Irish and by accepting Gaelic captaincies and privileges in addition to their English feudal rights.

The part of Ulster which lay to the east of the Bann and Lough Neagh (Counties Antrim and Down) had been conquered at an early stage by John de Courcy, who began his march north in 1177. He established fortified settlements at Newry, Downpatrick, Dromore, Carrickfergus and Coleraine, and his followers established themselves throughout the best agricultural lowlands of the two eastern counties. Attempts to advance into west Ulster failed, and the resurgence of Gaelic power which began in the late thirteenth century soon left only Newry, Carrickfergus, and an area south and east of Downpatrick with an effective English presence.

An important factor in this decline of English medieval influence in Ulster was the Bruce invasion from Scotland in 1315 and an increasing use by the Ulster Gaelic chiefs of 'galloglass'. These were professional soldiers from the western isles and highlands of Scotland who fought for land and pay in Ulster. Many settled but retained their distinctive identity. In Tyrconnell (County Donegal) the O'Donnells introduced McSweeneys, while the O'Neills brought over many McDonnells and other related families such as the McAlisters and McRorys. In a sense the Scottish Gaelic settlement in Ulster could be compared to the Anglo-Norman colony in south-west Ireland. Although the inhabitants of the Scottish isles and west highlands were often regarded as 'Irish', or at least to 'speak the language and have the habits of the Irish', the fragmented galloglass settlements were supplemented by an important movement of a section of Clan Donald to Antrim in the fifteenth century. This movement established in north-east Antrim a predictable extension of McDonald territory across the North Channel into a bridgehead that was threatening to become a Scottish equivalent to the Pale.

By the time Henry VIII acquired the English throne in 1509 the English colony in Ireland had survived two centuries of decline and contraction. Although the decisive struggle for sovereignty in Ireland between the English crown and the Gaelic Irish lords was not to come until Elizabeth's reign, the last years of Henry's reign, from about 1534 to 1547, are often seen as a turning-point in Irish history. Following an abortive rebellion of some Anglo-Irish led by 'Silken Thomas' FitzGerald in 1534, Henry had himself declared 'king' rather than 'lord' of Ireland and began spasmodic attempts to reconquer various parts of the country. His motive was the assertion of sovereignty rather than land confiscation and exploitation. At this time Henry's schism with Rome was complete, and his attempts to spread the Reformation through the Irish church became identified with this struggle for Tudor supremacy. In areas where Henry's writ ran, monasteries were dissolved and papal authority in the Irish church was officially disclaimed, especially with regard to the appointment of bishops. This reformation in Ireland was seen to be political rather than theological, and as such was largely rejected both by the Gaelic Irish and the Old English. From the start religion and politics were closely bound together in Ireland, and the Reformation was regarded as much an instrument of English power as a consequence of it.

When Henry's eldest daughter, Mary Tudor, came to the English throne in 1553 the Protestant dimension of Tudor rule in Ireland was temporarily diminished, for the new queen was a Roman Catholic. Married to Philip of Spain, Mary Tudor had re-established the connections between the papacy and the Irish church, but the attempts to extend the influence of English law in Ireland continued. Leix and Offaly (frontier areas just outside the Pale) were confiscated, renamed as Queen's County and King's County, and plans were drawn up for their plantation. Two-thirds of the total area was to be settled by Englishmen 'born in England or Ireland'. This plantation, which included the elevation of two military forts into the proposed towns of Maryborough and Philipstown, was in itself only a limited success. It did, however, herald a new era in which colonists were to be increasingly used as a deliberate means of extending English influence in Ireland. When Mary declared war on the French in 1557 fears that their Scottish allies would invade Ulster were increased. Mary's Lord Deputy in Ireland, the Earl of Sussex, suggested that a colonising force of 1,000 men should be planted in towns throughout Ulster as a means of neutralising the Scottish threat. These plans were postponed until Elizabeth's reign, when Sir Henry Sidney proposed yet another vague scheme to secure Ulster by means of a network of forts and settlements in 1567. However, the experience of Mary's plantation in King's County and Queen's County had shown how expensive such ventures could be. What Elizabeth wanted was a scheme to involve private enterprise and not crown resources. As a result, the subsequent proposals of Sir Thomas Smith and the Earl of Essex to settle Ulster in the 1570s involved private armies designed to conquer and settle.

Three fundamental methods of expanding English power were employed in Tudor Ireland: military conquest, plantation, and the 'civilisation' policy of persuading Gaelic lords to surrender themselves to English authority and accept crown grants of their clan territory. It was during the reign of Henry VIII that the most effective and skilful use of 'surrender and regrant' was made. Elizabeth's reign, on the other hand, witnessed a change in emphasis. It was characterised by the most successful of all the English military campaigns in Ireland, and also by the most extensive colonisation to occur in Ireland since the Anglo-Norman influx. During the Elizabethan period there was an increasing tendency for 'surrender and regrant' to be regarded as an expedient measure by both parties involved. The Gaelic chiefs became skilful in accepting crown grants and titles while in practice still retaining their Gaelic influence and privileges. At the same time it became increasingly clear that Elizabeth would cast aside the same crown grants to the Gaelic lords on the slightest pretext. If the experiences of the Irish lords in east Ulster during the private adventures of Smith and Essex were not evidence enough of this, the Anglo-Irish lords of Munster could also testify to similar unsettling events.

Proposals were made to allow a group of West Country adventurers to establish colonies and settlements in west Munster. The gulf between the Old English feudal lords and the new generation of Protestant Elizabethans was widening dramatically. The Catholic Old English felt their influence within the colonial system being eroded to the point of rebellion in 1569 and 1579. The subsequent confiscation of vast tracts of their land in Counties Kerry, Cork, Limerick and Tipperary was followed by the most extensive colonial project to occur in Tudor Ireland. Private ventures had proved ineffective, so the Munster plantation of 1586 to 1598 was to be an official enterprise on the grand scale. A theoretical total of 15,000 to 25,000 English 'civill loyal and dutiful subjects' were required 'to live in the service of Almighty God'.[3] Although actual settlement was slow at first, it has been estimated that as many as 15,000 English had arrived by 1598.[4]

The final years of the Munster plantation were contemporary with the opening years of the Elizabethan war with the Ulster Gaelic lords, O'Neill and O'Donnell. When Mountjoy became Lord Deputy in 1600 the war had developed a national character. Some of the Irish and Anglo-Irish chiefs of Munster and Connaught rallied to O'Neill and O'Donnell, and the long-awaited Spanish aid arrived in Kinsale in 1601. Defeat of the Spanish and Irish forces at the Battle of Kinsale marked the turning-point in the war. Hugh O'Donnell sailed to Spain and was succeeded by his brother Rory. O'Neill returned to Tyrone and resigned himself to a defensive war with an inevitable defeat as the outcome. The submission of O'Neill and O'Donnell in 1603 coincided with the death of Elizabeth, and with her death came the end of the Tudor dynasty.

Much to the dismay of the English servitors in Ireland, especially those such as Sir Arthur Chichester who had been instrumental in the conquest of west Ulster, the new Stuart monarch (James I of England and VI of Scotland) decided to treat the defeated chiefs favourably. The basis of O'Neill's and

O'Donnell's petition for a regrant of their surrendered lands (along with the claims of the other defeated chiefs such as Maguire and the McMahons) was that their disloyalty proceeded not from conspiracy but from 'hard usage' by the administration. In the regrants the Earls of Tyrone and Tyrconnell were compelled to accept only their own demesne lands as freehold estates. They were to receive a fixed rent from their subchiefs, who were also given the status of freeholders. However, the effective power of the Earls of Tyrone and Tyrconnell had been curbed. Military conquest had been completed in the very areas of west Ulster that even the Normans had been unable to penetrate. Symbolically, by 1605 all dioceses in Ireland for the first time had a bishop appointed by the monarch.

Any hopes entertained by the Earls of Tyrone and Tyrconnell that James I would prove to be tolerant of the Gaelic order in Ulster because of his Scottish origins were short-lived. Immense areas of termon land, traditionally set aside for the support of the Irish church, were being claimed by the Protestant bishops. In addition, the Earls of Tyrone and Tyrconnell were continually harassed by the Attorney-General Sir John Davies, the new Lord Deputy Sir Arthur Chichester, and other officials. Eventually Tyrone and Tyrconnell fled to the continent from Lough Swilly, accompanied by Maguire and scores of Gaelic subchiefs. This 'Flight of the Earls' in 1607 resulted in the eagerly awaited forfeiture of their estates to the crown. In a rather flexible interpretation of their extent, the confiscated lands were found to consist of almost all the 'temporal' or non-church land in Counties Tyrone, Armagh, Donegal and Fermanagh.

Within a year of the flight Cahir O'Doherty of Inishowen had been provoked into attacking Sir Henry Docwra's garrison at Derry. This revolt was quickly quelled and O'Doherty killed, but the result was that the government decided to reduce drastically the power of the remaining Irish chiefs in Ulster. The ultimate sanction of plantation was to be imposed. Inishowen was confiscated, and the remaining chiefs were forced to surrender their large estates and accept what would be offered to them in the plantation reallocation of land. By English law only the freehold estates of the Irish chiefs should have been confiscated, but it was argued that the Gaelic rights of the chiefs extended throughout all the six counties of Armagh, Cavan,

Coleraine, Donegal, Fermanagh and Tyrone. By 1608 all the temporal lands in these counties had been either confiscated by or surrendered to the crown, although many Irish chiefs were expecting considerable regrants of land.

Almost immediately on hearing of O'Doherty's death Chichester secured for himself a grant of the barony of Inishowen, and then conducted a preliminary survey of the escheated lands of Ulster. Although the principal servitors, especially Chichester and Davies, made certain of obtaining sizeable grants for themselves, they were enthusiastic about the need for a successful plantation in Ulster. This would have to involve a large number of settlers if the failings of the previous plantation attempts in Ireland were to be avoided. At this stage James I became increasingly absorbed with the idea of plantation, and also increasingly jealous that too much land might be granted back to the Irish. An official plantation project for Ulster was an attractive proposition. Besides extending the physical area, and the trade and resources of England and Scotland, a successful plantation would achieve stability in west Ulster, the area which had for so long been the most troublesome part of Ireland. In fact there were other equally powerful motivations. Rewards for military administrative services could be provided through grants of land in Ulster at little or no cost to the government. In addition, the ever-increasing population surplus within England and Scotland could be tapped off by investing this population resource overseas. With James established on the throne of England as well as Scotland, enthusiasm for plantation was heightened by the historical circumstances which provided a unique opportunity for a joint English and Scottish colonial venture in Ulster.

1

Ulster before the Plantation

Although during the Elizabethan war woodlands, buildings, crops and livestock had been wasted and ravaged by the 'scorched earth' policy of Mountjoy, large numbers of Irish remained throughout the areas that were to be planted. The continued presence of Irish alongside the settlers was to be an important influence on the progress of the plantation itself. In addition, there are other important reasons why the plantation cannot be studied in isolation from the pre-existing cultural framework. In the first place, some characteristics of plantation settlement are considered to have been introduced to Ulster by the colonists. If the degree of change is to be assessed (such as in building types, improved agricultural methods or the establishment of a market economy), then obviously these features must be compared against the standards of the pre-plantation Gaelic order. Secondly, when some of the superficially new proposals contained in the official plantation scheme are examined carefully, it emerges that many details of the plan were not so novel as might appear at first. The previous cultural environment was both a source of precedent and inspiration for the plantation scheme. In particular the Irish land divisions and their relationships to the Gaelic social hierarchy within the clan system provide an essential background to an understanding of how plantation land in Ulster was allocated.

The documentary sources from which a synchronic view of the Ulster landscape *circa* 1600 may be reconstructed fall into two major categories: English descriptive accounts and Irish texts. Irish texts such as the brehon laws present an idealised picture of the Gaelic order, while English accounts of contemporary Irish life also have associated problems of use and interpretation. The Irish laws were written during the Early

Christian and medieval periods and considerably predate the immediate pre-plantation era in Ulster. In addition, they refer to practices, structures, objects and territorial divisions which may have been characteristic of east rather than north-west Ireland. They do not allow for regional differences in tradition, and by inferring a uniformity of custom they can only be interpreted as representing a highly idealised view of society. Associated with the Elizabethan conquest and the subsequent plantation in Ulster under James there was a dramatic increase in the quantity and quality of English documentation. Much of this information is in the form of maps, surveys and written descriptions. These are often propagandist and require treatment with caution. However, when surviving artifacts or practices clearly of great antiquity supplement the documentary evidence, certain aspects of the pre-plantation order can be described with some confidence. Certainly some medieval influences from England and the Pale had filtered through to west Ulster by 1600, but this area was still the most 'Irish' and Gaelic part of Ireland. The Gaelic order had evolved slowly through centuries of close association between man and his physical environment. Agricultural practices, territorial divisions and other features of pre-plantation life may not have been solely determined by the physical landscape, but they did evolve in a manner that was extremely well suited to their environment.

1.1 *Physical landscape*

Concentrations of population had developed around Gaelic power centres in the valleys and plains of pre-plantation Ulster. The boundaries of these lowland clan areas were often loosely defined by the physical environment, particularly in upland and mountainous areas where cattle could only be grazed in the summer. The Sperrin Mountains represented the most significant physical barrier in central Ulster, effectively dividing the important septs in the Foyle basin in the north-west from those occupying the Lough Neagh basin to the east and south-east. The central Ulster basin around Lough Neagh was the greatest extent of lowland (Map 1). It was the fertile lowlands of this area, especially the hilly districts west and south of Lough Neagh, which became the heartland of O'Neill power in six-

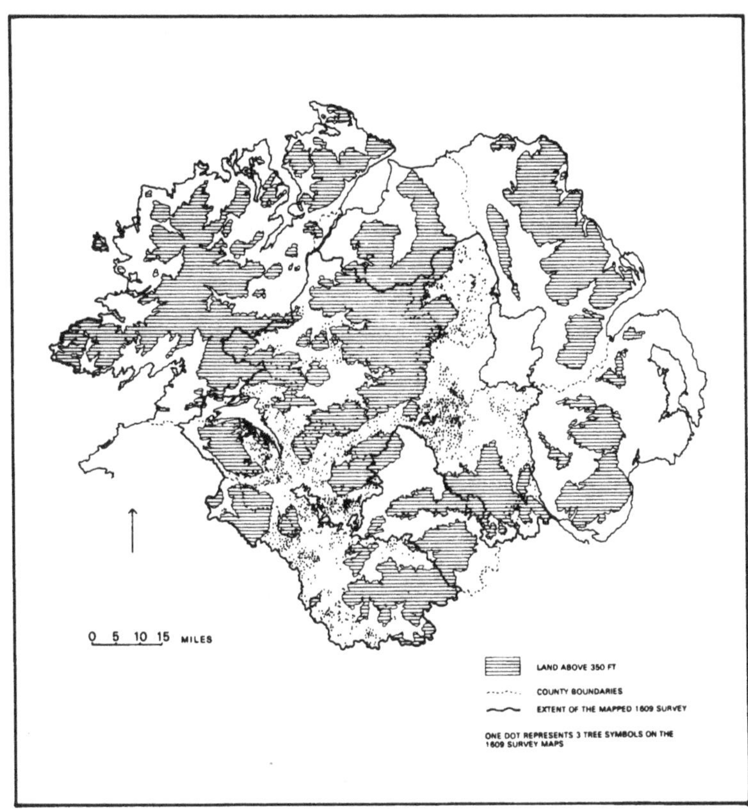

Map 1: *Pre-plantation woodland and upland in Ulster*

teenth-century Ulster. Of the other low-lying regions, only the Foyle basin and the Fermanagh/Cavan lowlands retained a concentrated and powerful resistance to English custom and supremacy. The lowlands of east Down and north Antrim were sufficiently close to England and Scotland to experience more directly the influence and power of the mainland. The rural population of Ulster both before and after the plantation was concentrated in areas where the soils were found to be most productive. No environmental factor affecting settlement was more important than the quality of the land. This quality was, of course, no more than the perceived usefulness of the land for agriculture.

In order that the settlement patterns of the seventeenth

century may be related to the physical landscape, it is necessary to establish first of all a relative measure of land potential throughout Ulster. Differences in the desirability of land from one locality to another did not depend on altitude alone. While the preferred areas of settlement were undoubtedly in the lowlands, local soil and drainage characteristics were also of

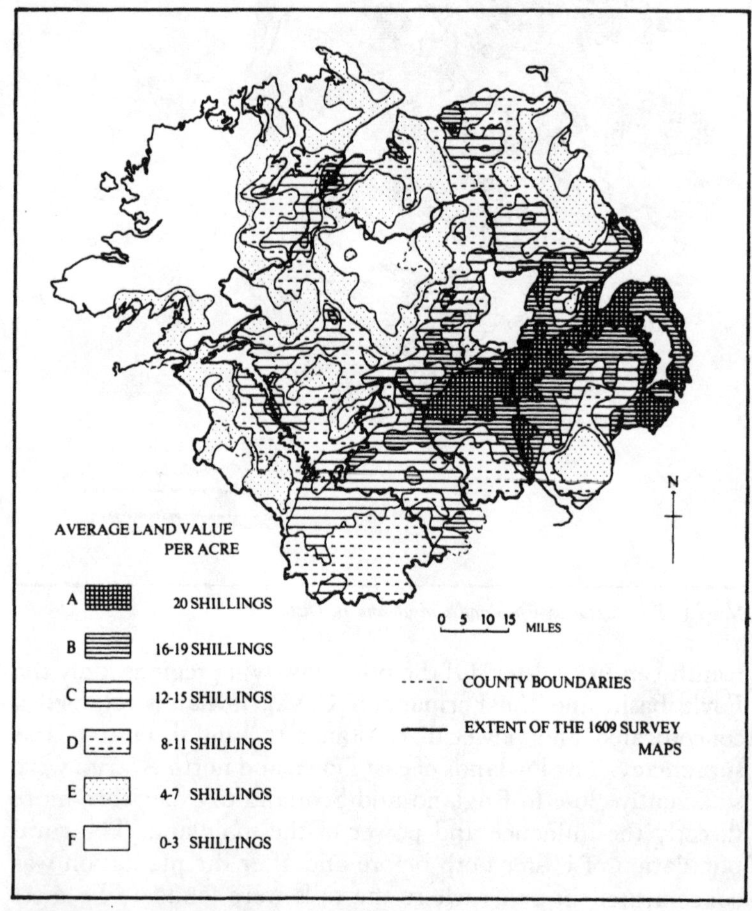

Map 2: *Land values in Ulster, c. 1860*[1]
The land-valuation totals for each Ulster parish in Griffith's *General Valuation of Ireland* have been divided by the parish area in statute acres to provide average land valuations in shillings per acre. These figures have then been plotted and isoplethed in terms of six valuation categories ranging from A (highest values) to F (lowest values).

critical importance. Quantification of the agricultural potential of land based on altitude would not account for poorly drained and unproductive lowland areas. In the absence of any suitable land-classification survey, the most pertinent data are contained in the land-valuation surveys of the nineteenth century. These surveys were compiled in the 1830s and 1860s to provide a detailed land valuation for taxation purposes. By dividing the total land valuation for any parish by its area, an average land valuation per acre can be calculated and used to provide a map of relative land values in Ulster (Map 2). The validity of using nineteenth-century criteria to indicate pre-plantation perceptions of land will be examined more fully below, but in general terms the areas of low valuations shown on Map 2 include both upland areas and the poorly drained lowland districts. In comparing, for example, the low valuations of the boggy shores of Lough Neagh with the extremely high valuations in the fertile Lagan valley and north Armagh, it must be remembered that the nineteenth-century surveys took into account factors other than soil characteristics. Accessibility to the land and proximity to markets inflated land values around towns and along the main lines of communication in the east. Land values are a particularly useful measure of the physical environment, since they assess the economic potential of the land rather than its actual physical characteristics. Man's economic behaviour is conditioned by his perception of the environment rather than its reality. Clearly perceptions of land usefulness have changed throughout the centuries; however, it is possible to make some assessment of the perceptions of land potential in the immediate pre-plantation period.

In 1609 Sir Josias Bodley conducted a survey of every barony in the six counties intended for plantation. The barony maps produced by this survey survive for Counties Fermanagh, Cavan, Armagh and Tyrone (see Map 1 for the extent of these surviving maps). Within each barony the surveyors mapped, by inquisition rather than by mensuration, the divisions of land which have since become known as townlands.[2] The individual Irish names of these small land units were also recorded; and they were usually estimated to contain sixty acres of profitable land each. In most of Ulster these townland units were known as 'ballyboes', although similar units were called 'polls' in Cavan and 'tates' in Fermanagh. In 1608 the ballyboe was described as containing 'one with another LX acres of arrable land medow and pasture'.[3] The attempt to define ballyboes, polls and tates as land divisions with a fixed area of sixty acres was quite misleading. Not only was that figure a serious underestimate of average townland size, but modern townlands which correspond to the ballyboes on the Bodley maps vary considerably in size. In general, large townlands contain poorer-quality land than the smaller townlands. This points to the emergence of ballyboes as land units which were not regarded by the Irish in terms of size, but rather as having a fairly standard economic or agricultural potential. The ballyboe was considered as the extent of land required to graze a particular number of cattle, or with more mixed farming the land required to support several families. While in reality the ballyboes were not of equal size, they were mapped as such on the Bodley maps. Therefore, when these ballyboes are identified on a true-scale map, certain areas emerge with a greater density than others. Map 3 shows the density of these early land units per square mile. If the assumption is made that these ballyboes had an approximately uniform economic potential, it would follow that Map 3 shows a pattern of relative land potential as perceived by the pre-plantation Irish in west Ulster.

In comparing Map 3 with the equivalent area in Map 2 showing nineteenth-century land valuations, several observations may be made. Despite the effects of land reclamation and woodland clearance, there is a broad measure of agreement between the high-density areas of townland units in 1609 and the areas of highest land valuations in the 1860s. However, one important contrast between these two patterns is the apparent absence in 1609 of much higher values in the east. This may have been partly because plantation surveyors had found that the townlands varied in size from county to county. Polls in Cavan were estimated to be smaller, having only fifty acres of profitable land, while some of the Armagh ballyboes in the east were estimated at 100 or 120 acres. This distorts the general pattern shown in Map 3 by increasing the density in the west. Bearing this problem in mind, it still appears probable that there was an actual change in perceptions between the seventeenth and nineteenth centuries. In a rural

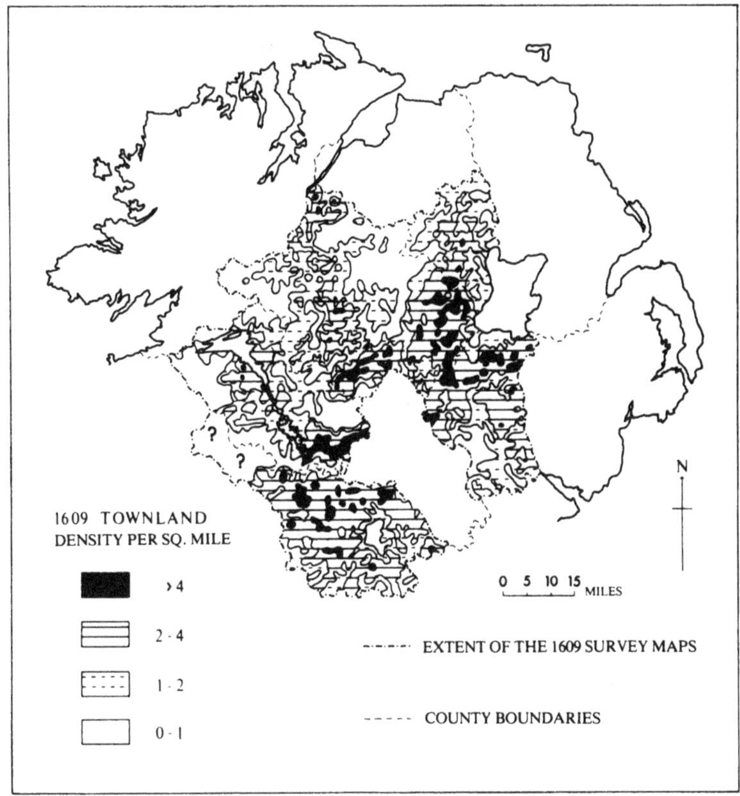

Map 3: *Townland density in Ulster, c. 1609*
Each townland recorded on the 1609 Bodley maps (P.R.O.N.I., T.1652) has been located on a true-scale map. The density of these townlands per square mile has then been calculated and isoplethed for four categories of density.

economy less dependent on external communications and the need to produce a surplus for export, the isolation of areas with fertile soils in the west need not have been a disadvantage.

Mountains, lakes and rivers can have changed little in three hundred years, but the distribution and extent of woodland and bog have been radically altered. These features were all mapped in considerable detail on the barony maps of the 1609 Bodley survey: mountainous areas with no permanent settlement were represented by shaded drawings of peaks devoid of territorial subdivisions; woodland by tree symbols; and bog or marsh by areas of rough cross-hatching (see inset to Map 4). Despite the fact that areas of lowland bog were regarded as a hindrance to military operations during the Elizabethan campaigns, only occasionally were vast tracts of bog mapped. In most cases only small pockets of bog are shown between townlands.

While some areas on the mountain fringes are depicted as continuous woodland with no territorial subdivisions, the overwhelming majority of tree symbols marked on the 1609 barony maps are shown within named townlands. The number of tree symbols contained within any individual townland on the 1609 maps varies from none to about eight. Indeed, the way in which these symbols are presented on the maps suggests that the townland's shape or area was not greatly affected by the presence of woodland, even in the most thickly wooded areas. Consequently there does not appear to have been any extensive lowland area where the density of wooded cover excluded Irish settlement. Rather the impression conveyed is that the woods were of an open and fragmented nature, even in the well-known forests of Glenconkeyne and Killetra to the north-west of Lough Neagh. The Civil Survey of 1654, which survives for the Ulster counties of Donegal, Londonderry and Tyrone, provides the first quantitative account of woodland distribution over a significant area.[4] Despite its post-plantation date, this survey is useful because the quantity of woodland is listed within each townland throughout the three counties. Rarely is more than a fraction of any townland described as wood, thereby confirming the fragmentary nature of the cover. The quality of timber can also be assessed, for the terms used usually describe underwood rather than profitable or 'timber' wood. In Donegal a total of 4,674 acres of such 'shrubby wood' or 'shrub and bog' are recorded, with no profitable woodland. In Tyrone 7,144 acres of underwood are listed (5,649 acres of this in the eastern barony of Dungannon), with only an additional 80 acres of 'wood'. Mention is made in Londonderry of some 6,355 acres of underwood, but in this case with a greater proportion (2,402 acres) of 'wood'. Of the better woodland in these three counties, almost all was recorded in the barony of Loughinsholin in south Londonderry (2,386 acres). This, of course, corresponds to the often referred-to forests of Glenconkeyne and Killetra.

The gradual but continuous process of woodland clearance

for cultivation which began in the Neolithic period had severely reduced the extent of primary (elm and oak) forests in Ulster by 1600. This process was accelerated by an increase in the other uses for timber, such as local demands for building material, charcoal for ironworks, bark for tanning, staves for barrels and smaller vessels, and even timber stakes for temporary field boundaries. Coupled with the flourishing export trade in Irish timber and the clearance of some woodland for strategic purposes during the Elizabethan war in Ulster, this meant that by the early seventeenth century much of Ulster's woodland cover was fragmentary, or of inferior scrubby vegetation characterised by thorns, ash, birch and alder. The largest and densest areas of woodland lay to the north-west of Lough Neagh and in the Erne basin, with significant areas also in north Down, in Killultagh in south Antrim, and in the Sperrin valleys. The drumlin belt of south-west Ulster contained woods of oak, ash and elm, but the more poorly drained areas south of Lough Neagh contained a greater proportion of species such as alder and willow. When the tree symbols marked on the 1609 Bodley maps are plotted on a true-scale map (Map 1) a clear pattern of woodland distribution emerges in west Ulster. While the reliability of these symbols as a quantitative representation of woodland may certainly be questioned, the pattern shown in Map 1 concurs with the distribution suggested by other cartographic, documentary and place-name evidence.[5]

1.2 *Irish land divisions and social structure: the Gaelic lordships*

The Irish laws describe a social system which was structured in terms of role into well-defined strata. While not completely contradicting this idealised ordering of society, the accounts and surveys by English observers do suggest a slightly different social order in west Ulster in the immediate pre-plantation period. Between the Gaelic lords and the broad mass of Irish peasantry at least two intermediate tiers can be readily identified. Each of these social levels was associated with control over a corresponding territory. In effect this meant a social structure closely interrelated to the hierarchical system of land divisions. It should be remembered, however, that the wealth of the Gaelic lords was not measured in terms of land but in the possession of livestock, mainly cattle. Patronage was provided by controlling the freedom to graze cattle, and economic control was exercised through the 'leasing' of cattle rather than land to the tenants. Anyway, individual and absolute landownership was not characteristic of the Gaelic system. Instead the land was owned collectively and was periodically redistributed, although in such a way as would provide continuity by giving the sept leader or chief first choice each time. Livestock was of key importance in the relationship between social structure and territorial divisions. Because of this all levels in the territorial hierarchy were flexible in size and without permanent boundaries. It was the application of English law to these pre-existing divisions that fossilized their extent, boundaries, and in many cases their Irish names.

Most of the counties of west Ulster had been shired in the sixteenth century on the basis of the extent of contemporaneous Gaelic lordships. O'Donnell's lordship of Tyrconnell and the territories of the Maguires, McMahons, O'Cahans and O'Reillys were broadly coextensive with the new counties of Donegal, Fermanagh, Monaghan, Coleraine and Cavan respectively. However, the principality of 'The O'Neill' (a title banned by English law) extended beyond the county of Tyrone into much of County Armagh. In 1584 O'Neill's territory south of the Blackwater was shired separately into County Armagh. County Tyrone was further reduced in 1613 when the barony of Loughinsholin in the north-east was added to Coleraine to form the new county of Londonderry. The eastern counties of Antrim and Down had been shired at an earlier stage. This was due to a continuous, if receding, English presence from Anglo-Norman times. In the late sixteenth century the remnants of the Old English colony were supplemented by the arrival of English adventurers in the vicinity of Newry and Carrickfergus. In 1594 much of the land around Carrickfergus was allocated to a mixture of new English adventurers and Old English families who had long-established connections with the town. The Gaelic lords in east Ulster became increasingly isolated as Elizabethan influence increased towards the end of the century. The movement of lowland Scots into east Ulster in the early years of James's reign (before the official plantation had begun) was a further indication that the supremacy of the Clandeboye O'Neills in the east had been brought to an end. To survive *in situ* the Irish in Antrim and Down clearly had to compromise with the new order.

One account of the principal Gaelic lords of Ulster in 1560 provides an interesting insight into the relationships between O'Neill of Tyrone, O'Donnell, and the lesser lords in Ulster, with no mention being made of the eastern Clandeboye O'Neills:

> O'Neile is the chiefest of the Irishry, and heretofore ought for the most part to be King of Ireland. . . .
>
> The people there are far more beast like and barbarous than the people of other counties. Lords under O'Neile: Magannyes, Magwyre, O'Cahan, McMahoun, O'Hanullan, Mack Cuvillin, Mack Donnell, consul of his Scots and galloglasses, O'Donnell is the second best lord in Ulster, and hath Lords under him as the said O'Neyle hath. . . . Lords under O'Donell; O'Dogherday, O'Byle, O'Gallihur, three Consulls, McSwynes, and divers others.[6]

By the end of the sixteenth century this description was no longer valid, for by then Maguire of Fermanagh was paying tribute to O'Donnell. In addition, the McQuillans and McDonnells of north Antrim, along with the Magennises of west Down, had joined the Clandeboye O'Neills in adopting positions almost independent of the west Ulster regime. This was perhaps best exemplified by the less than total commitment within Antrim and Down to the Gaelic cause during the Elizabethan war, and the understandable readiness of the east Ulster lords to compromise with the English authorities.

1.3 *The sub-chiefs (uirríthe) and their 'countries'*

Unlike O'Neill's lords, those listed above under O'Donnell were mostly tributary chiefs who controlled barony-sized areas within Tyrconnell. To the English observer the first division of the county in Ulster *circa* 1600 was into 'baronies'. A survey of 1608 found that the county of Coleraine contained three baronies, Donegal contained five, Tyrone five, Fermanagh seven, Cavan seven, and Armagh five: in all, thirty-two in west Ulster excluding Monaghan.[7] While these were all created from the territories or 'countries' of the tributary lords in Ulster, by no means had these *uirríthe* or sub-chiefs been made 'barons' in English law. One exception to this was Hugh O'Neill's father, who had been created Baron of Dungannon by Henry VIII in 1542.

Even the major lords in west Ulster had a secondary function: within their home baronies they exercised a degree of control similar to that of the *uirríthe*. This role within the Gaelic system involved the right to billet kerne (soldiers) and to collect rents or

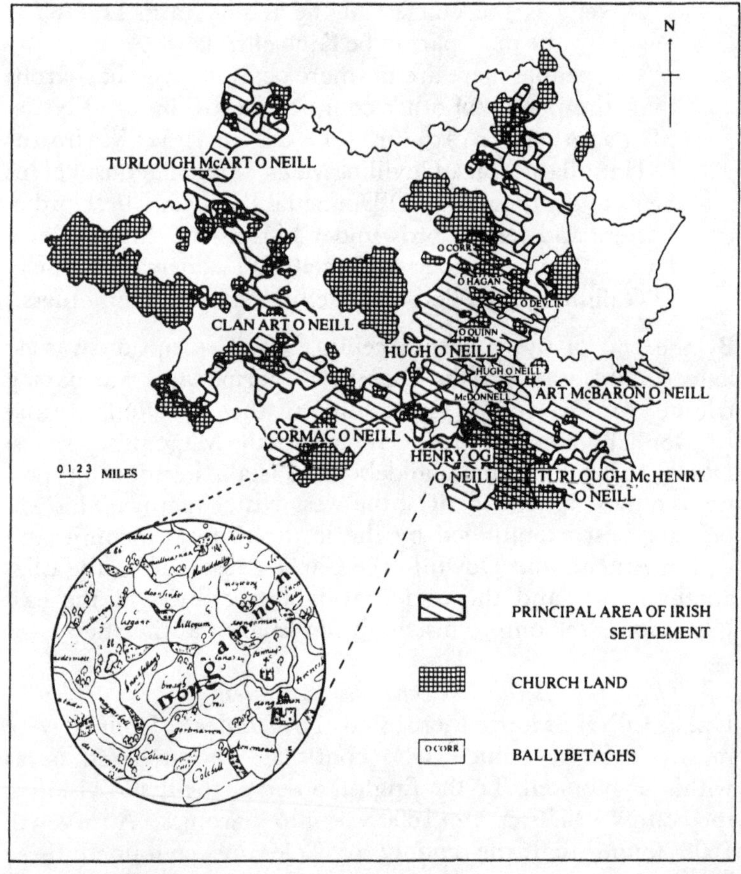

Map 4: *The Gaelic lordship of Hugh O'Neill*
Hugh O'Neill's lordship comprised all of County Tyrone, along with north Armagh and the barony of Loughinsholin, now in south Londonderry. The principal area of Irish settlement on this map has been assumed on the basis of pre-plantation townland density (Map 3). The inset of Dungannon ballybetagh (showing individual ballyboes) is from the 1609 Bodley map of Dungannon barony.

tribute from various septs within the barony. Inside Tyrone Hugh O'Neill exerted such a secondary economic and political control over his home 'country' of Dungannon. Hugh's brother, Cormac McBaron O'Neill, was the *uirrí* in the Clogher Valley, which he controlled as his territory. This area became Clogher barony, and similarly other baronies emerged from the 'countries' of the *uirríthe*, who in Tyrone were all closely related members of the ruling O'Neill clan (Map 4). In contrast, the *uirríthe* of Tyrconnell were not O'Donnells, but were the chiefs of the O'Dohertys, O'Gallaghers, O'Boyles and McSweeneys. Because the lords and *uirríthe* were dispersed throughout the lordships, each in his own respective country, a small number of dominant septs could maintain effective control over large areas.

1.4 *The sept leaders and their ballybetaghs*

Between the *uirríthe* and the lower strata of Irish society there was a substantial middle grouping responsible for the actual collection of rents from the broad mass of the farming population. They were also required to perform certain duties in return for the protection of the *uirríthe* (and a portion of the collected rents). Sir John Davies in 1606 described the social divisions in Ireland: 'There is first a general chieftain of every country or territory, which hath some demesnes and many household provisions yielded unto him by the inhabitants. Under him every sept or surname hath a particular chieftain or tanist, which has likewise his peculiar demesnes and duties.'[8] Sir Arthur Chichester listed the principal septs under Hugh O'Neill: 'The chief septs of this county are the O'Neales, and under them the O'Donnoles, O'Haggans, O'Quynes, O'Delvynes, O'Corres, the Clan-donnells, the Melans, and other septs which are warlike people and many in number.'[9] With the exception of the O'Mellans, who dwelt in the barony of Loughinsholin, the other six septs mentioned are those who were most closely associated with Hugh O'Neill's barony of Dungannon. The lists of Irish pardoned in Tyrone before the Flight of the Earls in 1607 included twenty-nine O'Neills, nineteen McDonnells, twelve O'Quinns, ten O'Donnellys, ten O'Devlins, nine O'Hagans, and two O'Corrs. Included in the group who fled with Hugh O'Neill in 1607 were two O'Hagans (one nicknamed 'Shane na

Ponty' — a rent-collector) and a Murtagh Quinn. Leaders of these various septs in the territory of Dungannon had particular traditional functions to perform. O'Devlin was sword-bearer to O'Neill, O'Hagan was the brehon or judge, O'Quinn was chief steward, and O'Donnelly was marshal. The McDonnells were a branch of the Scottish mercenaries who were powerful in County Antrim. Besides the ceremonial and military services provided by the sept leaders, their most important role was as middlemen in the collection of rents from the septs under their control.

The territorial unit controlled by a sept was known as a ballybetagh (Ir. *baile biataigh*: victualler's place) and in most cases consisted of sixteen ballyboes or townlands. The location and extent of some of these ballybetaghs or sept lands can be identified on the 1609 Bodley maps. On these maps groups of townlands are given ballybetagh names such as Ballyquin and Ballyokeuan, Ballyhagan, Revelinowtra and Revelineightra, and Donelowtra and Doneleightra, which identify those ballybetaghs occupied by the O'Quinns, O'Hagans, O'Devlins and O'Donnellys. Furthermore, ballybetaghs known to be the demesne lands of the chiefs are also shown, such as Hugh O'Neill's demesne lands of Dungannon. The survey of 1608 provides detailed information on the ballybetaghs or sept lands throughout west Ulster. Most of the baronies in Tyrone, Armagh and Coleraine were 'divided into ballibetoes and other quantities each balle[be]toe containing xvj ballyboes'. Similarly in baronies of Counties Fermanagh and Cavan ballybetaghs were ubiquitous, but there they consisted of sixteen townlands known as tates or polls rather than ballyboes. When the information for Counties Tyrone, Coleraine, Armagh, Fermanagh and Cavan is examined together, the ballybetagh consisting of sixteen ballyboes, tates or polls is found to be by far the most common subdivision of the barony (Figure 1).

There were also significant numbers of territorial units containing four, eight and twelve townlands, and these would appear to be the result of ballybetagh fragmentation. Indeed, in County Donegal the 'quarter' was the universal land denomination recorded in the 1608 survey. This 'quarter' was one-quarter of a ballybetagh but could be assumed equivalent to two, three or sometimes four townlands, presumably indicating

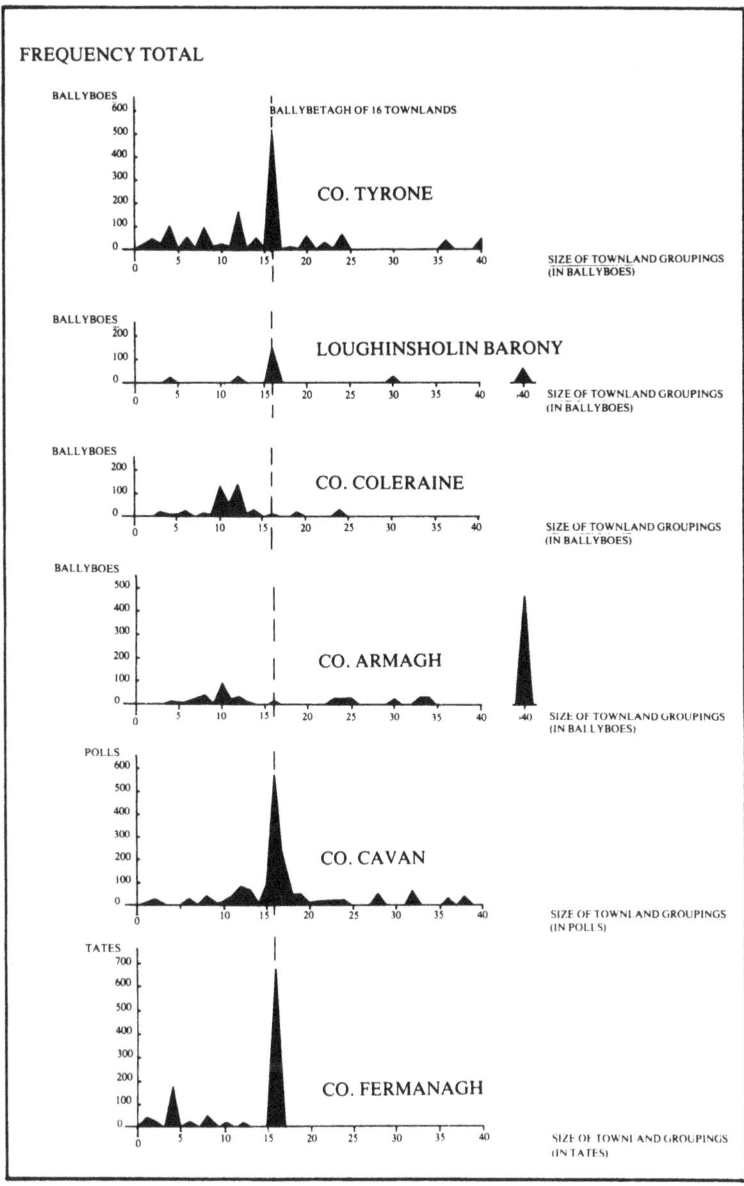

Figure 1: *The size of pre-plantation townland groupings*
Each townland grouping recorded in the 1608 survey was identified by a Gaelic place-name.

the former composition of ballybetaghs in that county. Throughout west Ulster in 1608 (excluding Monaghan and Donegal) there were only 42 subdivisions of the baronies recorded as containing more than sixteen townlands, while 119 ballybetaghs contained exactly sixteen. A further 214 land denominations contained between four and sixteen townlands, giving a total of almost 400 territorial groupings of townlands within the baronies. If these groupings of townlands, which had all been ascribed Irish place-names, are taken to represent ballybetaghs or sept lands with a politico-economic function, then an equivalent number of several hundred sept leaders in west Ulster must be inferred.

As much as 20 per cent of the total area of west Ulster was under ecclesiastical control in the early seventeenth century. These traditional church lands (known as 'termon' lands) carried with them rights of sanctuary and were undoubtedly useful as buffer zones between rival chiefs. Economically, however, the church lands functioned in the same way as secular lands, with ballyboes and ballybetaghs under 'erenaghs'. The erenaghs were the social equivalent of the sept leaders on temporal or non-church land, but collected rents and tribute for the church rather than the Gaelic lords.

1.5 *The Irish 'tenants' and their townlands*

All the sept lands throughout Ulster were made up of groups of small land units, each often equivalent in name and location to a modern townland. Because these townlands were used in plantation land grants, their extent and Irish names became fixed in subsequent leases and other legal documents. But before these townlands could be given legal status by the settlers, the plantation surveyors found it necessary to estimate their approximate size in acres. In Counties Tyrone and Coleraine the ballyboe was estimated to contain sixty acres of 'profitable' land. In practice the ballyboe could be almost any size from forty to 400 statute acres, depending on the quality of the land. This discrepancy between actual physical size and estimated size inevitably caused confusion in the early surveys. In Armagh the ballyboes in most baronies were also estimated to contain sixty acres, but in some baronies the estimate was of 100 acres, and in others 120 acres. The tates or taths of County Fermanagh and the polls of County Cavan were estimated to be rather smaller in the 1608 survey (tates at thirty acres and polls at twenty-four), but these estimates had been revised to sixty and fifty acres respectively by the time the plantation land grants were made in 1609. Although County Monaghan was not included in these surveys, Sir John Davies in 1607 described the ballybetaghs of Counties Monaghan and Fermanagh as being each 'divided into four quarters of land, and every quarter into four taths so as a bellibetagh containeth sixteen taths'.[10] The quarter ballybetagh, known simply as a 'quarter' (Ir. *ceathrú*), was a land division well known throughout west Ulster. However, as the ballybetagh did not always contain sixteen townlands, it was difficult for the surveyors to estimate an average size for its quarter. When the ballybetagh contained only twelve townlands, the quarter then would represent three rather than four ballyboes, and thus 180 rather than 240 acres by plantation estimate. In Donegal in 1608 the plantation surveyors estimated all quarters as 128 acres; but in 1609, when the plantation lands were granted, quarters were not given fixed area estimates (although in some cases their areas were taken to be 128, 160, 180, 220 and 240 acres).

While the term 'quarter' is self-explanatory, and the name 'ballyboe' appears to represent an area considered in the context of a pastoral economy (Ir. *baile bó*: cow land), the origin and meaning of the terms 'poll' and 'tate' or 'tath' found in Counties Cavan, Fermanagh and Monaghan are less clear. The terms appear English rather than Irish in origin, although naturalised long before 1600. In modern townland names the prefix *pol-* has a wide distribution throughout western Ireland, and the Irish *poll*, meaning 'hole' or 'hollow', is the generally accepted derivation. However, in Ulster more than half of all modern townlands with the prefix *pol-* occur in County Cavan or the approximately co-extensive diocese of Kilmore. Clearly in some of these Cavan examples the townland prefix *pol-* or *polla-* should be translated as 'the poll of...' On the other hand, the distribution of modern townland names with the prefix *tat-* is confined almost exclusively to the diocese of Clogher (Counties Fermanagh, Monaghan, and Clogher barony in County Tyrone), and this prefix cannot be confused with any other Irish word.

It is not clear if the occupants of these townlands were clustered within the townlands in kinship groups, or divided into classes of 'free' and 'unfree' as brehon law suggests. Some retrospective evidence of class distinction at this level is provided by the tax lists of 1660, which clearly divide the Irish occupants of townlands untouched by plantation settlement into two groups: 'farmers' on the one hand, and a great number of labourers or 'servants' on the other.[11] Indeed, in some cases the ballyboe itself was subdivided into six 'sessiaghs', although reference to this is rare. In Fermanagh the tate could also be subdivided into units with names apparently related to liquid or grain measures: 'gallons', 'pottles' and 'pints'. Generally the impression is given that the ballyboes were cohesive land units with an economic rather than a political function.

In 1608 a total of 4,691 ballyboes, tates and polls were recorded in Counties Armagh, Coleraine, Tyrone, Fermanagh and Cavan, with a further 685 quarters in Donegal. As a check for consistency with later surveys, the County Tyrone total in 1608 was 1,263 ballyboes, while the 1609 Bodley maps record 1,493 ballyboes, the 1654 Civil Survey 1,489, and the 1666 hearth-money rolls 1,250.[12] It is likely therefore that in the counties of west Ulster intended for plantation there was a total of approximately 6,000 proto-townland units.

1.6 *Pre-plantation settlement and house types*

The assumption that the ballyboes and other proto-townlands had a standard agricultural potential (say in terms of capacity to graze cattle) implies in turn that these land units had the potential to support a fairly uniform number of households. The density of townlands in 1609 illustrated in Map 3 therefore reflects pre-plantation population density, but this pattern becomes most relevant when the average population of the individual townlands is assessed. The absolute number of Irish in pre-plantation Ulster, or even rough estimates of population, are difficult to ascertain because of absence of any census for the period. In 1602 a pardon was granted by Elizabeth I to Turlough McHenry O'Neill of the Fews barony in County Armagh.[13] Included in this pardon is a list, supposedly of the heads of each household in the Fews, including the few females who were also 'tenants'. A total of 270 names are recorded for this barony, which contained 147 ballyboes according to the

1608 survey, or 143 ballyboes according to the 1609 Bodley maps. This suggests an average of about two households per ballyboe, in an area where the ballyboes were estimated to contain 100 acres rather than sixty acres by the plantation surveyors. Similarly, during the Elizabethan war Hugh O'Neill mustered some 2,000 men from the present area of County Tyrone, an area then believed to contain only about 1,300 ballyboes. In an intelligence report by John Dymmock in 1599 there is a breakdown of the strength of the Irish forces, including 'Cormoc MacBarron, the erl's brother, 300 [foot] 60 [horsemen]'. This meant that 360 men were drawn from Clogher barony with its 191 ballyboes of sixty acres each.[14] These estimates are, of course, fraught with problems of accuracy and reliability, but it can be stated with some confidence that ballyboes were not farms occupied by a single household. On average the estimates suggest two households per ballyboe, but this could only be regarded as a minimum figure, for it is not clear if an 'unfree' or landless class was included in the sources used. Many lowland ballyboes may also have been focal points for larger groups of families because of the seasonal movement of people with their cattle to summer pastures (creaghting). This practice involved movement between ballyboes and was widespread in pre-plantation Ulster. Besides implying that a large section of the population was mobile, it appears to indicate that some upland ballyboes had only seasonal occupation, while correspondingly greater numbers were based in the lowland ballyboes.

A minimal average of two or three families per ballyboe fits with the crude estimates of population for the period, and it is difficult to envisage a ballyboe with only sixty estimated acres of profitable land supporting groups of much more than seven or eight families without a considerable population pressure on the land. Indeed, there is little evidence for such pressure until after the plantation. A taxation list of 1660 provides some insight into the density of Irish settlement in unplanted areas, but presumably these were areas where Irish had settled in greater numbers to avoid the incoming English and Scots. Here the Irish-occupied ballyboes contained as many as ten or eleven families, with an average of about five.[15] If these townland settlements took the form of small clusters of dwellings, they could easily have expanded into the type of nucleated cluster known as 'clachans', given an increase in population or pressure for land. Apart from the possibility of 'clachan' settlements in west Ulster *circa* 1600, towns and villages such as those which existed in the parts of Ireland under Norman and Viking influence were virtually unknown. In east Ulster the Norman strongholds such as Carrickfergus certainly retained urban characteristics throughout the sixteenth century, but in the west the only town clearly marked as such on the 1609 Bodley maps was the ecclesiastical centre of Armagh. Other locations which may have given rise to a degree of nucleation were around other ecclesiastical sites such as Clogher, Downpatrick and Derry, and the English military forts at Omagh, Dungannon, Mountnorris, Charlemont, Mountjoy, Lifford and Monaghan. Contemporary maps and illustrations of these forts certainly indicate some clusterings of dwellings in the vicinity, and also suggest small nucleations adjacent to some of the castles of the Irish chiefs. At Lifford fort one description mentions 'some 80 houses set in a plain green upon the riverside, and compassed with an old ditch'.[16]

The collection of rents in kind by the Gaelic lords also suggests a centralisation of provisions which would be worthless without redistribution or export. Although a widespread market economy with urbanised weekly market centres did not exist, the economic and military functions of the chiefs would have required a number of persons in attendance, giving rise to some form of nucleation. Yearly and twice-yearly fairs were held at rural sites, but there were weekly markets at Dungannon and Cavan during the late sixteenth century. However, these nucleations were exceptional. In this context the English description of ballyboes in the plantation grants as the 'vil et ter' or 'town and lands of' can be understood against such apparently conflicting accounts of the Irish as never having made 'townships or villages'. According to Fynes Moryson in the early seventeenth century, 'They call it a town when they have compassed a skirt of wood with trees cut down, whither they may retire themselves and their cattle.'[17]

Such pre-plantation clustered and dispersed settlements in west Ulster consisted of various house types, ranging from stone-built tower houses to the most basic of shelters known as 'creats'.

With the exception of church buildings, construction in lime and stone was confined to the tower houses built by some of the lords and *uirríthe*. Clay or mud-walled houses were perhaps common in the lowland areas of mid and south Ulster. Irish 'coupled' houses are frequently referred to in the plantation surveys, the term 'coupled' indicating that the roof was supported by A-shaped timbers (pairs of principal rafter trusses). Contemporary illustrations and descriptions of these houses indicate that they usually had a hipped roof, were sub-rectangular in plan, and normally were without chimneys or internal partitions.[18] The walls were thick, either of earth and post construction with perhaps a wattle skin, or of mass construction in dry-stone or clay, and the open hearth was situated towards the centre of the house.

Beside the 'coupled' houses, contemporary accounts often refer to small beehive-shaped huts or 'creats'. Some confusion arose over the name given to the groups of people engaged in pastoral migration (creaghts) on the one hand, and their temporary timber-framed dwellings (creats) on the other: 'Some call them Creaughts, from the little huts they live in, which they build so conveniently with hurdles and long turf, that they can remove them in summer towards the mountains.'[19] The Irish *carraidheacht* (Mod.Ir. *creach*: a foray party; cattle and their caretaker) was variously anglicised in the seventeenth and earlier centuries as *creaght*, *crayte*, *keiriaght*, *kirriaght*, *kyriaghty*, *creaghting*, and *creatinge*; while *creata* (a timber framework; the ribs of a house or roof) was anglicised as *creats*, *crates*, *creaughts*, and *creets*. A number of seventeenth-century descriptions of creats confirm the widespread survival of a single-room dwelling with a circular plan, constructed with a light timber frame, thatched and wattled, and without chimneys. These creats were in some cases the dwellings of the 'creaghts', but in others were wattled dwellings clearly unconnected with creaghting. Some accounts of creats describe wattled structures of circular plan, but other sources refer to a construction method involving a ridge-pole supported at either end by upright timbers, suggesting timber-framed houses with rectangular plans.

Not only were these houses timber-framed in that they lacked walls of mass construction to support the roof timbers, but it is clear that the Irish 'coupled' houses were regarded by the plantation surveyors to have been 'timber' houses as well. The most obvious interpretation of this must be that the couples (principal rafter trusses) were supported by upright timbers, features now known as 'couple-feet' or 'crucks'. Certainly the native Irish cruck tradition which has survived in many parts of Ulster would have been much more widespread in the early seventeenth century. However, the extent to which this tradition was being superseded by coupled roofs supported solely by clay walls of mass construction in the pre-plantation period is not yet apparent. If the transition from timber-frame construction (which typified Celtic and Early Christian Ireland) to stone or clay mass construction (which dominates the present landscape) was initiated in the early medieval period, this transition had not been completed by the seventeenth century in west Ulster.[20]

1.7 *Pre-plantation economy*

The pre-plantation Irish in Ulster were essentially engaged in a pastoral, pre-market economy, with cattle providing the basic means of support for most families. However, the extent to which corn (in Ireland meaning oats) was grown should not be underestimated. There are numerous references to the burning and wasting of corn crops during the Elizabethan war in Ulster, and in a letter to Salisbury in 1607 Sir Thomas Phillips describes how the Irish in Tyrone have 'great plenty of corn' in an area where he 'did not expect to have seen so much'.[21] Another English traveller in the early seventeenth century described some of the practices he observed associated with this tillage:

> They use short ploughs amongst the mere Irish and draw their yokes by the horsetails which suddenly breaks their plough horses, and wears them clean out in a trice so they are never serviceable again. They burn their oats standing upon the stalk or reeds in the fields, and thereby lose the straw which might serve for many good uses. Where wood is plentiful they hedge in all their corn with stakes and bushes and pull them down in winter.[22]

Here the 'short' plough may refer to the length of the draught team, with horses side by side and tethered by their tails to a light wooden plough. 'Ploughing by the tail' was widely practised in Cavan, Tyrone and Fermanagh, but the plough involved may have been capable of little more than marking out furrows. More sophisticated wooden ploughs with iron coulters, iron ploughshares and flat wooden mould-boards with the ability to undercut and turn the sod were known in Ireland from prehistoric times, but the mould-board and use of horses rather than oxen for draught were probably introduced in the medieval period. Horse teams harnessed in tandem giving the 'long' plough were characteristic of the medieval use of heavy wooden ploughs in eastern Ireland. Contemporary apologists for 'ploughing by the tail' described it as a practice more suited for stony and mountainous grounds, with the horses forced to stop abruptly when an obstacle was encountered which might otherwise have damaged the ropes or plough.[23]

If 'ploughing by the tail' was as inefficient and as common as the contemporary English observers infer, it raises the question of the extent to which the ground had previously been prepared by spade cultivation. The one-sided wooden spade with an iron shoe (loy) is certainly of great antiquity in Ireland and was basically a foot-plough or sod-cutting and turning implement. An illustration *circa* 1600 of corn growing in an unenclosed field in the Barthelet map of Inisloughan, County Antrim, clearly shows the corn in ridges suggestive of spade cultivation. However, ploughed land was also worked into ridges some ten or twelve feet wide, separated by trenches which provided the soil for burying the seed.

After the corn was cut by means of the toothed sickle there were two methods by which the grain could be removed from the straw. The practice of 'graddaning' (or burning the straw from the corn) combined the threshing, winnowing and corn-drying processes, but was wasteful of the straw and has been taken to imply storage of the unthreshed corn in stacks, with graddaning as an expedient measure to obtain small quantities of grain for immediate use. The other threshing techniques, either using a wooden stick or 'flail' to beat the grain from the stem (with the straw laid on the ground) or 'lashing' the straw against a hard surface, were the processes normally associated with threshing in quantity.

The problem of whether corn was stored in unthreshed stacks, or the threshed grain stored in small straw-rope granaries, or indeed buried in the ground, is intensified by the absence of barns for grain storage. On this subject the list prepared by Sir Toby Caulfield as an account or '... Collection of Tyrone's Rents, from his flight in 1607 till 1 November 1610' is most enlightening.[24] Grain crops due to O'Neill and his exiled followers as rent 'in kind' in 1610 included 300 barrels of oats and 120 barrels of oatmeal, as well as twenty 'field cocks and wheat, by estimation 30 barrels ... 6 field cocks of oats, containing by estimation 6 barrels of oats, [and] ... 15 rick of oats, which yielded by estimation 40 barrels of oats'. While the oats were brought (and presumably stored) in barrels, oatmeal was brought in 240 'raskins' equivalent to 120 barrels. A raskin was a wooden but unstaved vessel, about the size of a firkin, made by scooping out a solid section of a tree, leaving the bark and about two inches of wood around the outside. As this account of O'Neill's rents was taken at Hallowtide, the field cocks and ricks of oats would then have been freshly harvested, and winter storage in this form is not necessarily implied. Despite kiln buildings described in the brehon laws and other Irish texts which indicate structures large enough to enclose both kiln and flailing space, pre-plantation kilns in Ulster were probably small pits, connected at their base by a narrow flue to a hearth area, but situated out in the open. The corn was dried by spreading out on a skin or wattle and straw mat which could cover the top of the kiln, and the whole might be covered with a removable sod-covered roof.

Hand-mills or querns were ubiquitous, but water power in the form of horizontal or 'Danish' mills was widely used for milling larger quantities of threshed oats. A description of one in County Down is interesting, for it not only describes the mill but also refers to graddaning and corn-drying kilns:

> Each townland almost had a little miln for grinding oats, dryed in potts or singed and leazed in ye straw, which was ye old Irish custom, the mealle where of called 'greddane' was very cours. The milns are called Danish or ladel milns, the axletree stood upright and ye small stones or querns (such as are turned with hands) on ye top there of; the waterwheel was fixed at ye lower end of ye axle tree and did run horizontale among ye water, a small force driving it.[25]

Besides oats, other crops were grown less extensively, but both wheat and barley were listed among rents due to O'Neill from 1607 to 1610. Wheat was not, however, commonly grown further west, and in Inishowen the crops were 'flax, oats and barley; wheat, rye or peas it hath none'.[26]

While the importance of oats in the rural economy was reflected in the rents collected by O'Neill, cattle formed the mainstay of O'Neill's wealth, his rents, and of the pre-plantation economy generally. The rent system in much of west Ulster was based on the number of cattle grazing in any area rather than on the actual occupancy of the land, and was paid at the rate of 1s per quarter year for every milk and calving cow. Allowing for the fact that the sept leaders responsible for collecting the rents were exempt, and could reserve a quarter for themselves, a total of £3,733 was due each year from O'Neill's territory of north Armagh, Tyrone and Loughinsholin.[27] At the stated rate of 4s per cow per year, this represented at least 18,663 cows in an area which contained 1,963 ballyboes of temporal land, or an average of 9.5 cows per ballyboe. This minimal estimate of the average number of cows per ballyboe is obviously unreliable. Another estimate in 1598 put the number of milk cows in Tyrone at 120,000 with three times this number of 'barren kine'.[28] However, this must be treated with some scepticism, for it would represent about sixty milk cows per ballyboe, a figure which conflicts with most other estimates. Niall O'Neill rented from Hugh O'Neill the castle of Newtown with five ballybetaghs (eighty ballyboes), for which he paid £130 a year. At the rate of 4s per cow per year, this represented 650 cows, or eight cows per ballyboe, and the rent remittal includes the clause 'with rents of so many tenants as feed 600 cows on the said lands'. A remittal by Henry McShane (O'Neill?) of £43 per 200 cows, and another by Brian Crossagh O'Neill of £40 for one ballybetagh of sixteen ballyboes, both suggest an average of some twelve cows per ballyboe.[29] In the Civil Survey of 1654 the average ballyboe size on the lands which had been reserved for Irish grantees in the plantation scheme for Tyrone was 53 acres, of which only 35 acres on average were recorded as profitable. Of these 35 profitable acres, about 22 were generally pasture of meadow, while 13 acres represented the average portion of arable land per ballyboe. According to Sir William Petty in 1672, a cow in Ireland required 2½ acres of pasture and meadow, so that 22 acres could only support about nine cows. On the other hand, the earlier plantation estimate of sixty profitable acres for each ballyboe (if taken to be all pasture) could support up to twenty-four cows. Probably on the basis that 'a cow's grass' was more often taken to be three acres, it has been asserted that the ballyboe and tate represented not sixty acres, but grazing for twenty cows.[30]

The wealth of the chiefs did not lie in their ownership of land, but rather in the possession of livestock. Land was let for grazing and sold in terms of cows, and even when monetary terms were used in the early seventeenth century there is some evidence to suggest that one milk cow was taken to be synonymous with £1 sterling. The ownership of cattle by the chiefs and the lending of stock to the 'tenants' was an extremely important element affecting territorial control. Occupation of the land involved a periodic redistribution among all sept members known to the English as 'gavelkind', but whether this redistribution occurred at the will of the chiefs or amongst kin after the death of a co-heir is not clear. Certainly one of the effects of frequent redistribution of land was to discourage permanent houses and fences.

With the only fences being in the form of low ditches and banks along the edges of cattle drove-ways and around territorial boundaries (along with wattled temporary fences around growing crops to protect them from trespass by cattle), there was a general absence of a pattern of permanent enclosure. Cattle were probably folded together at night, both in the lowland ballyboes and at the summer 'booleys' (upland pastures), but the contemporary descriptions of unenclosed or 'champion' land should be interpreted as indicating a landscape lacking a fixed field pattern of hedged fences rather than completely open and common land.

References to 'creaghting' (seasonal migration with cattle) are so numerous that the question only arises of the scale of those movements rather than the extent of the practice. It has been shown in Connaught that creaghting took place from lowland holdings to particular upland areas, most lowland townlands having their own associated upland pastures. In Ulster many pairs of ballyboes had the same names, with only the suffixes *-owtra* and *-eightra* distinguishing them. From the Irish *uachtar* (upper) and *íochtar* (lower), these may indicate ballyboes interrelated by seasonal migration. Booleying on lowland bogs in summer was also known. However, in some cases the contemporary accounts suggest that the movement involved large numbers of people, accompanied by the sept leaders. These movements could explain the occurrence of sept lands (ballybetaghs) with *-owtra* and *-eightra* suffixes, such as Donelowtra and Doneleightra, and Revelinowtra and Revelineightra (the sept lands of the O'Donnellys and the O'Devlins in east Tyrone). Creaghting in this sense was part and parcel of the pre-plantation rural economy, and so it must be distinguished from 'creaghting' for military and strategic reasons during times of conflict.

While the small 'Kerry black' cattle have been described as the only surviving 'native' breed, it would be misleading to suggest any uniformity of colour, skull shape or horn length for pre-plantation cattle in Ulster. However, in terms of size and milk yield all types of native cattle were commonly described as inferior to the breeds introduced by the planters. Just as there was an absence of barns for the storage of oats, so no separate byres were generally provided for housing cattle. Wintering cattle must have presented a problem, either from this point of view (for it is clear that man and beast shared the same shelter) or in terms of winter feeding. The lack of winter fodder heightened by the absence of sown grass and root crops created the necessity to kill off a large proportion of the calves that were essential to lactation, particularly bullocks, each autumn. It was the milk cow rather than the bullock which was the focal point of interest for the Irish, judging from the emphasis placed on the value of the milk cow in the Irish laws and texts. Certainly 'white meats' (milk, curds, cheese and especially butter) along with oatmeal formed the basis of the pre-plantation diet. Wooden vessels, both in staved form and hollowed out from solid wood, were used for the churning and storage of butter. While the reported storage of oats in pits in the ground may be questioned, the burying of butter in bogs is well recorded.

Among the goods listed as having been left behind by O'Neill and a few of his followers after the Flight of the Earls in 1607 were: 108 cows, 39 calves, 14 'steers', and 11 heifers; a collection of horses including 16 'garrons' (small work horses), 19 'working mares', 5 'plough mares', 19 'stud mares', 27 colts, and 2 'hackneys'. Other livestock listed were 82 sheep and 180 pigs (60 'hogs' and 120 'swine'). Rents due to O'Neill also included some 300 'mutton' and 72 'hogs'. In Armagh rents in kind mention hens as well as the above range of livestock, while Inishowen contained large numbers of cows, horses, sheep and swine. In 1600 a raid by the garrison at Derry reputedly returned from Inch Island with 2,000 sheep, 200 garrons and 250 cows.[31]

Although an increasing export trade in barrel staves from Ireland during the sixteenth century indicated a degree of woodland exploitation, the primary economic importance of the woodland continued to be in response to localised requirements for coopering, iron-making, fuel, building materials, wooden vessels, tanning, and the grazing of hogs. Flax was grown and linen materials woven in Ireland from an early period, but most of the garments worn were woollen. Sheep were shorn twice yearly (or had the wool pulled from their backs, according to some English observers), and the subsequent processes of spinning, dyeing and weaving were all well within the competence of each household group. Similarly, the rather more complex processes involved in the production of linen yarn were also domestic rather than specialised skills. This sequence of processes included 'retting' the flax (rotting in wet conditions); crushing or breaking thc core ('bruising'); hand-'scutching' the core out of the flax stems, leaving only the fibres; and spinning the yarn. Before the introduction of the 'low' or 'Dutch' wheel to Ulster in the mid-seventeenth century the linen yarn and wool were of poorer quality. All the processes involved in the production of the woollen mantle or cloak (the most characteristic garment of the period), and with linen weaving and spinning, were part of the domestic economy.

In spite of such domestic activities which suggest a great measure of self-containment and subsistence within the individual ballyboes, certain skills were specialised, and the economic function of the ballyboe cannot be regarded as a closed system. Perhaps the most important among such specialised occupations were iron-making, the finishing of iron agricultural and domestic equipment, wood-turning, and, of course, coopering, not only of large barrel- and churn-sized vessels, but of a range of articles down to small drinking-vessels (noggins). Clearly some specialised occupations were centralised, such as the manufacture of hand-mill or quern stones, but such centralised locations were fixed at the source of materials and not in urban centres. The finishing processes and distribution of many of the articles produced by specialist labour were in many instances itinerant rather then centralised, a factor indicative of a pre-market economy, where central places with a market function were not in evidence.

Besides the exportation of hides and barrel staves, there had been some trade in yarn and woollen mantles and rugs. Imports included salt, coal, iron, wine and luxury goods, primarily intended for the chiefs. The production of surplus agricultural produce was necessary to provide payment for rents, replacement implements and vessels, but also to support substantial numbers of economically unproductive persons such as the brehons, the bards, and the 'galloglass' mercenaries. This surplus may have been referred to in 1601: 'We have spoiled here good store of corn already.... We mean to it spoil it all... and then he [Tyrone] cannot keep any men this winter.'[32] The structure of the agricultural economy was not geared towards producing a surplus which could be sold at weekly markets, ultimately for export, in return for payment in cash. Certainly the rents collected by the chiefs in kind would have been useless without exportation or redistribution, and it can be asserted that a monetary system operated at the highest social levels. O'Donnell in Donegal was indeed known in Europe as the 'fish king' because of the massive trade he was engaged in with fish (herring and salmon) in return for wine. Items recorded among O'Neill's personal effects also indicate some degree of external trade and contact. Rents in money, or in kind with monetary equivalents, were, of course, inherent in the rural economic structure, at least between the sept leaders, the *uirríthe* and the chiefs. However, the extent to which a monetary system was present at the broad base of the pre-plantation social structure in west Ulster is questionable.

1.8 *The Flight of the Earls*

In September 1607 a group of Gaelic chiefs and their followers, totalling about a hundred persons, set sail for Europe from Lough Swilly in north Donegal. Foremost among them were the two Ulster earls, Tyrone and Tyrconnell, along with Cuconnaught Maguire of Fermanagh. They were not to return, and their departure has ever since symbolised the final collapse of the Gaelic order in Ulster. The events which led up to their flight began in 1603 when the nine-year war between Elizabeth and the Gaelic lords of west Ulster ended. During the campaigns the English had skilfully played off different lords against one another by holding out promises of 'regrants' of land or by supporting particular contenders for Gaelic chieftainships. The conclusion of the war when O'Neill and O'Donnell submitted in 1603 was followed by the regranting of land back, primarily to the defeated chiefs. This token of goodwill by the new monarch, James I, proved to be an unstable settlement from two points of view: firstly because of the angry reaction of the English servitors, who had been expecting some of the spoils of war for themselves; and secondly because of the continued discontent and jealousies among the Gaelic chiefs over the regrants.

From the point of view of the English servitors, both civil and military, any regrant of land back to the defeated lords was regarded almost as an act of betrayal. One military leader wrote of the settlement with Hugh O'Neill: 'I have lived to see that damnable rebel Tyrone brought to England, honoured, and well liked.... I adventured perils by sea and land, was near starving, eat horse flcsh in Munster, and all to quell that man, who now smileth in peace at those who did hazard their lives to destroy him.'[33] During the next few years the frustrated servitors increased their attempt to discredit and undermine the Gaelic lords in west Ulster. Their goal was to create untenable circumstances for O'Neill and O'Donnell so that their lands would be reverted to the crown.

No English servitors were more influential in this respect than Sir Arthur Chichester and Sir John Davies. Chichester had been placed in charge of the military garrison at Carrickfergus in 1599, taking the position vacated when his brother, Sir John Chichester, was killed in a skirmish outside the town in 1597. His contribution to the defeat of Hugh O'Neill was ruthless and decisive. Besides laying waste an area twenty miles around Carrickfergus, he completely subdued the Clandeboye O'Neills in Antrim and Down and moved west across Lough Neagh to help establish and then take control of the fort at Mountjoy in east Tyrone. These actions were crucial in the Elizabethan conquest of Ulster, and Chichester emerged as unquestionably the most able servitor based in Ulster. Indeed, for a while after the war it appeared that a Presidency of Ulster might be established, a post for which Chichester seemed the most probable candidate. However, O'Neill deeply resented moves to establish any central authority over Ulster and managed to have the event forestalled.

Although Sir Arthur Chichester became Lord Deputy of Ireland in 1605, he continued to be absorbed in Ulster affairs. Unlike Mountjoy (who died in 1606), Chichester was not pliable in his relationships with the Gaelic lords. He was intensely interested in the concept of plantation and already had started to acquire land for himself in south-east Antrim. Chichester's friction with the west Ulster lords was pragmatic, and as Lord Deputy he continued to espouse the cause of the disappointed Elizabethan servitors.

Sir John Davies, on the other hand, was motivated by a desire to extend the influence of English law and custom among the Irish. He was Solicitor-General in Ireland from 1603, and in 1606 he became Attorney-General. While also a keen advocate of plantation (and not without a desire for land himself), Davies was most concerned to destroy the quasi-independent status that had been re-established among some of the Gaelic lords, particularly O'Neill. This, and the persistence of Gaelic tenurial systems, he saw as a direct challenge to the authority of the state. By attempting to remove the dependence of the Irish on their lords and replace this with the status of 'free, natural and immediate subjects of his majesty', Davies was undermining the traditional authority of the lords. At the same time the Earls of Tyrone and Tyrconnell feared more specifically that he was gathering evidence of disloyalty against them for some pending indictment.

The basic problem associated with the absorption of the Gaelic lords into the English legal system of land tenure was related to the extent of the estates they should receive. If the entire area from which they had traditionally received tribute (their 'countries' or lordships) were granted, this would in fact greatly increase each lord's individual authority. Under Gaelic custom a chief or lord of a sept had certain privileges and rents due to him, but his power and wealth lay in the possession of livestock; the land itself was in the collective ownership of the sept. Certainly several of the Gaelic lords welcomed 'regrants' which gave them freehold and personal ownership of the land, but the drawback was that their subsidiary chiefs were then reduced to the status of tenants. A more important disadvantage of the 'surrender and regrant' system for the native population was that by their chief's acceptance of an estate in English law the whole territory could be forfeited to the crown on the misadventure of that chief or his heir. Indeed, the authorities were not above claiming additional land as forfeited to the crown on the basis of a chief's traditional Gaelic authority, even where no such grant in English law had been made.

In Cavan Sir John O'Reilly had accepted a 'regrant' of the county from Queen Elizabeth. Although he joined the Ulster earls in war in 1595, he died soon after, while his son Mulmory O'Reilly died at the Blackwater fighting on the English side. This meant that Mulmory's heir should have been in a favourable position under English title to inherit the county. However, Mulmory's son was eventually forced to accept only a small portion of land when the plantation allocations were made in 1610. Similarly in Fermanagh the lord of the county, Sir Hugh Maguire, died during the Elizabethan war. The county was subsequently divided between two cousins, Connor Roe and Cuconnaught Maguire. Cuconnaught considered himself entitled to the entire county, and this grievance led him to join the earls in exile. Connor Roe's possession of so much of Fermanagh was then conveniently found to be unjustified, and he too had to accept a smaller portion in the plantation allocation. Past experience in Monaghan, where the regrant to McMahon had led to confiscation and 'plantation' of the county in 1592, was one of the underlying causes of the outbreak of war in 1594. Sir John Davies's expedition in 1606 to Cavan and Fermanagh led to the widespread conviction that these two counties were to be treated in a similar manner.

In north-west Ulster the situation was rather different, although equally unsettled. Two Gaelic lords in Donegal had allied themselves with the English forces during the Elizabethan war. Sir Cahir O'Doherty had joined forces with Sir Henry Docwra in Derry on promise of the barony of Inishowen. And among the O'Donnells there had been a rival to Hugh O'Donnell for the chieftainship in Sir Niall Garve O'Donnell.

Sir Niall also supported Docwra's forces in return for a promise of the earldom of Tyrconnell. However, both Sir Cahir O'Doherty and Sir Niall Garve O'Donnell were to be disappointed when the regrants were made at the end of the war in 1603. Hugh O'Donnell had died in exile and was succeeded by his brother Rory. It was Rory O'Donnell who was chosen as Earl of Tyrconnell in 1603; and Sir Niall only received in compensation an estate around Lifford. The dominance of Sir Niall throughout Tyrconnell was so great in practice that he was able to take possession of most of the country's cattle and created great difficulties for Rory O'Donnell in controlling his earldom. Tyrconnell thus stood in sharp contrast to Tyrone, where Hugh O'Neill's authority was unchallenged. In 1607 neither Sir Niall Garve O'Donnell nor Sir Cahir O'Doherty joined with the earls in flight, both hoping that the new situation could be turned to their advantage. This did not prove to be the case, for Sir Cahir O'Doherty was goaded into an attack on the Derry garrison in 1608, after which he was killed during a counter-attack; and Sir Niall Garve O'Donnell was suspected of secretly supporting O'Doherty's rebellion and was imprisoned. Sir Arthur Chichester acquired for himself a grant of the entire barony of Inishowen, and the remainder of Tyrconnell was at the disposal of the crown.

While the flight of Rory O'Donnell and Cuconnaught Maguire into 'voluntary' exile in 1607 was predictable, the fact that Hugh O'Neill joined them was surprising. Although English authority and Gaelic jealousies combined to produce unstable conditions all around Tyrone, O'Neill's control over his lordship of Tyrone and north Armagh remained substantially unaltered and unchallenged. It was probably the legal manouverings of Sir John Davies which were of the greatest concern to Tyrone, and the issue which brought matters to a head was O'Neill's claim to include O'Cahan's county of Coleraine in the earldom. O'Cahan's position in relation to O'Neill was rather ambiguous: something between a sub-chief and a Gaelic lord. Davies encouraged O'Cahan to file a suit against O'Neill claiming independence from him, and this involved the summoning of both O'Cahan and O'Neill to London. In all probability it was O'Neill's conviction that other charges would then be brought against him which made him to decide to sail with O'Donnell and Maguire from Lough Swilly, even if his decision was taken at the last minute.[34]

The land confiscated as a direct result of the Flight of the Earls included the whole of Tyrone and Tyrconnell and half of Fermanagh. Subsequent confiscation and surrender left virtually all the non-church land in Counties Tyrone, Armagh, Fermanagh, Donegal, Cavan and Coleraine in the possession of the crown. The plantation of west Ulster could now be organised, but only after lands were set aside for the considerable number of Irish chiefs remaining (in anticipation of regrants), for the servitors in Ireland who had struggled for reward both in the Elizabethan wars and in subsequent years, and for the Protestant bishops who had claimed all the termon lands.

2

A Scheme for Plantation

Few of the areas chosen for the Tudor and Stuart plantations in Ireland were located in the prime agricultural and coastal trading regions of the east which would yield the greatest profit. Rather the plantations were westward extensions of already established areas of English authority in east Ireland. Conquest, subjugation and the imposition of English law in those Gaelic areas which were most threatening or resistant remained a dominant motivation. Just as the plantation of Leix and Offaly temporarily extended English influence beyond the Pale into central Ireland, so the Munster plantation was a deliberate attempt to reassert English authority in south-west Ireland where Old English power had become hibernicised. The Ulster plantation was no different in this respect. Only six of Ulster's nine counties were involved in the official scheme, and these were all west of the Bann, thereby excluding lands in Antrim and Down which offered the greatest potential for commercial exploitation.

To understand why the official plantation was confined to the western counties it is necessary to understand the chain of events in east Ulster which culminated in a tremendous influx of lowland Scots and English before the official scheme for plantation had emerged in 1609. This unofficial colonisation was the end product of a long period of attrition which not only resulted in north Down being colonised by lowland Scots, but also ensured the acquiescence of most of the remaining lords of the Old English, Irish and highland Scots in the parts of Antrim and Down untouched by the new wave of colonisation in the first years of the seventeenth century.

2.1 *Earlier English and Scottish colonisation in Ulster*

The early settlement history of Ireland is one of successive waves of colonisations throughout the pre-Celtic and Celtic periods. However, the story of English colonisation in Ulster begins in 1177 with the arrival of the Norman lord John de Courcy and more than 300 followers from Dublin. De Courcy commenced his campaign by defeating the first organised opposition he met at Downpatrick, and continued on a coastal route northwards, ultimately winning most of east Ulster for his followers. His best-known building enterprises were the castles of Dundrum in south-east Down and Carrickfergus in south-east Antrim, perhaps along with the medieval town of Downpatrick, which he expanded beside the existing abbey. Hugh de Lacy, who superseded de Courcy, was created the first Earl of Ulster in 1205. By the early fourteenth century many new towns and manorial centres had been formed throughout the earldom of Ulster, which by then comprised Antrim, Down and some northern parts of County Londonderry. However, Norman colonisation was not uniform throughout the earldom. Within Down a distinction may be made between the south-east of the county, where many surviving small castles or tower houses indicate areas of persistent Norman settlement, and the north-west, where earthen mottes suggest military outposts more characteristic of frontier settlement.[1] The English colonists held their lands in south Down in freehold, and their manorial system yielded an agricultural surplus for a flourishing export trade during the early fourteenth century. In Antrim, Carrickfergus became Ulster's most important port and medieval town, but in south Down important ports also emerged. Greencastle, completed in 1261 at the mouth of Carlingford Lough, Ardglass, and Strangford (an out-port for Downpatrick) were the most notable trade outlets in this area.

At no time, however, did the Norman conquest extend throughout the province of Ulster. A heartland of Gaelic power in north-west Ulster remained virtually intact throughout the medieval period. Indeed, in the early fourteenth century a period of Gaelic resurgence, coupled with the Bruce incursions from Scotland, almost annihilated the Norman colony in the east of the province. In the context of the later colonisations of east Ulster, it was the state of the Old English colony in that region at the beginning of the Elizabethan era which was to prove significant.

During the phase of Gaelic resurgence in the late thirteenth and early fourteenth centuries a branch of the mid-Ulster O'Neills had moved east into south Antrim and north Down. These O'Neills became known as the Clandeboye O'Neills after Aodh Buidhe (Hugh the yellow-haired) O'Neill, who died in 1283. Their territories in south Antrim and north Down became known as Lower and Upper Clandeboye respectively. Their principal power base was at Castlereagh, near Belfast, and this eastern extension of Gaelic influence effectively split the Norman earldom of Ulster in two. The besieged outpost of Carrickfergus was captured in 1384, after which it managed to remain under English control only through the payment of an annual tribute of 'black rent' for protection to the Irish chiefs.

There were two important territories in Antrim north of Lower Clandeboye which had emerged as distinct Gaelic lordships. These were the 'Glens' in the north-east and the 'Route' in the north-west. The dominant sept in the Route was that of the McQuillans, an hibernicised Norman family originally of Welsh stock. The Glens, however, had become totally dominated by highland Scots from those parts of the Scottish coast visible across the North Channel, namely the McDonnells. The McDonnells could lay claim to the Glens under English law through the marriage about 1399 of John Mór McDonnell of Isla to Marjory Bissett, the last surviving Norman heir to the territory.[2] The presence of highland Scots in such strength in Ulster was to prove a source of concern to successive Tudor monarchs.

South of the O'Neill territory of Upper Clandeboye in County Down the strongest vestiges of the Norman colony remained. Although they were extensively hibernicised and probably Irish-speaking, numerous families of Norman origin continued to resist the O'Neill expansion in south-east Down. Among these families were the Russells, Echlins, Audleys, Mandevilles, Whites, Smiths, Bensons, Jordans, Fitzsimmons, and most notably the Savages. The area that these Old English colonists dominated was south-east of a line between Dundrum and Downpatrick (the barony of Lecale) and included the southern portion of the Ards peninsula known as the Little Ards. During the fifteenth century the Savages had extended their influence throughout east Ulster, holding lands in many parts of Antrim and Down, but by the 1550s were only to be found as influential families at Carrickfergus and at Portaferry as lords of the Little Ards. Pardons granted to the Savages and their followers in the Little Ards in 1602 included many names with a *Fitz-* prefix, names such as Richard Savage FitzRichard, David Smith FitzDavy and Gerret Bane FitzSimmons FitzPeirs.[3] Norman patronymics were clearly still in use at the end of the sixteenth century.

The opening gambits of the Tudor attempts to reconquer east Ulster were a number of incursions by the Lord Deputy, Gerald Óg FitzGerald, ninth Earl of Kildare, in the early sixteenth century. In 1505 the previous earl had been granted custody of Greencastle, and by 1525 Gerald Óg secured Lecale and even marched north to attack and destroy the Clandeboye O'Neill castle at Belfast. However, this was only a temporary advance, for following the revolt and execution of the tenth Earl of Kildare, 'Silken Thomas' FitzGerald, the Geraldine influence in south Down virtually collapsed. In 1538 Lord Deputy Grey had to retake Dundrum castle from Magennis of Iveagh, and the new Tudor regime began to replace Old English authority in east Ulster. Of all the English Protestant soldier settlers who were to arrive in east Ulster from the middle of the sixteenth century, the most influential early newcomer was Sir Nicholas Bagenal, who came from Staffordshire with his Welsh wife in 1542. By 1552 Bagenal had been appointed marshal of the English forces in Ireland, built up the garrison town at Newry, obtained custody of Greencastle, and been granted large estates in south-west Down comprising the lordships of Newry and Mourne. His fortifications at Newry were strategically important in keeping open the routes of communication between the Pale and east Ulster. Bagenal was closely followed into south Down by Captain Andrew Brereton, who was sent from Dublin to Lecale with about 100 soldiers to 'quiet the country' in 1549. Brereton remained in Lecale well into the 1560s, when the name 'Andrew Brereton of Lecale' appeared in a list of persons willing to settle near Carrickfergus.[4]

At the same time as these new English settlers were arriving in County Down highland Scots in Antrim were increasingly giving cause for concern. The Scottish mercenaries or galloglass were an indispensable prop to the power of the Gaelic lords in Ulster, but the autonomous McDonnell colony in north Antrim became a national threat when Scotland's friendship with France became a formal alliance against England. When Lord Fitzwalter (shortly to become the Earl of Sussex) was appointed as Lord Deputy in 1556 Queen Mary stressed the importance of driving the Scots from their settlements on the Antrim coast. Following a successful military excursion against these Scots by the Earl of Sussex, Mary inquired about the possibility of an east Ulster plantation. To ensure the exclusion of the Antrim Scots Sussex decided that the places which would have to be settled were near the castles of Belfast, Carrickfergus, Olderfleet (Larne), at the mouth of the Bann, and throughout Lower Clandeboye. Sussex suggested that 1,000 men would be necessary to defend and cultivate this area, and that the queen should give each settler eight cows and distribute amongst them 1,000 horses, mares and colts. 'Northern' men and Welshmen were suggested as the most likely to be able to defend the country, and when they arrived they were first of all to build and settle in towns. Apart from the ports and inland towns thus created, the country was to be divided into townships and the inhabitants to have estates at a rent of 2d and 3d per acre.[5] No decision had been taken to proceed with this scheme when the war with France ended during the reign of Elizabeth. At this time the problem of the Scots in Ulster momentarily receded, and in 1565 Sussex was succeeded as chief governor by Sir Henry Sidney. During Sidney's period in office schemes for plantation in Ulster came flooding in. Humphrey Gilbert proposed a plantation with governmental patronage on the shores of Lough Foyle, and another suggestion by Sir Francis Knollys was that some of the soldiers due to be recalled from Ulster should remain, especially any who were good husbandmen, ploughwrights, cartwrights or smiths.[6] As a result of the latter suggestion, a list of some thirty-three persons likely to settle at Carrickfergus and elsewhere in Ulster was drawn up. Sidney himself suggested that a line of forts along the Antrim coast should be established and the interior planted with 2,000 'good and dutiful subjects'.

The reluctance of Elizabeth to proceed with any of these schemes was primarily due to the cost they would incur on her own purse. Her desire was that individuals should undertake and finance their own schemes, and to that end she approved the proposals of Captain Thomas Chatterton, Captain Nicholas Malby and Sir Thomas Smith in 1571.[7] Captain Chatterton, a native of Wiltshire, obtained a grant of almost half of County Armagh, including the territories of Orior and the Fews. Under the terms of this grant he was not permitted to lease any land to 'mere' (Lat. *merus*: pure; unmixed) Irish or Scots for a term longer than five years. Chatterton's lands contained 'ploughlands' of 120 acres each, and he was required to pay a rent to the queen of 20s per year for each ploughland. Every foot soldier in Chatterton's service was to obtain a ploughland of 120 acres, and every horseman 240 acres. In the event of his being unable to perform these conditions, the grant was to be surrendered. By 1575 Chatterton was absent in England, with little or nothing to be seen of his plantation on the ground. The force at Chatterton's disposal proved much too small, and in the following year his grant was revoked. Similarly, Captain Nicholas Malby was to settle McCartan's country known as Kinelarty in mid-Down on almost identical conditions to those laid down for Chatterton. Again, by 1575 this area was found to be 'desolate and waste', and Malby's grant was also revoked. However, the third of these 1571 schemes, that of Sir Thomas Smith, was the one most effectively pursued.

2.2 *Sir Thomas Smith's colony of the Ards*

The queen's principal Secretary of State, Sir Thomas Smith, managed to obtain a grant of the entire territory of the Clandeboye O'Neills in east Ulster at the same time as the grants were made to Malby and Chatterton. While Elizabeth certainly could claim under English law that Clandeboye was at her disposal through the ancient rights of the earldom of Ulster (which had passed by inheritance to the crown in the fifteenth century), the Clandeboye O'Neills had by now been established in the area for three centuries. Indeed, their current lord, Brian McPhelim O'Neill, had been knighted only three years previously for his service against Shane O'Neill. Smith acknowledged that the land he intended to settle would first of all have to be won. He proposed to begin by colonising the Ards peninsula and then to extend his colony gradually through Clandeboye by a process of conquest and settlement. The actual task of leading the colony was delegated to his natural son,

Thomas Smith, who in 1572 ill-advisedly prepared a booklet to advertise the venture and attract a retinue of potential colonists.[8] In this book Smith estimated that 300 men would be sufficient to defend the Ards, and he also explained that, as with the other contemporary grants, land was to be granted at the rate of one ploughland of 120 acres to each foot soldier, and two ploughlands to each horseman. The problem of the resident Irish was brushed aside by the assumption that once the Clandeboye lords were removed, the remaining Irish 'churles' or husbandmen would be so relieved of their oppressions that they would willingly live under, and farm for, the new colonists.

It is hardly surprising that the publication of this booklet caused widespread alarm among the Ulster Irish generally and Sir Brian in particular. Delays resulting from the need to placate him caused the assembled colonising force to dwindle to little over 100 men. The remaining colonists arrived with Thomas Smith the younger at Strangford and were led north to Newtownards, where they waited while Smith proceeded to Carrickfergus with the intention of negotiating with Sir Brian. These negotiations never materialised, and Smith's colony had to retreat south of Comber while Sir Brian stormed through Upper Clandeboye burning any buildings which could provide shelter around the abbeys and priories of Holywood, Bangor and Newtownards.

Despite these initial setbacks, the Smith venture proceeded cautiously with the assistance of some of the Old English of Lecale and the Little Ards. Some of the Savages certainly assisted this venture of Smith's (Henry Savage was killed in Smith's service during the early disturbances), and undoubtedly they saw the colony as a possible means of extending their influence northwards. Indeed, it was to a tower house owned by the Anglo-Norman Whites of Dufferin (Ringhaddy Castle) that Smith turned for shelter during Sir Brian's revolt in north Down.

Despite the apparent failure of the Smith venture, especially following the death of Thomas Smith at Comber in 1573, the grant for this venture was never revoked during the reign of Elizabeth. Rather it was overtaken by a parallel scheme for the colonisation of Antrim by the Earl of Essex in 1573, and by a renewed burst of enthusiasm by Thomas's father, Sir Thomas

Smith, in 1574. Under threat of confiscation, Sir Thomas procured a further band of 150 colonists headed by his brother George, Jerome Brett and Ensigns Harrington and Clark. This time more emphasis was to be placed on the construction of towns, and the centre-piece was to be a walled city called 'Elizabethia'. However, Sir Thomas Smith was obliged to relinquish any claim to Lower Clandeboye in south Antrim, as this area was crucial to Essex's scheme. Smith willingly backed the Essex undertaking, just as Captain Malby had joined with his own venture in Down when the Kinelarty colony in mid-Down had collapsed.[9]

2.3 *The Earl of Essex's colony in Antrim*

The determination of Queen Elizabeth not to expend any of her own resources on plantation schemes in Ulster was relaxed for her favourite, Walter Devereux, Earl of Essex, during his term of service in Ireland. In 1573 Essex proposed a joint scheme to colonise most of County Antrim, maintaining 600 soldiers for two years out of his own resources, along with 600 to be maintained by the crown. He was granted the northern half of Clandeboye that lay in County Antrim, except for the area immediately around Carrickfergus. Northern or Lower Clandeboye was intended for Essex and his own followers, with the remainder of the county for the remaining colonists. At an annual rent of 2d per acre each foot soldier was to receive 200 acres, and each horseman 400 acres. He was granted authority to build castles and forts, to incorporate towns, and make any laws necessary for his administration of the area.

In 1573 Essex sailed from Liverpool, but the fleet was scattered by a storm, and the arrival of the colonists at Carrickfergus was confused. Eventually Essex was able to muster 400 adventurers and more than 1,000 soldiers, but after a period of discouragement and lack of progress many of these potential colonists returned home. Their disillusionment was partly due to the apparent collapse of the Smith colony in County Down, and partly due to the continued unrest in Clandeboye created by Sir Brian McPhelim O'Neill. Between 1573 and 1575 there were several fruitless marches into the interior of the county, and in 1574 fresh adventurers were sent over. However, as yet nothing had been done to plant most of the area. A revised scheme was devised as a temporary expedient whereby a series of settlements around the Antrim coast were allocated to some of the principal adventurers. These were only reluctantly accepted, and indeed many of the settlements were never established. Eventually Elizabeth accepted that Essex had overreached himself in the venture, and the entire project was to be moderated. On the surrender of Lower Clandeboye, which Essex had hoped to retain for himself, and in consideration of the considerable capital he had invested and lost, Essex was granted the peninsula of Islandmagee in south-east Antrim. Despite replenishment of the dwindling forces and settlers at his disposal, Essex was only able to colonise successfully a small proportion of the area originally intended. This was the coastal strip of south Antrim from Belfast to Islandmagee; and indeed, many colonists preferred the relative security of the town and county of Carrickfergus, which had been retained in the queen's hands.[10]

In virtually all the sixteenth-century plantations in east Ulster freeholds were allocated by reassigning the pre-existing Irish land units. A common assumption was that these townland units consisted of 120 Irish acres of arable land and were known as 'ploughlands'. This may, however, have been a erroneous assumption based on English experience in the Pale, where the *seisreach* (ploughland) was indeed the equivalent of the modern townland. Throughout the O'Neill territories in Ulster the townland units of the early seventeenth century were known as 'ballyboes' and were assumed to contain only sixty profitable acres each. In Antrim and Down these ballyboes were also common, but it is possible that a few small areas may have had ploughlands through their earlier association with the Normanised arable parts of south-east Ireland. The only sizeable region of Ulster where modern townland equivalents of pre-plantation units are absent is the county of Carrickfergus. Instead the hinterland of Carrickfergus is comprised of much larger areas known as 'divisions'. The first 'division' of Carrickfergus was created in 1595 when about forty individuals were given strips of land known as 'alderman's shares' within what is today Middle Division.[11] These geometric parcels of land were set out without regard to the pre-existing territorial divisions, and were the only substantial allocation of land to colonists made in this manner. The persons who received these shares were partly Old English, including some Savages, and partly Irish; but for the most part they were Elizabethan English. The new English colonists became even more dominant in Carrickfergus county when the second and third 'divisions' were created in 1601 and 1603.[12]

When James VI of Scotland came to the English throne as James I on the death of Queen Elizabeth in 1603 the effect in Ulster was quite dramatic. As the first Stuart monarch on the English throne he was expected to be sympathetic to the recently defeated Gaelic lords of west Ulster. Certainly James did regrant them their traditional territories, much to the annoyance of the English servitors in Ireland, although this was to prove only a temporary gesture. The highland Scots in north Antrim could expect even more favourable treatment. A grant was made out almost as soon as James arrived in London of the entire territory of the Glens and the Route to Sir Randal McDonnell. Because of several defects in the patent for this grant, it was revised in 1604, and in the later version a clause was included which empowered Sir Randal to divide the area into manors of at least 2,000 acres each. A castle or strong house was to be built on each of these manors within seven years. This grant was particularly noteworthy because the various sixteenth-century plantation attempts in Ulster had referred only to the allocation of townlands to individual followers, and not to groupings of the townlands into manors.[13]

2.4 *The Hamilton and Montgomery plantations in north Down*

Besides the Catholic McDonnells of Antrim, a host of Protestant Scottish courtiers were expecting the accession of James I to present them with increased opportunities for aggrandisement. While most of these men had to wait for the official plantation to obtain their favours, two lowland Scots had particular designs on the Great Ards territory of north Down which had previously been part of the lands granted to Sir Thomas Smith. The first was an influential Ayrshire man, Hugh Montgomery, who had trading contacts in Carrickfergus. Through these contacts he devised a spectacular scheme to obtain lands in County Down.[14] Con McNeill McBrian O'Neill, the gullible lord of Upper Clandeboye, had been taken to Carrickfergus under a loose form of house arrest because of a drunken brawl between some of his followers and some English soldiers at Belfast. Hugh Montgomery's negotiated arrangement involved a faked kidnapping of Con and his transportation to London with the object of obtaining a pardon. In return for this Montgomery would obtain half of the north Down Clándeboye estate. This plan proceeded almost to complete fruition, but was modified at the last moment because another lowland Scot had entered the race.[15] He was James Hamilton, another native of Ayrshire, who had been teaching in Dublin during the first years of the reign of James I. While in Dublin, Hamilton had provided intelligence for James and, perhaps more importantly, was able to tempt the king with an offer of £1,700 in return for a grant of abbey lands in east Ulster. Hamilton suggested to James that the lands intended for Hugh Montgomery were too great for any single person to undertake. As a result, in 1605 an amended grant was made out in Hamilton's name. Under this new arrangement, Con O'Neill, Hugh Montgomery and James Hamilton would each receive one-third of the Upper Clandeboye estate. The area to be divided was supplemented by church land, so that the effect on Con O'Neill's and Hugh Montgomery's expectations was minimised. Con O'Neill's portion was to be in the north-west at Castlereagh, while Montgomery and Hamilton were to occupy the north-east of the county in the territory of the Great Ards. The sea coasts would therefore be 'possessed by Scottish men who would be traders'. Weekly markets were to be established at Bangor, Holywood, Greyabbey and Castlereagh, and Hamilton and Montgomery were to 'inhabit the said territory and lands with English and Scotch men'. They were also to procure English or Scots to settle as tenants on Con O'Neill's portion. The area within the Great Ards which Hugh Montgomery obtained lay to the south, that is the countryside around Comber, Newtownards and Greyabbey at the head of Strangford Lough. Hamilton's estates were to the north of these, along the southern shore of Belfast Lough from Holywood to Bangor and Groomsport.[16] Through these grants to Montgomery and Hamilton foundations were laid for the most concentrated and substantial colony of British to arrive in Ulster during the first half of the seventeenth century.

As well as Upper Clandeboye, James could feel confident that the remainder of Antrim and Down would be easily governed.

Besides the rapidly expanding Scottish settlements in north Down, English settlement had progressed in south Antrim, where much of the territory of Lower Clandeboye had passed from the Earl of Essex and his followers to James's deputy in Ireland, Sir Arthur Chichester. Elsewhere in east Ulster the Old English and Irish inhabitants had either resisted all attempts to be drawn into the earlier war with Elizabeth, or else had only momentarily succumbed to the attractions of rebellion. They opted rather to accept English authority as a means of strengthening their traditional resistance to the expansion of O'Neill power from Tyrone into east Ulster. It was with little difficulty therefore that James foresaw the process of unofficial plantation in east Ulster continuing, or at least could anticipate that the remaining Irish would live in a 'civil and obedient manner' under English rather than Gaelic law.

In west Ulster also considerable areas were to be excluded from the official plantation. For example, Inishowen in north Donegal had already been granted by 1608 to Sir Arthur Chichester. However, besides Antrim and Down, the only entire county of Ulster to be excluded from the official scheme was Monaghan. In 1591 land tenure in County Monaghan had been anglicised under the Tudor policy of 'surrender and regrant'. This was accompanied by the transference of extensive church lands to English servitors and by the retention by the crown of part of Farney barony, which in 1575 had been granted to the Earl of Essex. Nevertheless, the remaining area, which consisted of most of the county, was regranted by Elizabeth to Patrick McKenna and five leading McMahons. These Irish lords were to hold their lands under English law and pay rent to the crown, and many of the lesser Irish in the county were to be made freeholders. This establishment of an English tenurial system in Monaghan was to survive the Elizabethan war and was the principal reason why the county was not included in the official scheme. The Irish freeholders of Monaghan were not involved in the Flight of the Earls in 1607, so that their lands were neither confiscated nor surrendered.

Private plantations and the establishment of freeholders in Counties Antrim, Down and Monaghan had pre-empted the official plantation in the other six counties of Ulster. Ironically, the extent to which this had happened can be assessed by reference to the first of the plantation surveys in 1611.[17] It contains observations on the 'voluntary works' of James's grantees in Ulster outside the escheated counties, most of this progress having been made before the official scheme for plantation was drawn up in 1609. In County Down the survey noted eighty new houses on Sir James Hamilton's estate at Bangor, all inhabited by English and Scots. He was also reported to have brought out of England some twenty artificers for his building programme. At Holywood a further twenty houses inhabited by English and Scots were found on the Hamilton lands. The adjacent Montgomery lands were equally well settled, but this time with relatively fewer English. Newtownards then had 100 houses, 'all peopled with Scots'. Settlements in Down which had resulted from Tudor or earlier grants were largely ignored in this survey, but sundry British and Irish had 'resorted' to the seat of the bishop at Dromore. Captain Edward Trevor had built at Stranmillis and Malone near Belfast, where he had introduced some English families. Throughout south Antrim many English had obtained grants from the Lord Deputy, Sir Arthur Chichester. In that area of south Antrim between Belfast and Lough Neagh English settlers had established themselves at Lisburn, Muckamore and Templepatrick. At Belfast workers were engaged in the construction of Chichester's town, and many families of English, Scots and Manx were resident. Between Belfast and Islandmagee the Lord Deputy's lands contained many English, Scots, and 'civil Irish' (Lat. *civilis*: citizen; denizen). Islandmagee itself was found to be inhabited by English, Scots, and other 'civil' Irishmen, who 'can speak English and many of them do go in English habit'. In County Monaghan Sir Edward Blayney had completed Monaghan castle, which was in the king's charge, and had also built a bawn at Ballynelurgan. Sir Thomas Ridgeway had built a bawn in the same county at Glaslough, alongside which a town of almost thirty houses was recorded. In the barony of Inishowen in County Donegal Chichester had established a number of servitors, each of whom had built a strong house or castle, some having undertenants living close by.

2.5 *Precedents for the Ulster plantation scheme*

By 1608 various schemes were being considered for an official plantation in west Ulster. Many had been established through past experience in Ireland and abroad, not only because of the plantations in east Ulster, but also through the other Irish plantations in Munster, in Leix and Offaly, and in the various American colonial ventures. Throughout this period of expansion English theorists and philosophers of colonisation played an influential role in motivating sponsors, if not in shaping the form of the plantation.

The earliest period of colonisation by English adventurers in North America was largely one of unsuccessful experiments in the late sixteenth century. For example, the colony led by Drake, Frobisher and Raleigh to Virginia in 1585 shrank to a private venture, and they returned home in 1586. In the following year John White made another unsuccessful attempt to colonise Virginia. It was not until 1606, only a few years before the Ulster plantation, that the 'first' or 'London' colony of South Virginia was initiated. Jamestown was established, and the expanding colony was closely followed by a 'second' or 'Plymouth' colony in North Virginia in 1607. Despite disappointing starts in both, they were to be the first enduring English plantations in North America.[18] Private finance and sponsorship had characterised the early American and West Indian colonies, and in both the Virginian plantations of James's reign the London companies were subscribers. However, terms such as 'plantation', 'native' and 'colony' were used in connection with plantations in Ireland long before any English colonial ventures in America were undertaken.

The earliest of the Tudor plantations in Ireland began in 1556 when Queen Mary approved a scheme to plant the territories of Leix and Offaly. Leix was to be shired as Queen's County, and its principal fort was to become the town of Maryborough. Similarly, Offaly was to become King's County, with a garrison town at Philipstown. One-third of the total area was to be reserved for the displaced O'Mores, O'Connors and O'Dempseys, while the remainder of the county was to be 'planted' with English settlers. 'English' houses were to be built, military service was compulsory, and none of this land was to be sold or leased to any Irish. In the portion reserved for the Irish they were to hold their lands as freeholders, but no individual was to occupy more than two ploughlands or 240 acres. On the remaining two-thirds the English settlers were to pay 2d per acre rent for their land, and were obliged to keep at least one Englishman and no more than one Irishman for every ploughland held. The largest holding any English farmer could occupy was to be three ploughlands or 360 acres. However, the failure to attract sufficient numbers of English artisans and tenant farmers, along with the continuing frontier warfare with the displaced Irish, meant that the settlement did not endure or have any lasting effect on the balance of power in Ireland.[19]

Elizabeth's plantation of Munster (1586-98) was perhaps the most successful of all the sixteenth-century plantations in Ireland. Nevertheless, the defects of this scheme also led to the eventual failure of the project in terms of establishing an enduring English settlement of sufficient numerical strength to provide stability. Proposals for this plantation were finalised in a second or 'new plot' in 1586 and reflected Elizabeth's wish for Munster 'to be repeopled and inhabited with civile loyal and dutifule subjects'.[20] The grants in Munster were to be of four sizes: 12,000, 8,000, 6,000, and 4,000 acres. In the smallest, 4,000-acre grants there were to be planted (within seven years) two free-holders with 300 acres each, two farmers with 400 acres each, fourteen copyholders with 100 acres each, and a demesne of 700 acres. The remaining 500 acres were to contain at least twelve families on small tenures. This gave a minimum of thirty English families to be planted on each 4,000-acre estate. The larger grants of 12,000, 8,000 and 6,000 acres were to be divided and planted proportionally in the same manner. No grantee was to receive more than 12,000 acres, and produce from the estate could be exported free of duty for five years from 1590. It has been estimated that this scheme involved a theoretical total of 15,000 to 25,000 English, of which as many as one-third may have actually settled in Munster.[21] Even with this large number of settlers, English were still outnumbered by Irish and Old English. One reason for this was that the settlers were thinly spread on large estates over a very large area covering much of Counties Kerry, Cork, Limerick and Tipperary. English settlement mostly consisted of landowners, with Irish retained as subtenants and artisans. Indeed, Irish tenants would take farms on harsher conditions than the English, with greater profit for the landowners. When the Irish rebelled in 1598 thousands of settlers poured into the coastal towns and many returned to England. Although between the years 1603 and 1622 Munster was extensively replanted with English farmers, most of the land was still worked by Irish and Old English as before.

It has been estimated that during the seventeenth century some 100,000 persons sailed from Spain and Portugal to the Iberian colonies in Central and South America.[22] This spectacular movement of population in itself provided a motivation for the English government to compete so that England's naval power and trade routes could be expanded rather than blocked by the Spanish and Portuguese claims for monopoly. During the same period similar numbers of English were to cross the Atlantic to North America, but this movement was overshadowed by the even greater numbers from England and Scotland involved in all the Irish plantations. Just as the contempory Ulster and Virginian plantations were not considered separately, so there were connections between the Munster plantation and the earlier ventures in America. Sir Walter Raleigh on his return from the American adventure was to become one of the largest undertakers in the Munster plantation, and Sir Humphrey Gilbert, one of the most energetic plantation theorists, was also involved in schemes for planting Ulster, Munster and Newfoundland.[23] However, the influence of plantation theorists and philosophers can be easily overestimated. Strongly influenced by classical and Roman precedents, many extolled at length the virtues of honour and patriotism, and only a few recognised the more practical aspects involved.[24] The Elizabethan age was one of overseas expansion in the quest for new trade and markets, but colonisation could offer romance as well as profit. Writers like Richard Hakluyt on the theme of the voyages and discoveries of the English nation could tempt middling farmers with visions of vast expanses of virgin soil lying waiting for the English plough. In 1584 Hakluyt wrote his *Discourse of Western Planting*, which stressed the national benefits which would accrue from American colonies.[25] Although this work was enthusiastically received by Elizabeth, the sea war with Spain proved to be a more immediate drain on resources and surplus manpower. The war in Ireland, of course, proved an equally heavy burden during the last years of Elizabeth's reign. When the Ulster plantation was being considered, one of the most influential and best-known writers of the period, Sir Francis Bacon, applied his mind to the theme of plantation in Ulster. In 1608 he wrote that men were motivated by pleasure, honour or profit, and as no pleasure would be had, honour could be encouraged if the king were to grant titles as rewards to undertakers in Ulster. Profit could best be ensured by granting liberties in trade and estates at easy rates. Astutely he urged that care be taken in the selection of the personnel: it would be better that men of estate and plenty should be involved than the 'setting up' of those of low means.[26]

While those theorists who were not themselves directly involved in plantation ventures may have contributed little to the evolution of the scheme for the Ulster plantation, they do provide an insight into the social background which created the necessity for such a movement of population from England. Christopher Carlile, for example, observed that the needy and dependent could be transported from the crowded English towns and cities, thereby freeing the parishes from the burden of their support.[27] It was a widespread idea that colonies in the New World would provide an outlet for the surplus of unemployed who lived unprofitable lives 'oft-times to the disquiet of the better sort'. Certainly England at peace in the early seventeenth century was thought to be overpopulated, with poverty in the cities and land-hunger in the country. There was no shortage of persons willing to undertake plantation estates. Both the Munster and Leix/Offaly plantations were promoted as affording opportunities for the second and younger sons of landed families in England to obtain independent means of support. Indeed, the same argument was propounded by Thomas Smith in 1572 when he was promoting his colony of the Ards in County Down. Perceiving that the surplus of landed gentry and population generally had been exacerbated by the dissolution of the monasteries and abbeys and the associated increase in marriage and birth rates, he shrewdly recognised that younger sons could be persuaded to undertake plantation ventures.[28]

The union of the English and Scottish crowns in 1603 provided a unique opportunity for a plantation venture in Ulster which could be undertaken jointly by both nations. There were many reasons why James had become convinced by

1608 that a plantation in Ulster was both necessary and desirable. Of course, many Irish of the middle and upper social strata remained in Ulster. They would have to be accommodated if rebellion was not to be inevitable, but their estates and numbers could not remain as proportionately high as they had been in Munster, King's County and Queen's County. Besides the obvious trade and profit motives (and the high cost of keeping order in Ireland), there were a great many persons who seemed deserving of estates. A host of unemployed English soldiers, especially those who had served in Ireland, could justifiably claim rewards in land on the precedent of past experiences, as indeed could many English 'servitors' involved in the Irish administration. Among the younger sons and lesser gentry of England and Scotland who were pressing claims for estates abroad, Scottish court servants in particular sought favours in the form of estates in Ulster. The desire for land and self-aggrandisement went right down the social scale. Small farmers could be attracted by bigger and more productive farms, and especially by more secure tenure. Landless labourers could in turn be drawn by the possibility of upward social mobility by obtaining small holdings. For the latter, Ulster provided better alternatives than Virginia, where labourers had either to pay for their own passage or repay their debt through indentured service.

2.6 *Proposals for the official plantation*

Previous plantations in Ireland and abroad had provided the necessary experience to evolve a successful scheme for Ulster, even if the conditions would have to be made more stringent. The official scheme was to evolve almost entirely under the guidance of three English servitors in Ireland, along with King James and his ministers in London. The three leading figures in Ireland were Sir Arthur Chichester (the Lord Deputy), Sir John Davies (the Attorney-General) and Sir James Ley (the Chief Justice). The involvement of the Chief Justice and the Attorney-General in Ireland was significant, for it underlined the importance of replacing Gaelic law by English law in Ulster, and of establishing the king's title to the escheated' lands. After the Flight of the Earls in 1607 Chichester and Davies set out from Dublin in the following spring to survey the confiscated lands and gather evidence to justify their seizure. On the journey north Chichester learned of the O'Doherty revolt near Derry. Finding O'Doherty had died 'in rebellion', the Lord Deputy lost little time in obtaining a grant of the confiscated barony of Inishowen for himself. Later in 1608 Chichester dispatched Sir John Davies and Sir James Ley to London with the completed survey of the escheated lands. At the same time he forwarded certain 'Notes of Remembrance' concerning the plantation.[29] In this document Chichester seems to be a rather more temperate and cautious servitor than his earlier record might have suggested. His notes list many Irish lords and lesser freeholders throughout the escheated counties who had pretended or valid claims to retain their lands. He suggested that Counties Cavan and Fermanagh should be divided in the same manner as Monaghan had been under Elizabeth. Indeed, he noted many freeholders in Cavan, such as Captains Fleming, Tirrell and Tallbott, who were from the Pale and whose claims he suggested should be respected. In general, he felt that the first allocation of lands should be made to servitors and wards of the castles and forts under crown control. Officers who were poor in purse should be placed in the most exposed and dangerous positions. Once these servitors were settled and the favoured natives granted estates, the remainder of the land could then be divided equally. The Irish were to be prevented from migrating around the country with their cattle, were to settle permanently, and build houses 'like those of the Pale'. In contrast, Sir John Davies felt that the plantation would degenerate or be rooted out by the Irish unless the number of 'civil' persons planted exceeded the number of Irish.[30]

By the time Ley and Davies arrived in London King James had become absorbed by the idea of an Ulster plantation. His advisers had fired the monarch with such enthusiasm for the plantation that it had become almost a personal crusade. James decreed that Chichester was to abstain from making any promise of lands. Not a single acre was to be disposed of until all the surveys and certificates of the lands were returned to the council in London. Rumours of King James's personal interest in the project had reached Chichester, and he feared that the king was about to grant immense tracts of land to Scottish noblemen. Chichester had originally envisaged only undertenants coming from Scotland, but on learning of the king's intentions he had to be satisfied in suggesting that only small grants be made and that highland Scots would be excluded from the scheme. He stated that the land should not be granted away by counties to any one man, but that the division should be made amongst many. These portions were to be large enough for the undertakers to be attracted by the scheme, but the principal Irish must also be given grants and favours if they were to remain content.[31]

Many independent schemes and proposals were, of course, being put to the king at the same time. Lord Audley, father-in-law of Sir John Davies, offered to undertake a massive plantation of 100,000 acres covering all of County Tyrone. This would have involved a massive programme of building and plantation. However, the negotiations between the council in London, and Chichester, Ley and Davies in Ireland had already reached a stage where such grandiose schemes were recognised to be impractical. At this time James's Lord Chancellor in London was Sir Francis Bacon. Although Bacon was not to become involved in the plantation himself, he had written at length on the subject. One condition he promoted in his writings was included in the plantation scheme. This was the idea of village settlements: the manor-house on each estate was to draw its tenant farms into villages, and there were only to be a restricted number of corporate towns for settling artificers and tradesmen.[32]

The first tentative project for the official plantation was drawn up by Sir James Ley and Sir John Davies. This was made out for County Tyrone while the other counties were still being surveyed. There were to be several sizes of proportions, and the English and Scots obtaining them would be intermixed. These new settlers would be planted next to the rivers, with the Irish given freeholds on the plains, and servitors on the borders near the Irish. The distribution of the grants was to be by lottery. Under this proposal the number of proportions in Tyrone was estimated to be fifty-nine, besides ecclesiastical lands. Of this total, nine were of 2,000 acres, twelve of 1,500 acres, and thirty-eight of 1,000 acres. The project for Tyrone was soon expanded for the other counties, and a proposal entitled 'Collections of such Orders and Conditions as are to be Observed by the

Undertakers, upon the Distribution and Plantation of the Escheated Lands in Ulster' outlined the major conditions. These conditions formed the basis for the finalised plantation scheme, which was endorsed with several modifications in April 1610. If the 'Orders and Conditions' are compared with the finalised scheme of 1610, or with the intermediate 'Project for the Division and Plantation of the Escheated Lands', it can be seen that only a few alterations had been made in the last year of the scheme's evolution.[33]

2.7 *The finalised scheme*

There were to be three classes of grantees: English and Scottish undertakers (on whom the chief responsibility for the plantation was to fall), servitors (English crown servants in the kingdom of Ireland), and native Irish freeholders.

The principal conditions relating to the undertakers were as follows. The escheated lands of each county were to be divided into 'precincts' (baronies) and each precinct subdivided into three sizes of 'proportions' (estates): great, with 2,000 acres; middle, with 1,500 acres; and small, with 1,000 acres. These proportions were to include such bog and woods as were contained within each grant. Some of the precincts were to contain proportions for English undertakers, and others reserved for proportions allocated to Scots. In each precinct the chief undertaker was allowed 3,000 acres, but no others were to be allowed more than 2,000 acres. Produce could be exported for seven years free of tariffs, and necessary articles could be imported free of tariffs for five years. Timber from the king's woods in Ulster could be cut for building purposes.

In return for their proportions the English and Scottish undertakers had to fulfil the following conditions. Commencing in 1614, a rent of £5 6s 8d for every 1,000 acres was to be paid to the king. Undertakers of 2,000 acres were to build, within three years, a stone house and bawn; undertakers of 1,500 acres, a stone or brick house and bawn; and undertakers of 1,000 acres, a bawn. Within three years undertakers were to plant twenty-four able men of eighteen years or more, being English or 'inland' Scots, on every 1,000 acres. These must represent at least ten families. Of every 1,000 acres granted, 300 acres were to be held in demesne, with a further two fee farmers on 120 acres each, three leaseholders on 100 acres each, and four or more families of husbandmen, artificers or cottagers on the remaining 160 acres. Tenants were to build houses near the bawn for security and the making of townships and villages. Undertakers were to keep a convenient store of arms and take the Oath of Supremacy. The undertenants were also to take the oath and be conformable in religion. Undertakers were to be resident for five years or to have an agent resident. No land was to be demised to any Irish or anyone not taking the Oath of Supremacy. There were to be no uncertain rents.

These proportions were to be distributed either by agreement or let to the undertakers or their representatives before midsummer 1610. The undertakers or their agents were to take possession before Michaelmas 1610. One-third of the tenants were to be planted before 1 November 1611. The bawn and houses for one-third of the tenants were to be erected before 1 November 1610, and the remainder of the tenants' houses were to be completed within a further year. Each undertaker's stone house was to be finished within three years. All the articles concerning building, planting, residence and alienation of land were to be fulfilled within five years on a forfeit of £200 per 1,000 acres grant.

The servitors were to receive proportions on the same conditions as the undertakers, but with the following exceptions. They were to pay, after two years, a yearly rent of £8 per 1,000 acres if their tenants were Irish, or £5 6s 8d per 1,000 acres if the tenants were British. Their land could be let to Irish or British tenants, as there was no requirement to plant.

The Irish grantees were to observe the same conditions as the servitors, with the following exceptions. They were to pay, after one year, a yearly rent of £10 13s 4d per 1,000 acres and were to use tillage and husbandry after the manner of the English Pale.

Servitors and Irish were to receive their grants within the same precincts.

In each county there were to be market towns and corporations erected for the settling of tradesmen and artificers, with at least one free school in each county. There was to be a parish church erected within each parish, and one townland was to be set aside as glebe for every 1,000 acres granted.

Although these were the conditions under which the grantees

received their proportions, further alterations were made during the progress of the plantation. The most important of these adjustments related to the alienation of undertakers' land to Irish tenants. In 1622 Irish were permitted to become tenants on one-quarter of the undertakers' proportions. In fact, as the building and plantation programme had got under way very slowly, the stringent time periods allowed for completion had also to be relaxed.

3

Division and Allocation of the Land

3.1 *The area involved*

By choosing exile in 1607 the Earls of Tyrone and Tyrconnell were presumed guilty of treason. While they were accompanied by a great number of followers, most of the Gaelic lords in west Ulster stayed behind. Those who remained hoped that they could retain their own lands, or at least that they would be favourably considered in any regrants made. In fact the flight of Hugh O'Neill provided an eagerly awaited opportunity for James's government to confiscate or 'escheat' all the temporal lands of County Tyrone. Similarly, the lordship of Rory O'Donnell (Earl of Tyrconnell) fell to the crown, an area comprising most of County Donegal with the exception of Inishowen. The other large area escheated as a direct result of the flight was part of County Fermanagh. This had been held by Cuconnaught Maguire, the third most important Gaelic lord to choose exile. The remaining three baronies of Fermanagh were held by Cuconnaught's cousin, Connor Roe Maguire, but this area was soon afterwards surrendered to the crown by Connor Roe in expectation of a regrant. Just as this remaining part of Fermanagh had become escheated, so many other tracts of Armagh, Coleraine and Donegal were surrendered or confiscated. In Armagh the barony and city of Armagh were claimed by the archbishop. Oneilland barony in north Armagh had been forfeited after the flight, since it had been controlled by Hugh O'Neill. Soon afterwards the remaining Armagh baronies of Orior, the Fews and Tiranny were also confiscated or surrendered. Tiranny had been controlled by Sir Henry Óg O'Neill, who was killed in 1608 while fighting on the English side against O'Doherty. It was to Henry Óg's family therefore that Tiranny was eventually regranted. The Fews and Orior, which had been in the hands of Sir Turlough McHenry O'Neill and Sir Oghy O'Hanlon respectively, were reclaimed by the crown on the pretext that the almost forgotten Elizabethan grant to Captain Chatterton had never been revoked. However, Sir Turlough McHenry was to obtain a regrant of about half of his territory of the Fews.

When Sir Cahir O'Doherty rebelled and was slain near Derry in 1608 the only areas of west Ulster not at the disposal of the crown were the counties of Coleraine and Monaghan. With the seizure and imprisonment of Sir Donnell Ballagh O'Cahan, who was suspected of being implicated in O'Doherty's revolt, even County Coleraine could be added to the enormous escheated area available for plantation. By 1609 most of west Ulster was at James's disposal for the second time in a decade. Now, however, plantation rather than regrant was to be the design. But large areas of Ulster were excluded from the plantation scheme, most notably Counties Antrim, Down and Monaghan, where regrants or unofficial plantations had already taken place. In addition, vast tracts of land which had traditionally yielded rents and duties to the church were being claimed by the Protestant bishops. Nevertheless, virtually all of the rest of Ulster was now escheated and available for plantation. Surveys and inquisitions were necessary to distinguish church and temporal lands, and to facilitate the allocation of grants to the various recipients. Vested interests which would have to be considered included some British who already held lands in the escheated territory, and, of course, the many Irish lords and lesser chiefs who were expecting considerable regrants.

3.2 *The land surveys*

The vast areas of escheated land in west Ulster had not been previously mapped with any degree of accuracy. In fact the crown had obtained such unknown quantities of land that no division could be made until its extent was known in greater detail. The precedent of the Munster plantation had shown that a measured survey was impractical, even though lands around Carrickfergus had been parcelled out in measured strips in 1595, 1601 and 1603.[1] These divisions around Carrickfergus were on a much smaller scale and were facilitated by a uniformly sloping coastal topography, with strips running alongside each other inland from the coast. Such measurement and division throughout six of Ulster's counties would have been an almost impossible task, and such an exercise would have done little to distinguish the intermixed ecclesiastical and temporal land. Accordingly, a decision was taken not to measure the escheated lands 'to avoid His Majesty's further charge', but to conduct a survey which would enumerate the traditional local land divisions.

This first survey was conducted in 1608 by a commission sitting in Dungannon which included Sir Thomas Ridgeway, Vice-Treasurer in Ireland; Sir Oliver St John, Master of the Ordnance; Sir John Davies, Attorney-General; and Sir William Parsons, Surveyor-General.[2] Examining by inquisition each county in turn, they listed the temporal and ecclesiastical lands for each barony, not in acres but in ballybetaghs and the smaller townland units of ballyboes, tates and polls. Information was also collected on markets, fairs and 'fishings'. The townlands were to have the same bounds and quantities as were 'known, set out and used' at the time of the departure of the earls. So that grants could be made in acres, generally accepted size equivalents were applied. The ballyboe was taken to contain sixty acres of profitable land, except in some parts of Armagh where it was assumed to contain 100 or in Orior barony 120 acres. The 'quarter' in Donegal was of such a varied character that the totals were expressed in acres, these figures having been arrived at by an assumption that the quarter contained either 128, 160, 180, 220 or 240 acres of profitable land. The polls of Cavan were taken by the survey to contain only twenty-four acres, and the tates of Fermanagh thirty acres. Elsewhere the contemporary estimates found the polls to contain fifty acres, and the tates sixty acres. These estimations were applied to townlands which in fact varied enormously in size but whose average area was about 360 acres (approximately six times the estimated area). However, by assuming a fixed area, ballybetaghs of sixteen townlands could be taken to contain approximately 1,000 acres — the intended size of the smallest plantation estate. The 1608 survey then provided a list of the main ballybetaghs and other similar land units in each barony. Against each ballybetagh was entered the exact number of ballyboes, polls or tates that it contained. This meant that ecclesiastical land could be distinguished from lay or temporal land, the total area of land escheated could be assessed, and a scheme could be devised for the theoretical division of the temporal land among the different types of grantees. However, in practical terms the survey was inadequate for the purpose of making out grants of land. Besides omitting certain lands, it was only the number of ballyboes in each ballybetagh which was recorded, and not individual townland names, so that the identification of these areas remained imprecise. Even where grants of 2,000 acres would require the amalgamation of several ballybetaghs, the survey did not indicate which ballybetaghs were adjacent. Before grants could be made out a new and more detailed survey of the entire escheated area was needed.

A second survey, this one consisting of maps which showed and named each townland, was prepared under the direction of Sir Josias Bodley in 1609.[3] Colours and symbols were used to distinguish church from temporal land and to indicate groupings of townlands into ballybetaghs or intended plantation estates. These maps were prepared for each barony of the escheated counties by inquisition rather than by mensuration. Consequently the shapes of the townlands and the baronies as a whole were unreliable. However, care was taken to map the correct relationship of adjacent ballyboes. The earlier survey of 1608 had enabled an overall scheme to be evolved, while the second survey of 1609 provided the detailed information on local land units necessary for completion of land-grant documents.

3.3 *Church land*

The 1608 survey found that the six escheated counties contained 1,126 townlands or almost 75,000 acres of ecclesiastical land. This was composed of 794 townlands (48,158 acres) of termon and erenagh land, 92 townlands (9,240 acres) of mensal or bishops' demesne land, and 240 townlands (17,454 acres) of abbey, monastery, priory and friary lands (already in the king's possession through the Statute of Dissolution). The distribution of church land was not uniform, for while in Tyrone it amounted to almost one-quarter of the total county, in Cavan the proportion was less than one-tenth (Appendix 1).[4]

The greatest extent of church lands were termon or erenagh lands. These traditionally yielded duties and rents to the church, with erenaghs or sept leaders holding their territories under the bishop. For all plantation purposes termon and erenagh lands were regarded as the same, although termon lands had traditionally enjoyed privileges such as the right of sanctuary. The ownership of the extensive termon and erenagh lands became the subject of a considerable dispute. They were claimed by the Protestant bishops in addition to the mensal lands which had been the demesnes of the pre-Reformation bishops. In 1609 a number of jurors were appointed to examine the ownership of the termon lands. They found that the Gaelic lords had given these lands to the founders of the churches, who had in turn left them in the hands of several septs, who paid certain rents and tithes to the church. These septs had occupied the bishops' lands from time immemorial, and although the temporal lords received no rents from them, nevertheless the lands were found to be escheated to the king as they were not held by the bishops in demesne.[5] It was, however, eventually decided that the termon and erenagh lands should be granted in their entirety to the Protestant bishops.

Termon lands were dispersed throughout the dioceses and were claimed by the appropriate bishop for each diocese. There were five dioceses covering the escheated counties: Armagh, Clogher, Derry, Raphoe and Kilmore. In 1608 the three dioceses of Clogher, Derry and Raphoe were held by George Montgomery, Kilmore was held by Robert Draper, and Armagh by Henry Ussher. In 1610 Montgomery resigned the sees of Derry and Raphoe, in which he was replaced by Bruite Babington and Andrew Knox respectively.[6] Although absent in England for much of the period, Montgomery used his time there with good effect to press the bishops' claims to the termon lands. The diocese of Armagh extended beyond the county of Armagh to include the barony of Dungannon and part of Loughinsholin in Tyrone, so that the termon lands scattered throughout east Tyrone fell to Primate Ussher. The diocese of Clogher extended beyond Clogher barony in Tyrone to cover most of Fermanagh, Monaghan, and a small portion of south Donegal. Kilmore diocese was approximately coextensive with County Cavan, and Derry extended beyond County Coleraine into north Donegal to include Inishowen. The distribution of the termon lands throughout the dioceses was recorded in the mapped 1609 survey and again in the Civil Survey of 1654 for Counties Londonderry, Tyrone and Donegal.[7] In some areas the termon lands were very extensive, such as the large expanses of upland known as Termonamongan and Termonmagurk in Omagh barony which fell to the Bishops of Derry and Armagh respectively. Elsewhere the termon lands were fragmented, although the bishops' demesne or mensal lands were not so widely dispersed. In fact most mensal lands were located adjacent to the individual bishops' seats, so that almost all of this type of land was situated in three counties: Donegal (within which lay the seats of the Bishops of Derry and Raphoe), Tyrone (Clogher), and Armagh (Appendix 1). Monastery and abbey land was allocated in various ways. Much had previously been granted in freehold to soldier settlers before the plantation, some had been used to provide small estates for captains in charge of nearby military forts, and much was to be granted to the bishops. In addition to the termon, abbey and mensal lands of the bishops (now to be held by them in demesne) there were to be sixty acres of glebe in every plantation estate of 1,000 acres. Glebe townlands were to be assigned to the incumbent of each parish.

The vast territories granted to the bishops were intermixed with temporal land in almost every barony. Clearly if only Irish were to occupy these lands, they would prove a great hindrance to the plantation. Consequently George Montgomery, the powerful Bishop of Derry, Raphoe and Clogher, was delegated by his episcopal colleagues to confer with the commissioners on the feasibility of settling Britons on the bishops' land. The result of these negotiations was that the termon lands were to be planted with Britons at one-third of the rate required by the undertakers.[8] This meant that instead of ten British families required on every 1,000 acres, five families were to be settled on each 1,500 acres. Irish could, however, still obtain tenancies on church land, and in the later surveys which were made to inquire into the extent of British settlement no inquiry was made of the bishops' plantations. In fact the grants were much too extensive for the bishops to plant unaided by agents. It was necessary for them to let the lands in fairly large estates with conditions of plantation delegated to the lessees. The Archbishop of Armagh's land in Dungannon barony, which amounted to over

6,000 acres, was leased to only ten English Protestants. In one lease of sixteen ballyboes or 1,000 acres in 1614 the Primate required Sir Arthur Chichester to build four English houses of stone, brick or framed timber within five years and to settle in them four English families, while in a similar lease of twenty-eight ballyboes Sir Francis Roe was to build seven English houses and plant seven English families.[9] Many servitors and undertakers acquired church lands adjacent to their estates, and so the area opened up for potential settlement by incoming British farmers was greatly expanded.

3.4 *Servitors*

There were three types of individuals who could qualify for grants as servitors in Ulster: councillors of state, captains or lieutenants with military commands in Ulster, and English freeholders who already held estates in the escheated counties. Almost all servitors were paid officials of the state who had seen military service in Ireland, but the most important individuals in this group were the councillors of state. These councillors were leading figures in the English administration in Ireland, such as the Lord Deputy, Sir Arthur Chichester, who alone was permitted to obtain up to 3,000 acres. In fact his grant of Dungannon in the barony of the same name consisted of only 1,320 acres. Although this appeared to be a moderate acquisition, it should be remembered that in 1608 Chichester had been granted the entire barony of Inishowen after O'Doherty's revolt. In addition, Chichester also held extensive lands in south-east Antrim around Belfast and Carrickfergus. But the size of his Dungannon grant was compensated for in other ways. Dungannon's strategic importance was obvious as it was the former seat of Hugh O'Neill, but the 1,320 acres around the castle under Chichester's control was quickly expanded. A corporate town was to be established, to support which Chichester received 500 acres adjacent to the town. In addition, he obtained a lease of 960 acres of adjacent church land from the Archbishop of Armagh (and his principal tenants leased another 750 acres of the same). The free school to be established at Dungannon provided yet another 700 acres, so that in total some 4,230 acres around Dungannon was to be controlled by Chichester and a few of his local freeholders. The other councillors of state, such as Lord Audley, Sir Thomas Ridgeway (Treasurer), Sir Richard Wingfield (Marshal), Sir John Davies (Attorney-General), Sir William Parsons (Surveyor) and Thomas Jones (Lord Chancellor), could each receive no more than 2,000 acres each. Only councillors of state could obtain undertaker estates as well, an option which was taken up by most, with the notable exception of the Lord Deputy. In Dungannon barony, where Chichester had selected his own portion, several other councillors also had obtained estates: Sir Thomas Ridgeway and Sir Richard Wingfield each received 2,000 acres, while Sir William Parsons obtained 1,000 acres. Both Ridgeway and Parsons had also obtained undertaker estates in Clogher barony. Lord Audley and his son-in-law, Sir John Davies, took out estates as undertakers in Omagh barony as well as their servitor estates in Armagh and Fermanagh. The Lord Deputy's youngest brother, Sir Thomas Chichester, obtained a small servitor estate of 500 acres in Kilmacrenan barony, and Sir Thomas Ridgeway's brother George obtained a small undertaker estate in Clogher barony.

The early recommendations concerning the lands to be given to servitors had suggested that they should be mixed with those of the Irish grantees in baronies on the plains. The servitors' proportions should lie along the border of these baronies for the security of the neighbouring undertakers. Chichester felt that the poorer captains and officers who had served in Ulster should be placed in the positions of most danger. Although servitors were only required to build on their estates and not to plant with Britons, their estates were not simply rewards for service. Their role was intended to be strategic; clearly they were best suited to dwell among the Irish grantees and oversee them.

In all, nine baronies in the escheated counties were set aside for servitors and native Irish grantees. In Armagh Orior barony was reserved, in Tyrone Dungannon barony, and in Donegal the barony of Doe and Fanad (Kilmacrenan). Four baronies were set aside for servitors and natives in Cavan: Tullyhaw, Clanmahon, Tullygarvey and Castlerahan; and two in Fermanagh: Clanawley and the barony of Coole and Tirkennedy. In the projected county of Londonderry no distinct barony was reserved, but Sir Thomas Phillips obtained some 3,000 acres around Limavady and Castledawson. This substantial grant among the London companies' lands was partly in lieu of the surrender of his interests around Coleraine, and partly through his continued wardship of the fort at Toome. A list of the servitors and their estates throughout the plantation is given in Appendix 2.[10]

The men in command of the forts and garrisons across west Ulster often received grants of adjacent land as servitors, even when such forts were in baronies set aside for undertakers. In Omagh barony Captain Edmund Leigh was the custodian of Omagh fort in 1608 when the adjacent abbey lands of Omagh had already been granted to him. The custody of the fort was transferred in 1609 to John Leigh, who with his brother Daniel obtained an adjacent grant of 330 acres as a servitor. Other fort lands were granted as servitor proportions to the men in military charge. Sir Francis Roe was constable of Mountjoy Fort in Tyrone, and Henry Adderton was constable of Mountnorris in Armagh, for which they each obtained estates of 300 acres. Elsewhere the custodians of forts or other Englishmen who had already obtained freeholds or developed sites in the escheated area were granted servitor estates in the appropriately reserved baronies. Sir Henry Folliott, who had held 1,000 acres around Ballyshannon and Donegal town, was granted a servitor estate of 1,500 acres in Fermanagh. Sir Richard Hansard, who had invested and built around his military charge at Lifford, and Captain Henry Hart, who had held custody of Culmore Fort from 1604 to 1609, were each granted estates in Kilmacrenan. Two other freeholders in north Donegal (Sir Ralph Bingley, who had held over 1,000 acres in Inishowen, and Basil Brooke, whose freehold was of former abbey land) also obtained servitor estates in Kilmacrenan.

In Cavan the proportion of the county allocated to servitors and natives was much greater than elsewhere. Four of the seven baronies in the county were reserved in this manner, and the Cavan servitors were granted a total of 19,050 acres, or just over one-third of all the servitors' lands throughout the escheated counties. This high proportion of land (where plantation was not required) was to prove an important factor in the distribution of plantation settlement. Indeed, many of the Cavan servitors turned out to be either English 'recusants' or Palesmen who were Roman Catholic. In his 'Notes of Remembrance' in

1608 Chichester had recorded that there were many freeholders in the county.[11] Among these were Captain Garrett Fleming, Captain Richard Tirrell and Walter Talbott, whose purchases of lands from the Irish were to 'be respected'. Tirrell was granted a servitor's estate of 2,000 acres in Tullygarvey barony, Talbott obtained a joint estate with Hugh Culme of 1,500 acres in Tullyhaw barony, and Fleming (Lord Slane) retained his extensive lands in the undertakers' barony of Clankee. These servitors were all recorded in the Cromwellian Book of Survey and Distribution as 'recusants' or 'Irish Papists', as were many others in the county, such as Lawrence Dowdall and Luke Plunkett (Earl of Fingall), who had purchased servitor estates from the original grantees.[12]

3.5 *Irish grantees*

One aspect of the plantation which particularly concerned Chichester was the allocation of land to the Irish. It was largely as a result of his representation that they were not to be scattered among the undertakers as in the Munster plantation. Instead they were to be given freeholds in baronies reserved for servitors and Irish. Chichester also felt that the commissioners were not realistic in only providing for a small number of Irish, although by 1609 he agreed that only the principal septs controlled more than a ballybetagh (1,000 acres) and that most of the lesser sept leaders would be content with two or three ballyboes. The allocation of land to the Irish involved grants of estates to the principal Gaelic lords of approximately the same size as the grants made to servitors and undertakers. The broad mass of sept leaders who had previously held ballybetaghs under the Gaelic order were given one or two ballyboes each in freehold. A total of 280 Irish obtained plantation land grants in the escheated counties, but of these only twenty-six were provided with estates of 1,000 acres or more. A list of these major Irish grantees is given in Appendix 3,[13] while a summary of all the crown grants to individuals of the different clans is provided in Appendix 4.[14]

In 1610 the Lord Deputy and commissioners were instructed to allocate land to the Irish so that the area distributed would amount to 58,000 acres or thereabouts.[15] It seems from Appendix 4 that this calculation related only to large grants intended for the greater Gaelic lords. A further 37,000 acres were to be granted in smaller lots to several hundred lesser Irish lords and sept leaders. This inclusion of many middle-ranking Ulster Irish was recognised as a very necessary expedient by Chichester, who particularly stressed the expectations of the Irish 'freeholders' in Cavan. The baronies in which these Irish grantees obtained their lands were, of course, the same as those listed for the servitors, but with several important additions. There were a few Gaelic lords whose claims for regrants were sufficiently strong to enable them to retain most of their original territories. Sir Turlough McHenry O'Neill achieved the largest individual grant of all when he was reallocated 9,900 acres of the Fews in south Armagh. The remainder of this barony was intended for Scottish undertakers. Similar exceptions were made for two other Gaelic lords, Connor Roe Maguire and Sir Henry Óg O'Neill. Connor Roe Maguire had surrendered his half of Fermanagh following the escheatment of the remainder of the county on the flight of his cousin, Cuconnaught Maguire. However, instead of being regranted three complete baronies as he had hoped, Connor Roe had to be content with most of Magherastephana barony. Sir Henry Óg O'Neill had died in the English service during O'Doherty's revolt in 1608, and his family had therefore a strong claim to his territories, which covered Tiranny barony in Armagh and part of Dungannon barony in Tyrone. Consequently they were granted to Sir Henry's kin.

When the names of the clans obtaining the most land are considered, it is clear that the dominance of the O'Neills was well established, for they obtained about one-third of all the land allocated to Irish. Only the O'Reillys of Cavan, the Maguires of Fermanagh, the O'Cahans of Coleraine and the McSweeneys of Donegal were also to obtain large grants. Most clans received land within the same county that they had earlier occupied, albeit in the reserved servitors' and natives' barony. The apparent dominance of O'Neills in the grants did not mean, however, that Hugh O'Neill's authority had been simply transmitted to his immediate successors. Instead many of the O'Neills who had obtained large grants were of related, but competitive, septs from Armagh and Tyrone. Rory O'Donnell's flight ended the dominance of the O'Donnells in Tyrconnell, and it was the McSweeneys and O'Boyles who were to be the chief beneficiaries in Donegal.

The area granted to native Irish was 94,013 acres, or some 20 per cent of the escheated territory, much more than the total granted to the servitors with whom they were supposed to share baronies. Of course, this was not the total area which Irish tenants could occupy. Under the terms of the plantation Irish tenants could obtain leases on any freehold land granted to Irish and also on servitors' lands, church land and school, college or corporation lands. In fact only the lands granted to undertakers and the London companies were intended to be exclusively settled by British tenants.

The regranting of almost one-quarter of the escheated lands to Irish grantees was somewhat tempered by the fact that several tracts were only to be held for the grantees' lives. Thus Art McBaron O'Neill's estate of 2,000 acres in Orior was to pass to Lord Audley on the death of Art and his wife. However, in due course the importance of this was by-passed by events surrounding the 1641 rebellion and the subsequent confiscation of virtually all Irish freehold land by the crown.

3.6 *English undertakers*

Seven baronies were set aside for English men of means who would undertake to build defensive structures and plant British settlers in return for estates of 1,000, 1,500 or 2,000 acres. The fertile barony of Oneilland in north Armagh was the area most coveted by the applicants. This barony was reserved for English undertakers, and the other six baronies similarly allocated were Lifford in Donegal, Loughtee in Cavan, Clogher and Omagh in Tyrone, and Clankelly and the barony of Lurg and Coolemakernan in Fermanagh. In the temporal lands of these seven baronies a total of fifty-one estates or 'plantation proportions' were granted. The list of these estates contained in Appendix 5[16] shows that two were of 3,000 acres (only the principal undertaker in each barony was allowed an estate of this size); twenty-one estates were of 2,000 acres; eleven of 1,500 acres; and seventeen of 1,000 acres. These fifty-one estates involved a total area which was estimated to be 81,500 acres.

By 1609 lists of applicants for the estates had been drawn up in England.[17] Groups of applicants, often from one region, were arranged in consorts under a leading man of rank. Details of wealth and annual incomes were provided as an indication of their ability to finance their undertakings. Most of these applicants were men of moderate means, with an average annual income in the region of £200. Only a minority were peers of the realm. However, not all the individuals who received undertakers' estates in Ulster were to be found among these lists of applicants. Fourteen estates were granted to men already involved in Ireland as servitors, or to their kin. Indeed, six English undertakers' estates were granted to men who had also obtained proportions as servitors in other baronies. Those applicants who received grants did not necessarily remain grouped in the consorts that they had originally appeared in. Nevertheless, there was often some connection between the grantees in each barony. For example, all the grantees in Lurg and Coolemakernan barony were from Norfolk or Suffolk, while in Omagh barony the grantees consisted of George Tuchet (Lord Audley), two of his sons, and two sons-in-law. By 1619 all but one of the undertakers' estates in Omagh barony were owned by Audley's son and heir, the Earl of Castlehaven. The other proportion belonged to Sir John Davies, Castlehaven's brother-in-law.

In 1609 Lord Audley had proposed to the plantation commission that he would undertake 100,000 acres of County Tyrone in an elaborate plan to establish thirty-three estates with a castle, town and thirty families in each.[18] This proposal was clearly beyond Lord Audley's means, but it must have impressed the commissioners, for his consort acquired four estates in Omagh barony amounting to 9,000 acres, along with his grant as a servitor in Armagh, and the reversion of 2,000 acres in Orior which were only to be held by Art McBaron O'Neill for life.

Several of the leading servitors who extended their influence beyond small servitors' estates in Ulster were of the Elizabethan tradition of West Country adventurers. Both Chichester and Ridgeway were, for example, from Devon. Yet the new English undertakers coming to Ulster were from East Anglia and the Midlands rather than the West Country. The counties of origin are known for twenty-seven of the thirty-seven grantees who had no previous Irish connections. More than half came from East Anglia (eight from Norfolk, five from Suffolk, and one from Cambridgeshire). A further seven came from the Midlands (three from Staffordshire, two from Nottinghamshire, one from Leicestershire, and one from Shropshire). The other six whose origins are known all came from miscellaneous southern counties. It would be wrong, however, to suggest that the links between the undertakers' estates and their home localities in England were anything other than tentative. Not only were many of them already resident in Ireland as servants of the crown, but the rate of turnover in plantation estate ownership was high. By 1619 only twenty-nine of the fifty-one estates remained in the hands of the original grantees. Thirteen of the estates which changed ownership were acquired by individuals who had not been original grantees elsewhere in Ulster.

3.7 *Scottish undertakers*

Compared with the English undertakers, the Scots appeared to have received more land, for they had obtained fifty-nine estates throughout nine baronies. However, the average size of the Scottish-owned estates was smaller. Five chief undertakers obtained 3,000-acre estates, while the other estates were composed of seven of 2,000 acres, ten of 1,500 acres, and no less than thirty-seven of the smallest size, 1,000 acres. In total the Scots were granted 81,000 acres, marginally less than the 81,500 acres granted to English undertakers. Most of the nine baronies set aside for Scottish undertakers were around the periphery of the escheated counties. The Scottish baronies were Portlough, Boylagh and Banagh (in Donegal), Mountjoy, Strabane (in Tyrone), Knockninny, Magherabov (in Fermanagh), Clankee, Tullyhunco (in Cavan), and the Fews (in Armagh) (Appendix 6).[19]

The fact that so many of the Scottish estates were of the smallest size reflects the lower income of most Scottish undertakers. Although some of the chief undertakers were extremely wealthy, the average income of the ordinary Scottish undertakers was probably less than £150 per annum.[20] The 1609 lists of Scottish applicants did not provide any indication of individual wealth, but anyway only eighteen out of almost eighty original applicants actually obtained estates. James used his influence to persuade several of the most influential Scottish noblemen to become chief undertakers. In his final selection it became clear that many wealthy townsmen were rejected in favour of middle-ranking Scottish lairds with experience in handling landed estates. Besides the nine chief undertakers who were all titled, eleven of the ordinary undertakers were also knights of the realm.

The vast majority of the Scottish undertakers came from the central lowland belt, especially the Edinburgh/Haddington area in the east and the Renfrew/north Ayrshire area in the west. Apart from a few undertakers from the east coast of Scotland north of Fife, the only other area from which significant numbers were drawn was the extreme south-west of the country between Dumfries and Portpatrick.[21] Once again, any assumption that these source areas indicate regions which were to influence the course of later plantation settlement cannot be accepted. As with the English undertakers, many Scots had sold their patents even before viewing their lands in Ulster. By 1619 thirty-three of the fifty-nine Scottish undertakers' estates had changed ownership. However, in this rapid turnover only a small fraction of the Scottish estates were acquired by English.

3.8 *London companies*

Joint-stock companies such as the Virginia Company or the East India Company had been set up to involve the considerable wealth of the London merchants and guilds in colonising schemes before 1610.[22] As lists of English and Scottish undertakers were being prepared it became clear that the involvement of the London companies could ensure the success of the Ulster plantation. While Scottish merchants were rejected as undertakers in favour of lairds with experience in handling landed estates, the wealth of the city of London had to be harnessed if the costly task of developing the towns of Derry and Coleraine was to be successful. The London companies were to obtain a region in the escheated territory with the highest potential for commercial development.

In 1610, following negotiations aimed at securing the city's involvement, a corporate body of London aldermen, merchants and representatives of companies was created. This body was to be called 'The Society of the Governor and Assistants, London, of the New Plantation in Ulster, within the Realm of Ireland'. It was not until the late seventeenth century that this body became known as the 'Irish Society', although this term is convenient to use here. This early Irish Society was to be the governing body of a joint-stock company formed for the specific purpose of the Ulster plantation. The membership comprised a court which was to meet at the Guildhall in London with a governor, deputy governor and twenty-four assistants who would represent a cross-section of the city's interest.[23] John Rowley and Tristram Beresford were appointed by the society as its agents in Ulster, and they set about the task of reconstructing Derry and Coleraine. The city of Londonderry was to have 4,000 acres reserved on the Donegal side of the Foyle, and Coleraine to have 3,000 acres on the Antrim side of the Bann. These 'Liberties' of Londonderry and Coleraine were the only lands in the county to be governed directly by the society. The remainder of the county was to be divided into estates and allocated to specific London companies, allowing, of course, for church land, Irish freehold land, and for certain lands granted to Sir Thomas Phillips. The new county of Londonderry consisted of what had been O'Cahan's country (County Coleraine), but was also to include the Liberties of Coleraine and Londonderry across the Bann and Foyle respectively, and the barony of Loughinsholin which had formerly been regarded as part of County Tyrone.

A levy was imposed on fifty-five London companies to provide some of the finance necessary for the venture. By 1611 only eighteen of these companies had indicated that they would be willing to accept land, but before any land could be allocated, several private interests in the county had to be settled.[24] A number of English men had already built and settled around the garrisons of Coleraine and Derry. Their interests were to be bought out, but at Coleraine the investment by Sir Thomas Phillips had been so substantial that he was to be offered extensive estates in the heart of the county as a servitor. The allocation of the county land to the individual companies did not proceed until 1613 when the report of two commissioners sent from London was made.[25] These men, George Smith and Matthias Springham, found that the society's agents had spent a great deal of money with little to show for it. Smith and Springham divided the county into twelve proportions, and the fifty-five companies who had financed the undertaking were grouped into twelve consorts, each led by one of the twelve principal London companies. Very few of the lesser companies retained any interest in the plantation, and in practice it was the twelve leading companies which were to be responsible for the twelve proportions. Each company received 3⅓ ballybetaghs of land, or an estimated 3,210 acres (at the rate of sixty acres to a ballyboe and sixteen ballyboes to a ballybetagh). Some of the estates were rather fragmentary, but their size was about twice that of most of the undertakers' estates elsewhere. Although the London companies were obliged to build and plant their estates on terms equivalent to the undertakers', their plantations were not typical of the other counties. The larger estates and the exploitation of the companies' resources by many of their agents meant that only in County Londonderry did the 'characteristic' plantation village around a bawn become ubiquitous. Even in terms of the time scale involved in plantation, building work had been progressing on many undertakers' estates for two or three years by the time most London companies first sent representatives over to view their newly acquired estates in 1614. A list of the estates granted to the London companies is given in Appendix 7.[26]

3.9 *Other lands allocated as college, school, town and fort land*

Certain tracts of fort land were regranted as servitors' estates for the custodians of the military garrisons. These men were, by definition, servitors. However, some of the forts were intended to be the sites of corporate towns. Where grants of fort land had been made to the constables of these particular garrisons, their land was frequently retained in lieu of corporation land.

The plantation scheme included proposals for a corporate town to be erected in almost every barony and a free school in each county. Of twenty-seven such towns proposed between 1609 and 1611, only sixteen were incorporated during James's reign. Land was to be allocated to each town to provide burgess and common land for the townsmen. Rents from the remainder would help finance the urban development and building programme. In most cases the principal servitor or undertaker in each barony was the recipient of the crown grant of these corporation lands. The 300 or 400 acres they each received was usually adjacent to the proposed town. Two towns were to have special charters; they were to be incorporated at an early stage and to enjoy enormous tracts of land. These were the Irish

Society undertakings at Derry (becoming Londonderry) and Coleraine, which were to have 4,000 and 3,000 acres respectively.[27] Of the proposed towns listed in Appendix 8[28] which succeeded in gaining incorporation, only Strabane, Armagh and Limavady had no land granted for their support. Another anomaly was the allocation of 250 acres to the proposed town of Virginia in Cavan with no associated incorporation following. The remainder of the corporate towns had land set to them in one of two ways. Firstly there were those which were granted corporation land in the manner originally envisaged in the plantation project. Secondly there were towns which were to be sited at military forts, such as Omagh, Mountjoy, Charlemont, Mountnorris and Ballyshannon. These garrisons each had associated 'fort' land granted to their wardens. It seemed that these grants were not intended to be just small servitors' estates, but somehow the fort land was to serve in place of corporation land. Indeed, in 1610 many of these parcels of land were being described as 'fort and town' land.[29] Excluding the 7,000 acres granted to the Irish Society for the Liberties of Londonderry and Coleraine, 3,318 acres were allocated as corporation land and a further 2,230 acres as fort land where the forts were intended to become corporate towns.

In each county a free school was intended for the education of the second-generation colonists (Appendix 9).[30] Only in Londonderry, where a school was built in 1617, does no crown grant of land appear to have been made.[31] Elsewhere a total of 2,645 acres was set out to support the schools and schoolmasters, even though only a few school buildings were actually constructed before the reign of Charles I. In the early years of the plantation a servitor or undertaker normally received a crown grant of these school lands. Sir Arthur Chichester ensured that the Tyrone 'royal' school intended for Mountjoy was build at his town of Dungannon. In Fermanagh Lord Burley secured (at least temporarily) the lands intended for a proposed school at Enniskillen or Lisgoole. His school was built at Lisnaskea, and it was not until 1643 that the Fermanagh royal school was transferred to Enniskillen. Ownership of all the school lands was transferred in 1626 from individual landlords to the Lord Primate of Armagh.[32] This established church control of the schools and of the appointment of schoolmasters.

In Dublin the Irish post-Reformation university had been functioning long before the 1610, but it was to benefit substantially from the Ulster plantation. Trinity College, Dublin, was to be granted very extensive estates in Armagh barony amounting to 6,000 acres. In Tirhugh barony, County Donegal, the college land amounted to 4,000 acres; and there was a further 2,400 acres in Clankelly barony, County Fermanagh.[33] In total this 12,400 acres of college land, added to 2,645 acres of school land and 12,548 acres of fort and corporation land, made no less than 27,593 acres allocated to the 'minor' grantee classes.

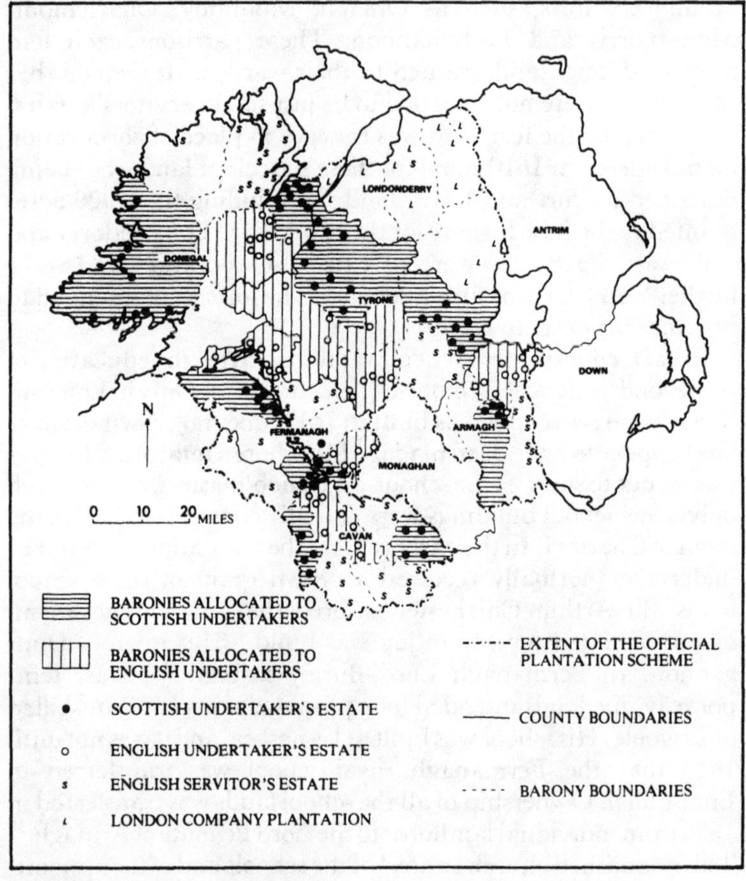

Map 5: *The official allocation of plantation lands in Ulster, c. 1610*[34]

3.10 *The area and quality of the plantation grants*
Patents for plantation land grants were made out by listing the Irish territorial denominations to be included, rather than by defining boundaries. In this way the ballyboes and their Irish names were given legal status and became fossilized as townlands. The estimated area was obtained by multiplying the number of townlands in the patent by the estimated townland area. To the plantation commissioners most ballyboes contained only sixty acres of profitable land, although in Armagh some were taken to extend to 100 and 120 acres, and the polls and tates of Cavan and Fermanagh were sometimes thought to be smaller than sixty acres. In total the area indicated in the plantation grants by this means of assessment was 459,110 acres. However, the real extent of the six escheated counties was 3,690,714 statute acres. These six counties contain over 11,000 modern townlands, giving an average townland size of 330 acres, so that the actual size of an Ulster townland was approximately five or six times the area estimated by the plantation commissioners.

It has been possible to identify positively 64 per cent of all modern townlands with ballyboes, polls or tates allocated in the plantation. Although many plantation estates were found to include townlands not mentioned in the patents, it was not the 'containments' that led to discrepancies between the actual and estimated areas. Rather this was because of an underestimation of the size of the ballyboe, and a misinterpretation of its nature. The ease by which modern townlands can be identified in plantation grants is not consistent throughout Ulster. Hardly more than 50 per cent of modern townlands can be identified in Fermanagh and Donegal, while in Tyrone the rate is in excess of 80 per cent. Many of the unidentified townlands are in very poor mountainous areas, largely uninhabited during the plantation period, or are scattered townlands in the lowlands where modern names have replaced the earlier Irish ones.

The general pattern of land allocation is indicated in Map 5, while in Table 1 the areas allocated to each class of plantation grantee may be compared. Discrepancies in actual size between estates of the same nominal area may be explained largely by the inverse relationship of townland size to land quality. The poore the land, the larger the ballyboes, for they were economic ur

Table 1: *Areas granted to the different grantee classes*

Grantee class	Area indicated in plantation grants		Identified modern townlands		
	Acres	%	Townlands	%	Statute acres
English undertakers	81,500	18	1,267	17	418,110
Scottish undertakers	81,000	18	1,232	17	406,560
London companies	38,520	8	572	8	188,760
Church	74,852	16	1,338	18	441,540
Servitors	54,632	12	994	14	328,020
Irish natives	94,013	20	1,301	18	429,330
College	12,400	3	157	2	51,810
School, town & fort	15,193	3	266	4	87,780
Irish Society	7,000	2	151	2	49,830
Total	459,110	100	7,278	100	2,401,740
Unidentified modern townlands			3,938		1,288,974
Total			11,216		3,690,714

without a fixed size. Individual townlands could vary enormously in size depending on their agricultural potential, and so estates also varied in extent according to their location. Many undertaker estates, intended to contain contain only 1,000, 1,500 or 2,000 acres, in fact contained tens of thousands of statute acres. Two 1,000-acre estates in Tyrone provide an interesting comparison: that of Gortaville, situated in rich agricultural land, contained in reality only 1,851 statute acres, while Eden, which was located on marginal land in the Sperrin Mountains, included 46,814 statute acres.

Despite the fact that all grantee classes and individual grantees obtained more land than their grants indicated, there is no evidence to suggest that this was the result of discrimination in the allocation of land; rather it was inherent in the method adopted for distribution. Those who were most favourably treated obtained their favours overtly in terms of the absolute numbers of ballyboes received. As with townland size, so the actual areas of estates were inversely related to land quality. Sixteen ballyboes of small extent but of high-quality land were easier to colonise and more profitable than sixteen ballyboes containing a larger area of poor land. Thus the difference between the actual and theoretical area of a plantation grant was not a good measure of its desirability. The relative attractiveness of plantation estates depended rather on the quality of land obtained, even though this advantage was modified by a related decrease in the actual area.

Each of the 11,216 modern townlands in the six escheated counties can be placed in land-valuation categories from A (highest values) to E (lowest values).[35] The breakdown of the number of townlands granted to each grantee class for these categories is provided in Table 2. These data are also presented

Table 2: *Frequency matrix of townland valuations and grantee classes*

Grantee class	Land value categories (townlands)						Total (townlands)
	A	B	C	D	E	F	
English undertakers	168	108	335	421	185	50	1,267
Scottish undertakers	70	103	276	389	191	203	1,232
London companies	14	41	159	197	119	42	572
Church	165	179	294	281	198	221	1,338
Servitors	56	100	257	235	219	127	994
Irish natives	54	118	399	386	208	136	1,301
College	24	17	40	36	16	24	157
School, town & fort	48	64	94	32	19	9	266
Irish Society	35	46	50	9	7	4	151
Total identified	634	776	1,904	1,986	1,172	816	7,278
Unidentified	200	313	803	1,016	652	954	3,938
Total (townlands)	834	1,089	2,707	3,002	1,824	1,770	11,216

in a frequency-distribution graph (Figure 2) from which a visual assessment of the quality of land allocated may be made. Irish grantees did not obtain land of any poorer quality than the other

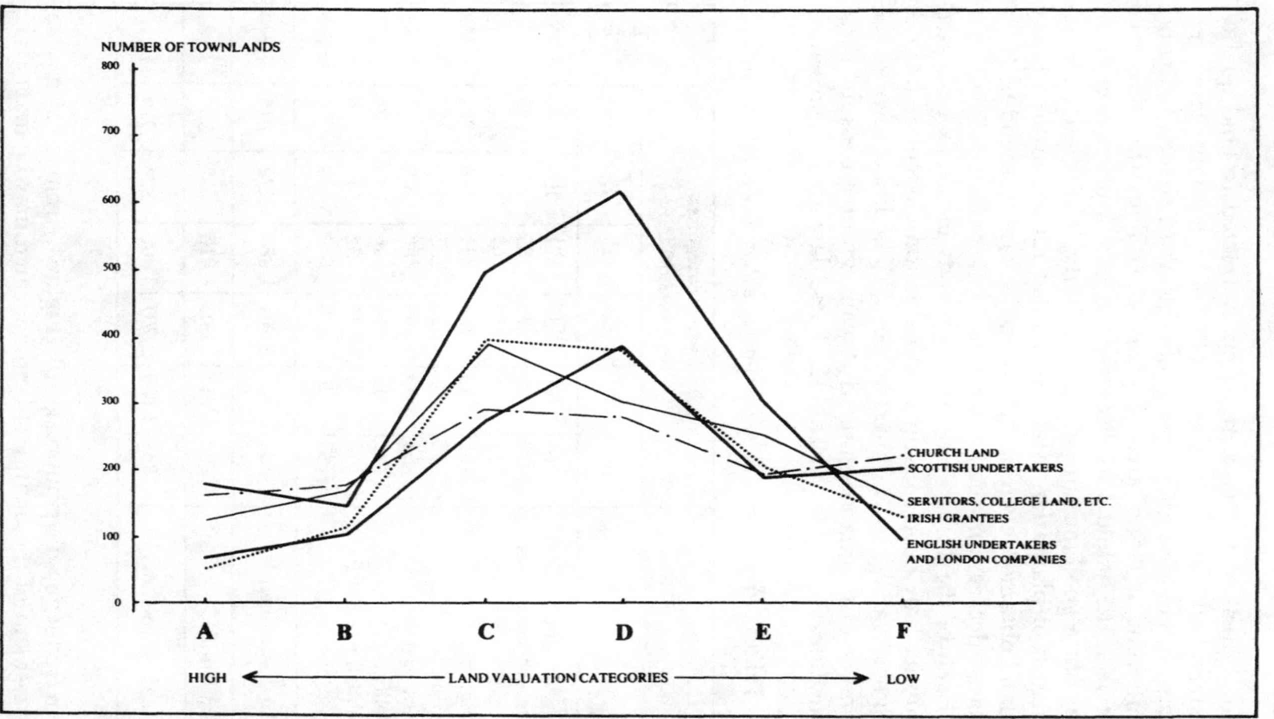

Figure 2: *Land values of townlands allocated to each plantation grantee class*

grantees. In fact only English and Scottish undertakers and London companies 'peak' at land-valuation category D, while the others, including the Irish, 'peak' at the higher land-valuation category C. If any general observation may be made, it is that the Scottish undertakers obtained proportionately fewer high-valuation townlands, and more low-valuation townlands, than those obtained by English undertakers. The variations in land quality were essentially due to the character and disposition of the baronies allocated to the various grantee classes. English undertakers obtained the particularly lucrative lowlands of Oneilland in north Armagh. Church land was reserved in every barony, so all types of land were acquired by the bishops. The Irish grantees obtained their land along with the servitors, and no deliberate manipulation of land quality in the allocation of land may be inferred.

3.11 *Change in the social order: 'new lords for old'*

At every level the plantation land divisions reflected pre-plantation territorial units. Ballyboes, polls and tates became the basic land units which the undertakers leased to their tenants as townlands. The plantation estates of 1,000 acres or sixteen ballyboes were often equivalent in size, name and location to Irish ballybetaghs. Precincts or baronies in turn were formed from what had been the Irish chiefs' territories or 'countries'. Just as the hierarchy of plantation land divisions in Tyrone was a reflection of pre-plantation land divisions, so the plantation social structure mirrored that of pre-plantation Irish society. The principal undertakers in each barony held a comparable position to the Irish chiefs, the ordinary undertakers to the sept leaders, and the undertenants and cottagers to the Irish farmers. Even within each barony it was generally the principal undertaker who obtained the ballybetagh which had been the personal demesne of the Irish chief. In Tyrone this transference of power took place in each barony. In Clogher barony the principal undertaker, Sir Thomas Ridgeway, obtained ballybetaghs which included Sir Cormac McBaron O'Neill's castle at Augher. In Strabane barony the Earl of Abercorn obtained the ballybetaghs around Turlough McArt O'Neill's castle of Strabane. Hugh O'Neill's 'country' of Dungannon had been divided to form Mountjoy and Dungannon baronies. In

Mountjoy barony the principal undertaker obtained the lands associated with one of O'Neill's most influential septs, the O'Devlins (Revelineightra and Revelinowtra). In Dungannon barony Sir Arthur Chichester obtained Hugh O'Neill's own castle and demesne lands of Dungannon, thus reflecting at every level Hugh O'Neill's pre-plantation social standing. As Lord Deputy, Chichester symbolically was positioned in the place formerly occupied by the The O'Neill. As the 'principal servitor' of Dungannon barony, Chichester obtained a status equivalent to that which had been enjoyed by Hugh O'Neill in his own 'country'. As a servitor in the proportion of Dungannon, Chichester even obtained O'Neill's own castle and demesne lands. Around Chichester in the barony which had formerly been the heartland of Gaelic Ulster were positioned many leading councillors of state.

As far as the new order throughout the escheated counties was concerned, what appeared on the surface to be a radical upheaval had so far been little more than a substitution of new lords for old, with a general adoption of pre-plantation land divisions. Although only about 20 per cent of the escheated land was granted to Irish native grantees, Irish tenants were to be allowed to remain on all church, servitors', college, school, town and fort land as well (in all about 57 per cent of the escheated territory). It was not until the English and Scottish undertenants and cottagers began to arrive that most Irish began to perceive the effectiveness of the change.

4

British Settlement in Ulster, 1610-70

The lands intended for plantation consisted of 162,500 acres granted to English and Scottish undertakers and 38,520 acres granted to the London companies. Undertakers and London companies were all required to plant their lands with a minimum of twenty-four adult males from England or lowland Scotland for every 1,000 acres received. Each quota of twenty-four men was to represent at least ten families.[1] In theory this meant that at least 3,900 adult British males were to be planted on the undertakers' estates within three years. The London companies were required to plant with the same density of colonists, giving an additional 925 adult males to the projected total, making 4,825 in all. The Londoners, however, did not obtain their patents until several years after the undertakers, so they could not be expected to plant within the same deadline. Other British colonists were anticipated, not only on the servitors' estates but also in towns such as Londonderry and Coleraine. Although the projected numbers of the townsmen were unspecified, Irish were to be excluded from the corporate towns. It could be argued that some of the land reserved for the maintenance of the corporate towns was also intended for plantation, particularly when these townlands were conjoined with undertakers' estates and assigned at the same crown rents. An attempt was also made to involve the 48,158 acres of termon land granted to the bishops in the plantation scheme. It was suggested that their lands should be planted at a compromise rate one-third that of the undertakers, i.e. eight adult British males for each 1,000 acres. However, only the lands allocated to the undertakers and London companies were to be continually surveyed and examined throughout the plantation period to assess the progress of colonisation, while the other lands were largely ignored. In a muster of British males in the escheated counties in 1618 it was observed that 4,728 men ought to have appeared if the plantation rate of twenty-four men per 1,000 acres had been observed on 197,000 acres.[2] Clearly even by 1618 it was felt that only the lands of the undertakers and the London companies were specifically intended for plantation.

4.1 *The population data*

Once the undertakers had taken out their patents *circa* 1610, surveys were carried out to inquire if they had fulfilled the plantation requirements relating to settlement and building. The articles of plantation required the undertakers to have all their tenants planted by November 1611, and at the same time they were given three years to plant their full quota of adult males.[3] This time period proved insufficient, as the surveys of Lord Carew in 1611[4] and Sir Josias Bodley in 1613[5] both showed. James I was intensely displeased at the slow progress of the plantation, but extended the time allowed so that the requirements were to be met by the end of August 1616.[6] A second survey by Sir Josias Bodley is believed to have been carried out in 1616, but with the exception of a few fragmentary reports on individual London company estates, nothing further is known of it. This survey must nevertheless have again indicated an unsatisfactory situation, for a royal proclamation in 1618 stated that a new deadline had been set at 1 May 1619, by which time all Irish were to be removed from the undertakers' estates.[7] Captain Nicholas Pynnar's survey of 1618-19[8] showed that, for the first time, a substantial number of the undertakers had fulfilled the plantation conditions. However, many Irish still remained on the estates. Few landowners would remove the Irish unless alternative British settlers were at hand. In 1621 it was decided that one-quarter of the undertakers' estates could be set apart for Irish. A final plantation survey was conducted in 1622, which also recorded the number of Irish families still resident on each plantation estate.[9]

The numbers of British on each plantation estate may therefore be compared for four plantation surveys: those carried out in 1611, 1613, 1619 and 1622. These data are supplemented by two surviving musters of adult British men, listed under various undertakers and servitors, in 1618[10] and *circa* 1630.[11] Finally several detailed sources survive as taxation lists for the mid-seventeenth century. These hearth-money rolls,[12] poll-tax lists[13] and the 'census' of *circa* 1659[14] all provide settlement information not on the basis of landed estates but at a much more detailed townland level.

Population data relating to British settlement have been extracted from the surveys and musters up to 1630 and tabulated (Appendix 10). From this information distribution maps of plantation settlement in Ulster have been prepared (Maps 6 and 7).

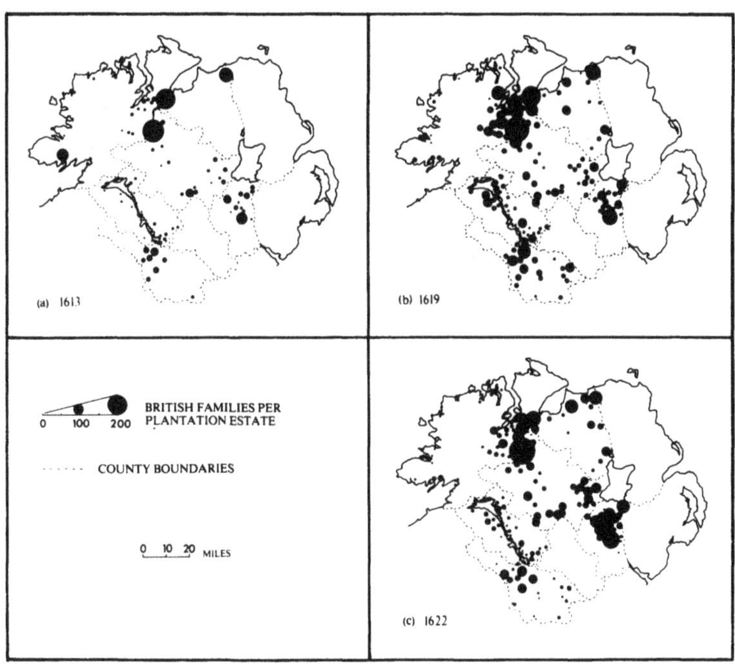

Map 6: *British plantation settlement in Ulster based on the plantation surveys: (a) 1613, (b) 1619 and (c) 1622*

4.2 *The emerging settlement pattern, 1611-30*

When the pattern of British settlement in Ulster is compared for 1613, 1619 and 1622 in Maps 6(a), (b) and (c), it is apparent that colonisation was more successful in certain areas. The distributional pattern had become especially well defined by 1622 when several preferred areas of settlement had emerged. The first was in mid-Ulster, to the south and west of Lough Neagh. In

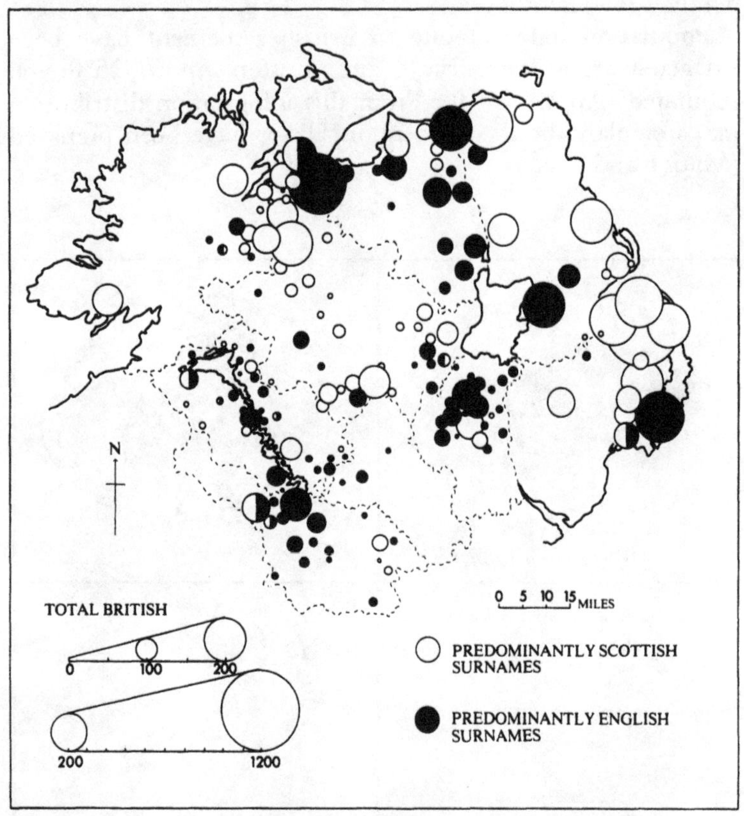

Map 7: *English and Scottish settlement in Ulster based on numbers and surnames recorded in the muster rolls, c. 1630*

particular north Armagh, east Tyrone, and the Clogher Valley in south Tyrone were densely settled. A second area which attracted a great number of colonists was the Foyle basin in north-west Ulster; many colonists settled in and around Londonderry and Strabane. Other areas also proved to be consistently attractive to British settlers, although on a less dramatic scale. Foremost among these areas of secondary importance were mid-

Cavan, the Erne basin, the lower Bann valley and north-east County Londonderry.

The distributional pattern of British settlement which emerged in Ulster between 1613 and 1622 is confirmed yet again by the data of the 1630 muster rolls (Map 7). Here, however, comparative statistics are also available for church land and for Counties Antrim, Down and Monaghan. Many areas which had a consistently poor colonisation record had been intended for plantation. A great number of undertakers' estates which were situated on lands of relatively poor quality were unable to attract or retain significant numbers of colonists. This relationship between areas of successful colonisation and good agricultural land may be observed by comparing the settlement maps with the map of land values (Map 2). Nevertheless, other factors besides land quality may also have influenced successful colonisation. Plantation estates adjacent to ports with easy access to and from the main channels of communication were obviously favourably situated to receive settlers. As Irish settlement had previously been concentrated in those areas which were now being most densely settled by English and Scots, the removal of the Irish could not have proved more than a temporary obstacle to British settlement. Some accounts of the plantation refer to colonisation in terms of the 'efforts' of the undertakers, but the settlement pattern appears to conform primarily to the distribution of high-quality land. Although this suggests that the undertakers' role was passive, undoubtedly some were financially more able to manage their estates and to transport tenants. However, those undertakers who were best able to plant were generally the chief undertakers in each barony, and as such obtained their grants in the most favourable locations. Little successful colonisation occurred on the marginal land, in areas isolated from the main centres of colonial expansion.

The plantation surveys indicate that on the poorer, isolated estates the tenants were highly mobile and often left the land shortly after they had arrived. This internal population movement served to rationalise the population distribution in terms of land quality. Despite little overall change in the total plantation population between 1619 and 1622, many isolated areas of poorer agricultural land suffered a substantial population decline in these years. Elsewhere, especially in the lowland

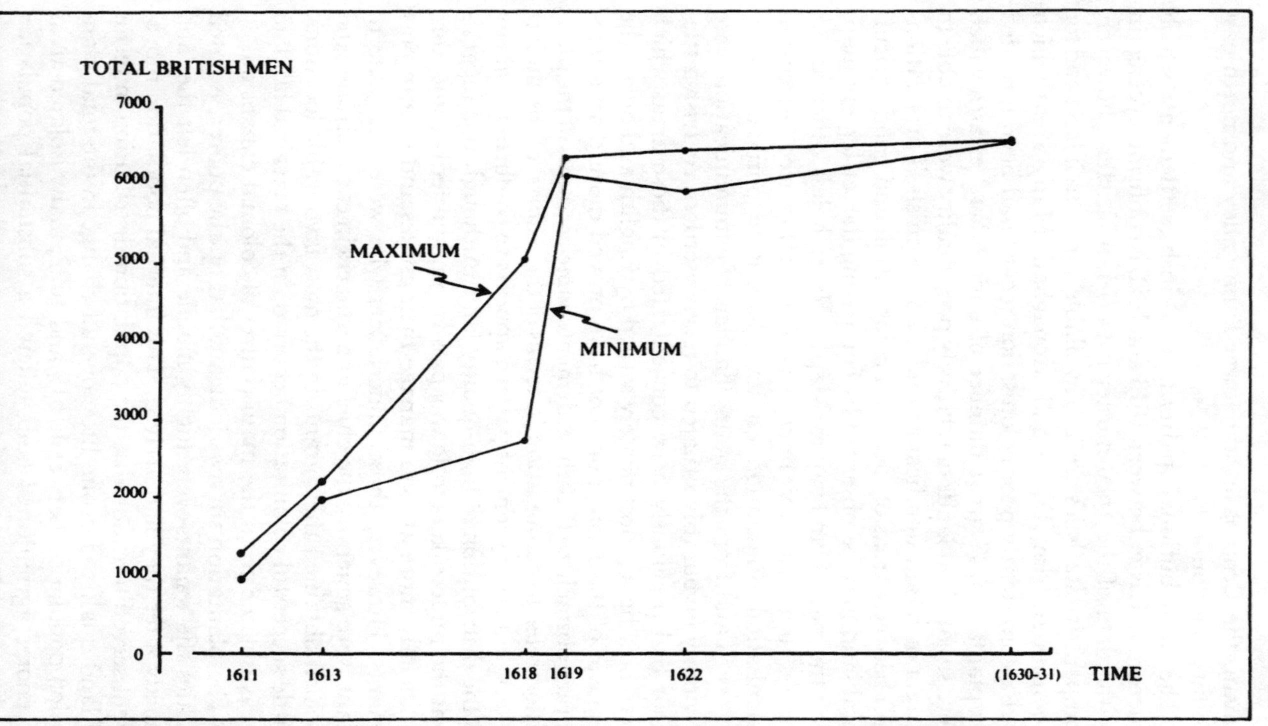

Figure 3: *British population totals on the plantation estates based on the plantation surveys and musters, 1611-c. 1630*

centres, the plantation population increased proportionally. The pattern of these differential changes in the settlement pattern from 1619 to 1622 suggests that centripetal forces were operating in internal population movements during this period.[15]

Evidently the population distribution of English and Scottish settlers had established into a coherent pattern *circa* 1622, indicating that the greatest influx of colonists had occurred by then. When the totals of adult British males on the plantation estates are plotted against time for 1611, 1613, 1618, 1619, 1622 and 1630, the main period of population increase appears to have been just before 1619 (Figure 3). The general pattern shows a slow rate of increase up to 1614, a rapid increase between 1614 and 1619, followed by stabilisation and, in some cases, decline from 1619 to 1630.

4.3 *The uneasy balance: British and Irish settlement patterns to 1670*

Although plantation studies rarely extend beyond 1641, colonisation continued spasmodically throughout the seventeenth century. Documentary sources of the mid-seventeenth century are considerably more detailed than the earlier surveys. In particular the hearth-money rolls of the 1660s and the poll-tax lists (collated in a 'census' of *circa* 1659) provide the first detailed information of Irish and British settlement at townland level. The pattern of British settlement in Ulster in the 1660s conforms closely to distributional patterns found in 1622 and 1630. The turmoil of the 1640s can have had only a temporary effect, and indeed in many parts of Ulster the British population appears to have increased substantially between 1630 and 1670. After the 1641 rebellion and the Cromwellian confiscation of land, considerable areas of land which had previously been Irish-owned were opened up for colonisation.

Because the distribution of the British population in Ulster *circa* 1659 has been shown in Map 8 in proportionate terms (of the total population), it follows that the distributional pattern of Irish settlement is the converse of this. Strictly speaking, this is not accurate, for the areas with the highest proportions of British were also the most densely settled areas. The Irish were to be found in greatest numbers in the moderately good agricultural land which had not yet been inundated by colonists. But

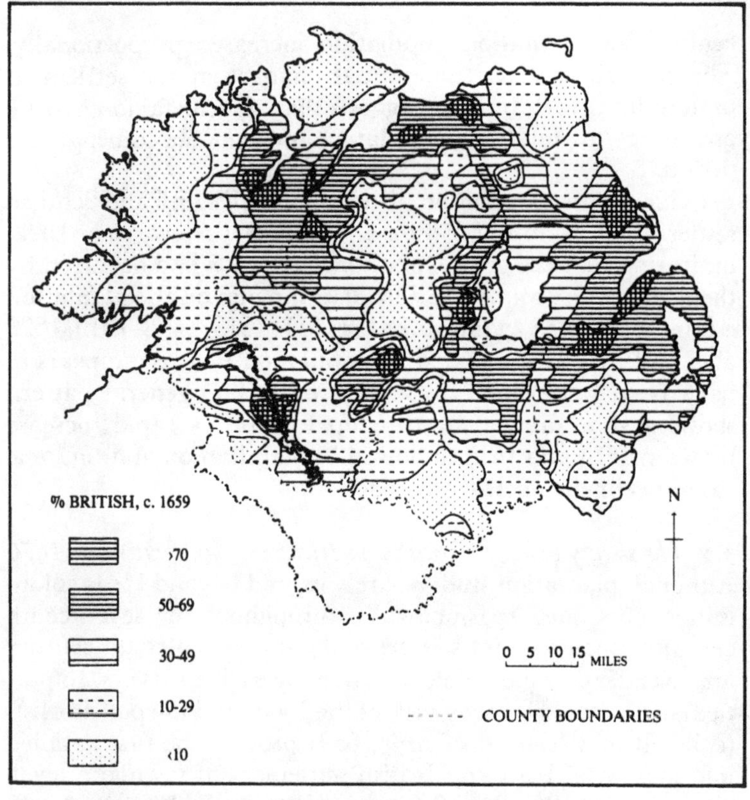

Map 8: *British settlement in Ulster, c. 1659*
The percentage of British in each parish has been calculated from the census of *circa* 1659 for Counties Antrim, Armagh, Donegal, Down, Londonderry, Fermanagh and Monaghan, and the values then plotted and isoplethed. Comparable statistics for the County Tyrone parishes were obtained by adjusting the numbers of British- and Irish-owned hearths recorded in the hearth-money rolls of 1666 by correction factors. These factors were based on a comparison with the fragmentary poll-tax cover which survives for some Tyrone parishes, and this adjustment removes the socially selective imbalance inherent in percentages derived from the hearth-money rolls alone.

although sparsely distributed, it was the poorer areas that the Irish occupied in almost exclusive proportions, especially in the west of the province. The general pattern of British settlement in 1659 conforms closely to the present-day pattern of politico-religious groupings in rural Ulster. Not only was an equilibrium between British and Irish settlement established early in the

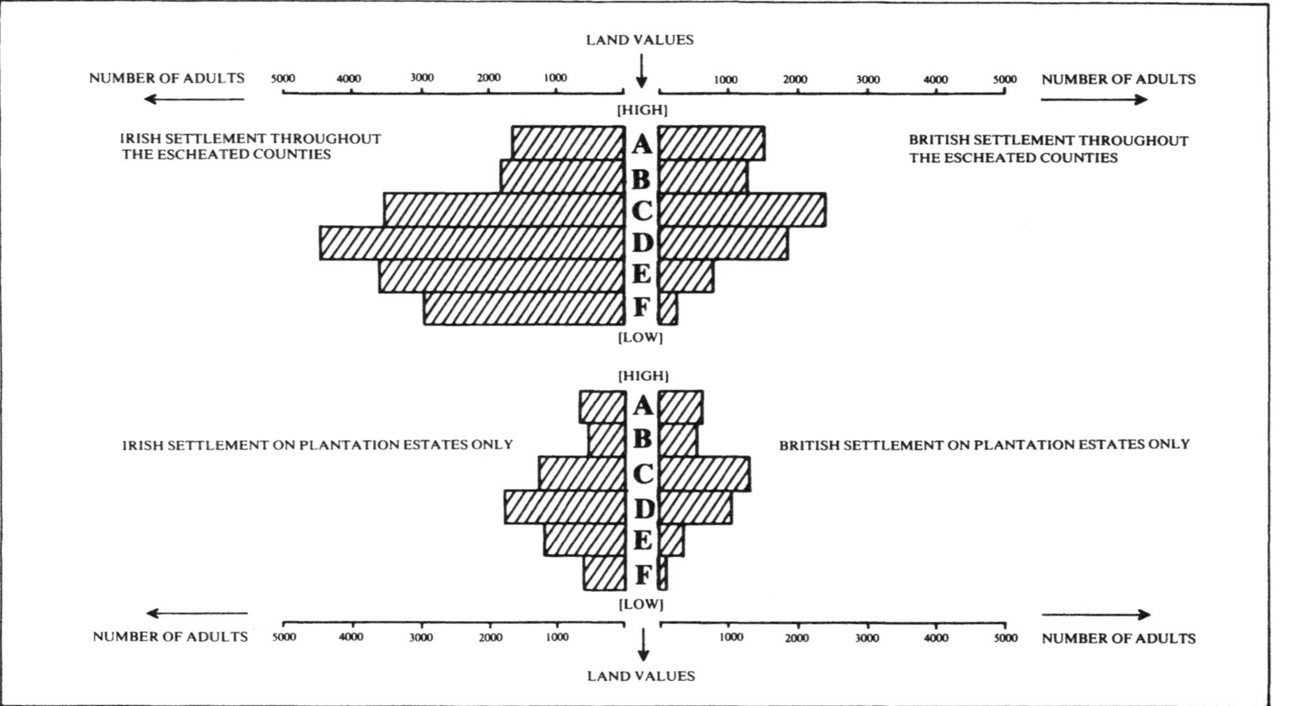

Figure 4: *Land values of townlands occupied by British and Irish, c. 1659-1667*

plantation period, but the areas of most intense colonisation correspond closely with the distribution of fertile lowlands, especially in areas adjacent to the coastal plains of the north and east. The colonisation of Antrim and Down cannot be divorced from that of west Ulster where the official plantation scheme applied. Despite the absence of population data for east Ulster before 1630, it can be assumed that the pattern of British settlement in Antrim and Down had been established as early as, if not before, that in the escheated counties.

Because the hearth-money rolls and the census of 1659 enable individual townlands to be identified, it is possible to examine in detail the hypothesis that English and Scottish settlers occupied better land than the Irish. When the land values of the townlands are examined against British or Irish settlement (Figure 4) it is clear that British settlement on the best land, even on the plantation estates, was numerically matched by Irish settlement. However, very few British occupied the poorest lands, and their totals 'peak' at land-valuation category C, compared with the Irish settlement, which 'peaks' at category D. The absence of British from the poorer areas was much more marked than that of the Irish from the best townlands.

While Figure 4 does illustrate that British occupation of the best agricultural land was not exclusive, it would be misleading to suggest that all the rich lowlands of Ulster had developed a mixed or integrated settlement pattern. There were lowland areas where British settlement had become virtually exclusive. Even localities which appeared fairly mixed were prone to the development of segregated pockets of British and Irish. However, there were also many areas which recorded both British and Irish occupants within the same townlands. One way of illustrating the extent of settlement segregation is to examine the 1659 census in detail. In part of County Armagh 75 townlands were occupied exclusively by 554 British adults, while another 112 townlands were mixed, providing in them a total of 709 British and 685 Irish. In contrast, the same region contained a further 2,554 Irish in 286 townlands, apparently to the exclusion of all British.

Some pockets of segregated Irish settlement did coincide with inferior land quality in the lowlands, and in the 1660s Irish were to be found in many of the plantation towns. Few of the town-dwelling Irish were named in the hearth-money rolls, being for the most part poor artisans.

Under the conditions of the plantation Irish were permitted to settle on church land, servitors' estates and those estates granted directly by the crown to Irish freeholders. The removal of many Irish chiefs and sept leaders to their new allocations involved a small fraction of the population, but the total removal of Irish from undertakers' estates was not a practical proposition. Pynnar recorded many Irish on the undertakers' estates in 1619 and concluded that their presence was not totally undesirable, because of the 'greater rents, paid to them [the undertakers] by Irish tenants who graze. If the Irish pack away with their cattle, the British must either forsake their dwellings or ensure great distress on the sudden, yet the cohabitation of the Irish is dangerous.'[16]

Similarly, repeated representations from the London companies' agents stressed that until British tenants could be found to farm each townland it was senseless to eject the Irish. However, concern about the continuing presence of Irish was reflected in the survey of 1622, which included, for the first time, an estimate of the numbers of Irish families on each plantation estate. Considerable numbers of Irish were resident and, as in the situation *circa* 1659 (Figure 4), often outnumbered the British tenants. According to the 1622 survey, there were not only 866 British families living on the Tyrone undertakers' estates, but also a further 1,199 Irish families.[17] British settlement was, of course, not restricted to the undertakers' estates but was also present on the servitors' and ecclesiastical land by 1630. A pattern of segregation of British and Irish settlement, based primarily on economic factors such as land quality and distance from market centres, clearly existed in the 1660s. But such a pattern had already been established by the early 1620s when the British colonisation had reached its optimum numerical level.

In 1621 it was suggested that the Irish could remain on the undertakers' estates.[18] By 1628 legislation was finally passed to enable grants to be reissued with higher crown rents, but allowing the undertakers legally to take Irish tenants on a reserved quarter of their estates:

> The patentee shall keep three-quarters of his lands

> occupied by Englishmen, and shall keep two freeholders and two leaseholders at least in every 1,000 acres of his demesne. . . . If this is broken, except in favour of mere Irish who are artificers, it shall be lawful for us to seize unto our hands such parts of the three-quarters as are let to mere Irish. . . . All the mere Irish, except they are artificers, shall be removed from the three-quarters reserved before 1st May 1629. On the other quarter of their estates the patentee may have Irishmen and let them leases for 21 to 41 years, or for three or four lives. These natives to live and build together, and not be dispersed, and to be conformed in habit and usage.[19]

Inquisitions were then held to determine what land had already been let by the undertakers to the Irish and which townlands were most suitable for the proposed Irish 'quarters' of the estates.[20] Almost without exception the reserved quarters were the poorest and most isolated sections. Indeed, many of the townlands which were the 'most fit parts to be let to the natives' were precisely the same townlands as had already been leased to Irish tenants.

From surviving inquisitions, in conjunction with the 1622 undertakers' certificates (which in some cases name the townlands let to British tenants),[21] it is possible to reconstruct the pattern of Irish/British segregation at townland level within two adjacent estates. The estates of Ballyconnolly/Ballyranill and Ballyloughmaguiffe, which between them straddle a section of the fertile Clogher Valley in south Tyrone, provide an almost complete picture of Irish and British settlement *circa* 1628. Map 9 clearly shows how British settlement within these estates was focused around the plantation centres of Aghintain and Ballynelurgan (Fivemiletown) in the valley basin. The lands which were let to and reserved for Irish were essentially those townlands which bordered on the surrounding uplands. The 1666 settlement, mapped from information in the hearth-money tax returns for the same townlands, indicates the continuity of the detailed settlement pattern in this area between the 1620s and the 1660s. The effect of the 1628 legislation was really to institutionalise the economic segregation which had already taken place.

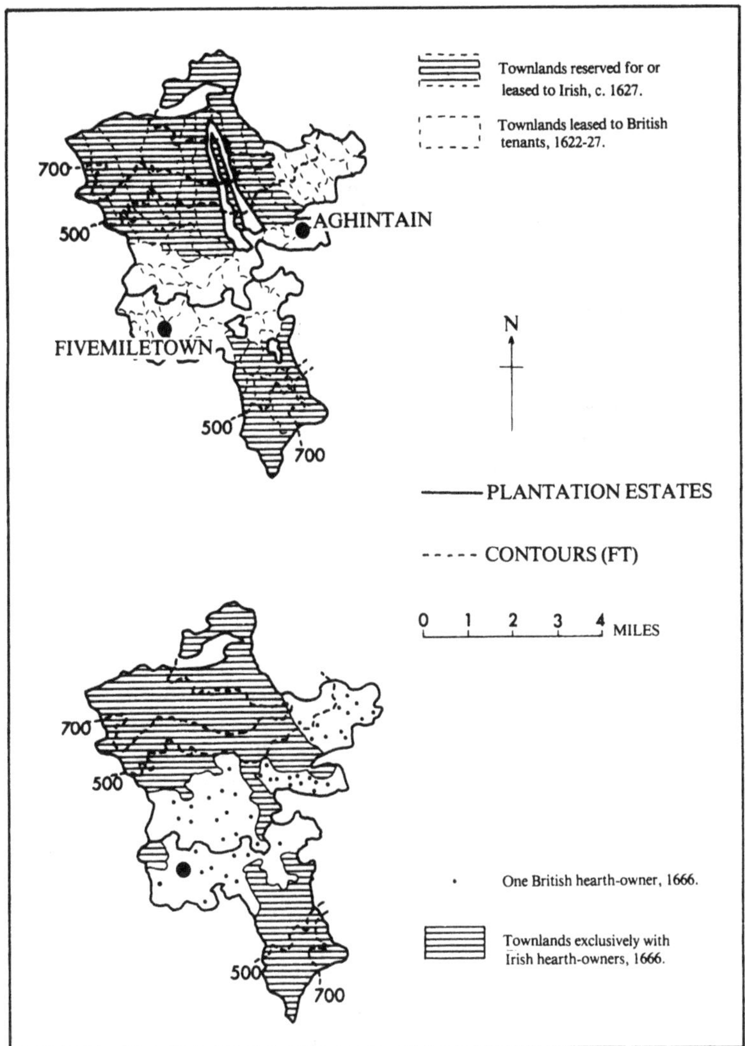

Map 9: *British and Irish segregation on two plantation estates in County Tyrone*
The northern estate is Ballyconnolly/Ballyranill (2,000 acres), originally granted to Edward Kingswell but owned by Sir William Stewart in 1619. The adjacent estate in the south is Ballyloughmaguiffe (1,500 acres), originally granted to Captain Edney but owned by Lord Burley in 1619. (The tenants found clustered at Aghintain in the 1620s had dispersed by 1666, leaving the village deserted.)

4.4 *Population estimates*

Both the plantation surveys of 1619 and 1622 indicate the presence of over 6,000 adult British males on the plantation estates. A total provided by Pynnar for his 1619 survey is of 1,974 families, making 6,215 men with arms.[22] However, when his totals are checked against the numbers he recorded on the individual estates, only the adult male total corresponds (at over 6,000). In fact Pynnar recorded some 2,700 British families, and his own lower total was probably a summation of the numbers of freeholders, leaseholders and cottagers, omitting many undertenants. Although Pynnar had found 6,215 British men in the escheated lands, he also noted that there were 'upon occasion, 8,000 men of British birth and descent for defence'.[23] The 1622 survey supports Pynnar's initial conclusion that there were just over 6,000 British men on the plantation estates. Both these surveys only recorded the numbers of British resident on the lands allocated to servitors and undertakers. It is the muster rolls of *circa* 1630 which provide the most comprehensive account of British settlement throughout Ulster during this period. Listed in this source for the first time are the names of British settlers on church land, and also the great numbers present in Antrim, Down and Monaghan. The musters record about 6,500 adult males settled on the undertakers' and servitors' estates alone, but to these must be added another 700 recorded on church lands, and 5,500 in Counties Antrim, Down and Monaghan. In all, about 13,000 British adult males are recorded in the 1630 musters for Ulster, but even this total must be further supplemented. In several areas, such as Kilmacrenan and Tirhugh baronies in County Donegal, the servitors did not 'appear' with their tenants. In fact even more significant omissions occurred at Carrickfergus and Belfast in County Antrim. These were certainly the largest settlements for which no returns have survived, and a figure of 1,500 would be a conservative estimate of these unmustered British. This would give a total of some 14,500 British men throughout Ulster in 1630.

There is no basis for any further estimate of the plantation population until *circa* 1659 when a 'census' was compiled from poll-tax returns. Table 3 contains the county totals of British and Irish for all the Ulster counties except Cavan and Tyrone. To the total of British listed here must be added an estimate of

Table 3: *British and Irish in Ulster, c. 1659*

County	English & Scots	Irish	Total
Antrim	7,074 (45%)	8,965	16,039
Armagh	2,393 (35%)	4,355	6,748
Donegal	3,412 (28%)	8,589	12,001
Down	6,540 (43%)	8,643	15,183
Fermanagh	1,800 (25%)	5,302	7,102
Londonderry	4,428 (45%)	5,306	9,734
Monaghan	434 (11%)	3,649	4,083
Total	26,081 (37%)	44,809	70,890

some 4,300 for Cavan and Tyrone, giving more than 30,000 English and Scots in Ulster at this time. While the 1630 musters may not have been as comprehensive as the 1659 census in actually recording all the British present, they did clearly indicate that the totals were of adult males. The 1659 census, on the other hand, is rather ambiguous as to what its totals represent. Certainly the census returns were not of total population. By comparing the census returns in Counties Antrim, Londonderry and Donegal with the contemporary hearth-money tax returns for the same areas, it is apparent that a multiplier of about 2.2 would have to be applied to the numbers of British-owned hearths to make the totals comparable with the 1659 census. In County Tyrone, although the census has not survived for this county, there are several fragments of the original poll-tax lists. When these are compared in turn with the hearth-money rolls for the same areas, it is clear that the poll-tax lists were indeed used to compile the 1659 census. It is also apparent that these totals do not represent, as originally intended, all adult persons (both male and female) over fifteen years. Instead only adult males were recorded, along with their wives when married. The females recorded were wives or widows, and adult single females were usually excluded. A total of 30,000 English and Scots recorded in these terms would represent only about 20,000 adult British males, a total which nevertheless was a considerable increase on the 1630 estimate of 14,500. Any exercise to project these figures to provide an estimate of the total British population would substantially increase the margins of error, and would require a greater understanding of the nature of colonial family size and household structure than is possible at present.

Against the evidence of these surveys, musters and the census must be set the contemporary estimates of population in Ulster. In 1638 the Scottish Covenanters believed that there were 40,000 Scottish men in Ulster,[24] while Sir Thomas Wentworth estimated in 1639 that there were 100,000 of the Scottish nation in Ireland.[25] These estimates were not based on any surveys and can only be interpreted as being unreliable exaggerations, but exaggerations that were mild in comparison with the thoroughly discredited accounts of the enormity of the 1641 massacre of Protestants in Ulster (which ranged from 20,000 to 100,000).

Fluctuations in the colonial population size between 1630 and 1659 would, of course, be expected, but the apparent increase over this period points to the 1630s as being an important period of influx. The upheaval of the 1641 rebellion and its aftermath could hardly indicate the 1640s or even the early 1650s as a period of colonial expansion in Ulster. Scots in particular entered Ulster during the 1630s in increasing numbers.[26] One report from Scotland in 1635 stated that 10,000 had passed through the port of Irvine on their way to Ireland in the preceding two years.[27] Although this was again probably an exaggeration, and many returned without permission to embark, the report does testify to the substantial exodus from Scotland at this time.

4.5 *Phases of influx and colonisation*

Several distinct phases of colonisation emerge from a consideration of the population data of Ulster from 1610 to 1670:

(a) 1610 to 1615. This was a period of slow initial colonisation with hesitant undertakers introducing tenants to their estates. In limited areas such as north Down there was a considerable build-up.

(b) 1615 to 1620. During this period there was a rapid increase in the number of settlers. With a considerable amount of internal population movement a distinct settlement pattern developed which was related to the economic environment.

(c) 1620 to 1630. Stagnation in the rate of influx and high internal mobility led to a decline in the colonial population in certain less favoured areas.
(d) 1630 to 1641. Continued rationalisation of the British settlement pattern, but associated with a marked increase in the migration of Scots to Ulster.
(e) 1641 to 1654. The rebellion and its ensuing turmoil proved to be only a temporary setback to the continuing process of colonisation. Undoubtedly many Protestants were killed, and many more fled to more secure parts.
(f) 1654 to 1670. Following the reconquest, the Cromwellian and Restoration resettlement of Ulster continued. During this period it is likely that English rather than Scottish settlers played a significant if not dominant role.

The first and second of these phases of colonisation were almost exactly paralleled in the contemporary colonisation of America. In a muster of the inhabitants of Virginia in 1624 the dates of arrival of the English settlers are given.[28] From 1607 to 1617 the rate of increase appears to have been very slow, but from 1618 to 1622 the American colony expanded at a greatly increased rate. The obvious inference is that the late increase in colonisation of both America and Ulster was due to an increase in centrifugal migration forces at the common colonial source. The reasons for mass population movements from and within England in the early seventeenth century are complex, but it is likely that agricultural and social changes were of greater importance than dearth or famine. Similarly in Scotland small farmers were leaving the lowlands in great numbers because of rack-renting rather than because of general subsistence crises.[29]

It would be misleading to suggest that the movement of English and Scots to Ulster which occurred spasmodically from 1610 had petered out by 1670. If anything, the colonial processes were intensified, although no comparable population data are available for almost a century after this date. The 1659 census reveals that only about 32 per cent of the total population in Ulster was of English or Scots extraction, yet by the mid-eighteenth century an absolute majority in religious terms may have been achieved.[30] Indeed, many areas which in 1659 were recorded as being exclusively Irish were in the following decades to become extensively settled by British. While some of this change was due to assimilation and religious conversion, there clearly were major periods of colonial influx after 1670.[31]

5

The Processes of Colonisation and the Development of English and Scottish Localities

The colonisation of Ulster was undertaken by English and lowland Scottish settlers in a competitive manner which often enabled the two groups to retain their national identities. As the areas of predominantly Scottish settlement which emerged were not coextensive with the lands allocated to Scottish undertakers (and likewise with the areas of English settlement), a unique opportunity is provided to examine the processes of colonisation involved in the development of English and Scottish areas of settlement. It is possible to distinguish even in present-day Ulster areas where the inhabitants display characteristics which are specifically English, Irish or Scottish in origin. Thus, if the Irish element is abstracted, it is possible to observe which localities are essentially 'English' or 'Scottish'.

5.1 *Surviving English and Scottish localities in Ulster*

In using cultural phenomena to ascertain the national origin of the population in a particular area, a principal obstacle is the fact that many cultural traits (which may be of English or Scottish origin) were disseminated rapidly throughout populations of mixed origin. However, in Ulster three criteria may tentatively be used: dialect, surnames and religious denomination, as these were not amenable to transmission between large groups with conflicting national origins.

As far as dialect is concerned, there are three basic linguistic groups which contribute to present-day speech patterns in Ulster: Irish Gaelic, Ulster Scots and Ulster Anglo-Irish. The two primary English dialects of Ulster, called the north-eastern or Ulster Scots dialect and the mid-Ulster dialect, are considered to have originated from the seventeenth-century dialects of south-west Scotland and the north-west midlands of England respectively.[1]

Although the two main Protestant denominations in Ulster — Presbyterian and Episcopalian — have been broadly associated with Scottish and English settlement respectively, it should be remembered that although Presbyterianism was a dominant philosophy among the early Scots settlers, it only became established as a distinct religious denomination in Ulster during the later seventeenth century, when it then spread rapidly throughout many areas of Scottish settlement.[2] This

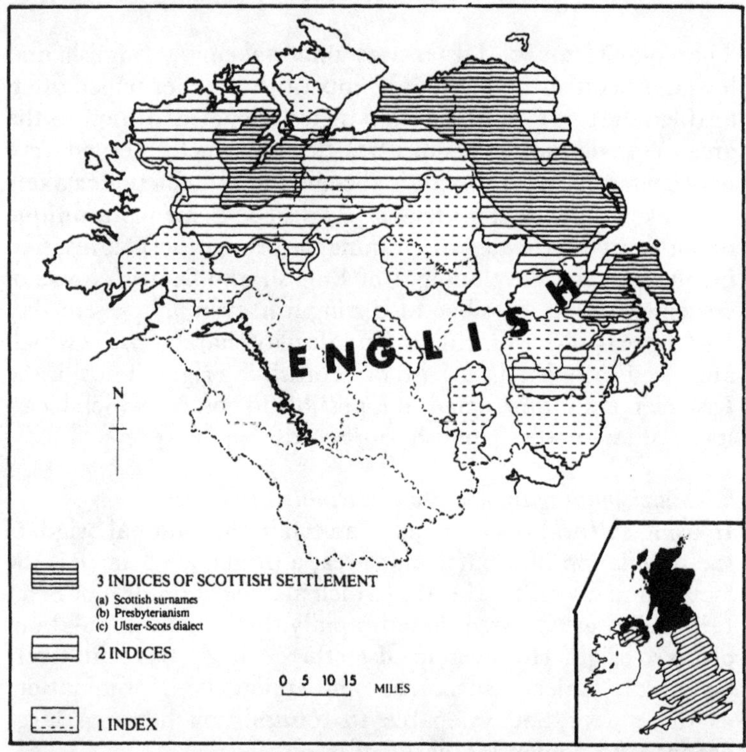

Map 10: *Scottish and English settlement and cultural areas in present-day Ulster*[3]
The territorial units used for the construction of this map are: *(a)* rural districts, for British surnames, i.e. Scottish surnames comprising more than 50 per cent of the British surnames in the electoral lists: *(b)* baronies, for religious denominations, i.e. more than 50 per cent of the Protestant population recorded as Presbyterian; *(c)* the extent of the Ulster Scots dialect as mapped from fieldwork evidence by Gregg (1972). Some areas in the extreme west and south of the province are not included in the assessment of Scottish traits, i.e. where fewer than 15 per cent of all surnames are of British origin and less than 15 per cent of the total population are Protestant.

means that especially in the interior of the province many Scots may not have become Presbyterian. Furthermore, many English did not conform to the Established Church, and there has been relatively less social resistance to intermarriage between Protestants of differing denominations than between Protestants and Roman Catholics. However, despite these limitations, the core areas of English settlement have remained Anglican and the core areas of Scottish settlement Presbyterian, so that their relative distributional strengths within Ulster may be cautiously used as an index of national origin.

While dialect and religious denominations have both been subject to processes of assimilation, surnames do provide a more stable and representative index of national origin. The problems associated with the use of surnames in this context are not those of transmission between English and Scottish settlers, but rather of identifying which surnames are of English and which of Scottish origin. A consensus of the surname, religious and dialect evidence strongly suggests that the present-day 'British' settlement in Ulster is comprised of two major components: an outer area to the north-east, north and north-west where the non-Irish population is primarily of Scottish origin, and an area in mid and south Ulster where it is predominantly of English origin (Map 10). In general, the pattern of Scottish settlement shown in Map 10 contains at its core the area of Ulster Scots dialect which has in the recent past been shrinking at the expense of the Ulster Anglo-Irish dialect.[4] On the other hand, the fundamentalist revivals of the mid-nineteenth century in Ulster may have resulted in an expansion of Presbyterianism at the expense of the Anglican church at the zones of contact, while in the core areas of English settlement the same revival resulted in an increase in the numbers of Methodists. Consequently many peripheral Scottish areas display the characteristic of Presbyterianism alone among the three indices of Scottish settlement considered.

5.2 *Seventeenth-century patterns of English and Scottish settlement*

Present-day English and Scottish localities in Ulster become most relevant to plantation studies in the context of English and Scottish settlement continuity since the seventeenth century. But in defining the extent of English and Scottish localities in the seventeenth century, it is only possible to examine two of the three criteria used above, as obviously an examination of seventeenth-century Ulster dialect is not possible. However, the present dialects of Ulster represent, to a large extent, fossilized versions of seventeenth-century speech in England and Scotland,[5] so that even they must represent a considerable degree of continuity.

The spread of Presbyterianism in Ulster had by the late seventeenth century resulted in the formation of many Presbyterian congregations throughout the major areas of Scottish settlement. The distribution of these earliest congregations conforms closely to the notion that there were four core areas where Scottish settlers were dominant: north Down, South Antrim, the 'Route' area of north Antrim and north-east Londonderry, and the 'Laggan' area of the Foyle basin in north-east Donegal and north-west Tyrone. These areas are precisely those of the first four presbyteries of Presbyterianism in Ireland, and from which Presbyterianism continued to spread territorially during the seventeenth century. Included in the articles of the plantation was a condition that the undertakers and their tenants should be conformable in religion (to the Established Church). As the colonisation of Ulster by both English and Scottish settlers was well advanced before Presbyterianism was introduced, the spread of this movement was rather restricted initially to areas which had a predominance of Scottish settlement, where the channels of communication with Scotland were strong, and where adherence to the Established Church was not rigidly enforced. Hence the use of religious denomination to distinguish areas of English and Scottish settlement is not a substantially more reliable technique for the seventeenth century than for the present day.

Surnames not only enable the identification of areas of Scottish settlement, but they also provide positive identification of English-settled areas. There are two periods in the seventeenth century (the 1630s and the 1660s) for which it is possible to examine the surnames of the British inhabitants throughout most of Ulster. The 1630 muster rolls list the names of all the British adult males present on each large landowner's estate, while the hearth-money rolls of the 1660s provide the names of all hearth-owners in most of Ulster. Map 7 shows which estates contained predominantly English or Scottish settlers in 1630. The areas of Scottish settlement indicated on this map coincide with the areas of Presbyterianism in the seventeenth century, although some areas in mid-Ulster appear to have also had a majority of Scottish tenants. Areas of English settlement in County Londonderry, north Armagh, south-west Antrim and Fermanagh support the assumption that most non-Presbyterian British were of English stock. In places these 'English' settlers included Welsh and Manx men. Besides the Welsh recorded among the Dungannon inhabitants in 1622[6] there were considerable numbers of Welsh surnames in the 1630 muster roll for the Donegal estate of Captain Robert Davis. These names included Evans, ApEvans, Griffiths, Lloyd, Davis, Jones, Thomas and Williams. The same settlement was described as 'Welsh Towne' in the Civil Survey of 1654.[7]

Besides the obvious similarities between the seventeenth century and the present day, in terms of the relative distribution of English and Scottish settlement, several important changes may be distinguished. County Londonderry appears in the seventeenth century to have been predominantly English rather than Scottish, with few Presbyterians and mostly English surnames, while south Tyrone apparently contained a relatively higher proportion of Scots. The precise pattern of English and Scottish surnames in 1630 can be confirmed by using the hearth-money rolls. Here again it may be observed that in the seventeenth century the English and Scottish localities of Ulster were similar to those of the present day, with the exception of County Londonderry, which was English rather than Scottish, and south-west Tyrone, which was Scottish rather than English.

Certain processes of colonisation are suggested by these settlement patterns. When the present English and Scottish localities in Ulster are considered in relation to the source areas of the settlers, their location and extent appear to be consistent with the notion of colonial movements rationalised by distance, convenient points of entry, and channels of communication. However, in the seventeenth century the relative disposition of the two national groups was somewhat different. With respect to the seventeenth-century English settlement of most of County Londonderry, it is necessary to invoke the concept of direct plantation (i.e. the introduction of settlers by the landowners of particular estates) in order to explain the presence of English settlers in an area adjacent to Scotland and isolated from convenient English entry points and core areas of settlement. A similar explanation may be used to explain areas of Scottish settlement in the baronies of Fews in Armagh and Mountjoy in north-east Tyrone and, of course, the Welsh settlement in Donegal. Since the seventeenth century these culturally isolated communities have largely been assimilated and submerged or have retreated as the distinct blocks in Ulster have developed. The concept of direct plantation, thereby equating the nationality of the landowner with that of the tenants is, however, not sufficient in itself to explain the distribution of English and Scottish settlement areas in Ulster, even in the seventeenth century. When the distribution of surnames in Ulster in 1630 is compared with the areas allocated to English and Scottish landowners (Maps 7 and 5) it is apparent that Scottish settlement in north-west Donegal extended beyond the area allocated to Scottish undertakers, while in south Tyrone Scottish settlement predominated in an area originally allocated to English undertakers. With the exception of this problematic area in south Tyrone, the location and extent of the English and Scottish settlement areas in Ulster in the seventeenth century may be satisfactorily explained by reference to either or both concepts of colonisation outlined above: direct plantation of settlers by the landowners, or the colonial spread of settlers from convenient points of entry. Thus when an area of Scottish landownership also had good communications with the Scottish mainland, for example in the Foyle basin or in north Down, persistent core areas of Scottish settlement emerged. Likewise in south-west Antrim and north Armagh, where English landownership coincided with good communications with England, persistent core areas of English settlement emerged.

5.3 *Ulster ports as colonial entry points*

Clearly the relationship between a plantation estate and a convenient port would have had little significance in terms of seventeenth-century colonisation if the sole process involved had been the direct plantation of settlers by landowners. However, in order to explain the settlement patterns of Ulster in the seventeenth century it is also necessary to envisage a process of colonial spread from points of entry by settlers who had not been specifically introduced by plantation undertakers. This concept is supported by the distribution of British *circa* 1659 (Map 8), which shows that colonisation was most successful on the coastal plains of the north and east. As Ulster was being colonised from two primary source areas (south-west Scotland to the north and east, and England to the south-east) all colonial entry points were not equally convenient to both groups of incoming settlers. The ports on the north coast, Londonderry and Coleraine, were more convenient for Scottish settlers rather than English. Clearly some English had travelled to Londonderry, but this was a movement of settlers primarily intended for English-owned estates in the neighbourhood.

A report of the Surveyor-General of Customs in 1637[8] provides an indication of the relative importance of the different Ulster ports at that date. The custom duties due at each port (including duties due from their subsidiary 'creeks') are given in this report, and most important appears to have been Londonderry with a custom duty of £1,259. Second in importance, although only just so, was Carrickfergus with a duty of £1,137, and these were followed by Bangor (£992), Donaghadee (£644), Strangford (£437), Carlingford (£244) and Coleraine (£244). These figures express the relative importance of the major Ulster ports in 1637 and in turn provide an indication of the strength of their hinterlands or spheres of influence. The primary areas of influence adjacent to the ports are important in terms of colonial processes, for the hinterland also represents the area which would be initially colonised from that port acting as an entry point to settlers (if they were to spread and colonise in a manner observed in other colonial situations). The sphere of influence in this sense which is of particular interest is that around the port of Londonderry. Despite the development of Derry by Londoners, and the well-documented presence of English settlers there in the early seventeenth century, Scots were numerically dominant in the city by the 1630s. According to the 1637 customs report, the English there were 'weak and few in number . . . the Scots being many in numbers, and twenty to one for the English'.[9] Not only was Londonderry situated so that it was a convenient entry point only for Scottish colonists, but its hinterland at this time extended well into south Tyrone and in fact included much of north-west Ulster. Therefore in the early seventeenth century south Tyrone was subject to Scottish colonial pressures emanating from the focal point of Londonderry even though this part of Tyrone had been allocated to English undertakers. It may be postulated that under these pressures Scottish settlement expanded, accelerated by the subsequent takeover of several English-owned estates in south Tyrone by Scottish undertakers. The same reasoning may be applied in County Londonderry, where similar pressures in the north of the county may have occasioned a change to Scottish landownership of several London company estates.

In 1637 some of the custom rights of the port of Carrickfergus were sold to Belfast, then merely one of its subsidiary 'creeks'.[10] This event heralded the rapid growth of the port of Belfast in the mid-seventeenth century. Carrickfergus was soon eclipsed as the major port and entry point for English colonists in east Ulster. By the late seventeenth century Belfast had become the distribution point for great numbers of English settlers who spread up the Lagan valley across the already English-settled estates of north Armagh and into south Tyrone.[11] Consequently during the seventeenth century there was an important change in the port orientation of south Tyrone. Belfast was in direct competition with Londonderry for the trade of this area, and hence the colonial pressure in south Tyrone was once again to come from English sources.

The changes in the extent and position of the English and Scottish localities in Ulster between the seventeenth century and the present may be explained partly by an initial introduction of settlers to isolated areas by landowners (as a product of the plantation system of land allocation) and partly by the colonial spread of English and Scottish settlers from different points of entry, with the relative importance of the ports changing significantly with time. These two processes sometimes operated in concert, and sometimes in opposition, but their relative importance in the development of English and Scottish localities has also changed with time, direct plantation being more important in the early stages of colonisation.

5.4 *The processes of colonisation*

An explanation of the development of English and Scottish

localities in the seventeenth century requires the use of at least two basic concepts of colonisation which have already been outlined: the introduction of tenants by the landowners of particular estates (direct plantation), and the spread of settlers from the major ports of Ulster (colonial spread). The basis of most colonial process studies has been that migration between two points is a function of the distance between them. Distance really refers to accessibility, not only in terms of physical separation, but in the social and political possibilities of movement and settlement between two areas. Therefore, given a uniform economic surface open to colonisation, the density of settlement should reflect the direction of colonial spread, as physical distance is an important factor. In studies of colonisation in Sweden theorists such as Hägerstrand, Olsson, Morrill and Bylund have identified many such processes of colonisation.[12] Bylund considers that if the ages of settlements are isoplethed, downslope gradients provide the direction of colonial spread. However, settlement density in Ulster was more often a reflection of the economic variability of the land being colonised.

Several plantation historians have alluded to a colonial-spread type of colonisation in Ulster. Hume refers to English spreading up the Lagan valley from Belfast Lough, pressing across north Armagh and into south Tyrone.[13] Braidwood also refers to English spreading along the Lagan valley and fanning north into the barony of Massereene in south Antrim. Scots are also stated by Braidwood to have encroached into County Londonderry from Antrim to the east and 'through Derry city, a natural port for Scots immigrants'.[14] However, the idea of a radial spread of settlers extending from initial points of entry meets with several obstacles in its practical application to the colonisation of Ulster in the seventeenth century. Bylund's concept of colonial spread in the 'clone model' involves a genetic increase of settlers so that each new generation would seek new land as close as possible to the mother settlement. In Ulster the total colonisation was well advanced within the time span of one or two generations, so the idea of colonial spread by genetic increase cannot be accepted, although settlement spreading rapidly from entry points should result in a similar distributional pattern.

On the other hand, a factor which undoubtedly did affect the settlement pattern as it would have been expected to develop through a process of colonial spread was the nature of the plantation scheme itself. The plantation requirement for each undertaker to plant or colonise his estate with ten families of English or lowland Scots for each 1,000 acres resulted in an initial direct plantation of many colonists without particular regard to distance from any convenient port or colonial entry point. The Scottish undertaker of one of Tyrone's most successful plantation estates, Lord Ochiltree, had by 1611 introduced a considerable number of followers to his estate via Islandmagee in east Antrim.[15] Had these colonists arrived at the same entry point and not been specifically destined for this plantation estate, it is doubtful that they would have had to travel as far as County Tyrone before selecting a suitable area for settlement.

Besides the operation of these two basic colonial processes, it must also be observed that there was a considerable degree of internal migration within Ulster. In 1619 Pynnar's survey stated that tenants were leaving the land in Omagh barony because their tenancies were weak and uncertain.[16] Other instances of internal movement are recorded in the surveys, such as the 1622 survey of Cavan which relates that many of the Scottish tenants of Sir Henry Piers 'had left that land (as we were informed) were gone to dwell in the Clandeboyes from where they came'.[17] Indeed, when the population changes indicated on the surveys between 1619 and 1622 are examined in detail, it would appear that that there were large-scale population movements from poorer to better agricultural land, and from isolated to more central areas. The direction of much of this internal migration is contradictory to that which would be expected if the observed intermingling of English and Scottish tenants was the result of colonial spread. Internal migration within Ulster must therefore be regarded either as part of the continuing process of colonial spread, or as a separate colonial process occurring after direct plantation.

There are, then, three basic processes by which an individual colonist in Ulster may be expected to have arrived at any observed location. In the first place, the colonist may have been introduced directly from England or Scotland to a plantation estate by the landowner or an agent acting on his behalf *(direct plantation)*. Secondly, the colonist may have moved to Ulster via any of the points of entry as a free agent, that is seeking the best and nearest land to his entry point and not being bound to settle on any particular estate *(colonial spread)*. Thirdly, the colonist in question could have originally arrived and settled elsewhere in Ulster, only later moving to the observed location. This process *(internal migration)* may only be regarded as separate and distinct from that of colonial spread if the internal migration was subsequent to the direct plantation of the colonist in a location which he found untenable, and the direction of movement was contradictory to the concept of colonial spread.

5.5 *Colonial processes observed in Tyrone*

To observe the nature of the different processes of colonisation it is necessary to examine a group of undertakers' estates in detail. In the context of the development of English and Scottish localities in Ulster, the central position of Tyrone is of crucial importance. Today north Tyrone is essentially a contact zone between the two major units of British settlement, and in the seventeenth century Tyrone represented an area which requires the use of all concepts of colonial processes in order to explain the development of English and Scottish areas of settlement. A careful examination of surnames at this scale is necessary because of the greater accuracy required in establishing detailed English and Scottish settlement areas, especially if their delineation is to enable observations concerning the colonial processes involved in their development. Besides the muster rolls of *circa* 1630 and the hearth-money rolls of 1666, a third source of settler surnames is available for Tyrone. This is a collection of certificates prepared by individual undertakers or their agents to enable the compilation of the 1622 survey.[18] These certificates list the tenants' names and survive only for Counties Tyrone and Armagh. In fact these 1622 undertakers' certificates provide the first county-wide list of British settlers anywhere in Ulster. The surnames of the plantation population of Tyrone were therefore recorded on three separate occasions: in 1622, *circa* 1630 and 1666. Some of the surnames were clearly of lowland Scots origin (Hamilton, Stewart and Crawford) while others were clearly of English origin (Barlow, Cornewall, Perkins and Penlington).

Besides these readily identifiable names there were many like Wilson, Smith or Young which could have been of either English or Scottish origin.

The importance of accuracy and consistency prohibits using the predominance of one national grouping in any particular area to assume the origin of the remaining doubtful surnames. Indeed, the dominance of English or Scottish surnames on any estate cannot be taken to indicate total English or Scottish settlement, for the mixing of English and Scots is a basic assumption in the colonial-spread process. To avoid many of the numerous pitfalls inherent in the use of surnames as an index of national origin all British surnames recorded in Tyrone for the seventeenth century were collected into a single list. It was arranged alphabetically, and, without reference to location within the county, the names were classified as English, Scottish, or miscellaneous (not identifiably English or Scottish).

The reliability of surnames as an index of national origin can be tested by examining lists of seventeenth-century British surnames which consist of people whose national origin is already known. A register of the names of all the passengers travelling from London to Virginia in 1635 contained only sixteen names in a total of 239 (6.9 per cent) which could be classified as Scottish.[19] From English parish registers 2,000 surnames of recorded baptisms between 1590 and 1630 were obtained from each of the following areas: Chester (Cheshire),[20] Audley (Staffordshire),[21] Southampton (Hampshire),[22] Tor Bay (Devon)[23] and St Olave's (London).[24] The proportions of these names which could be classified as Scottish in each instance were 16.6 per cent (Chester), 4.5 per cent (Staffordshire), 7.4 per cent (Hampshire), 1.0 per cent (Devon), and 16.3 per cent (London). Thus, even in the ports of London and Chester where the incidence of Scottish names was highest, the proportions were small. In contrast, the *Irish Patent Rolls of James I* contain the names of 125 persons 'of the Scotch nation or descent' resident in Ulster.[25] In this list 80 per cent of the surnames could be classified as Scottish. These test results enable a confident assumption that those areas of Tyrone which in the seventeenth century had a higher proportion of Scottish surnames among the British tenantry also represented areas of predominantly Scottish settlement.

In the baronies of Tyrone allocated to Scottish undertakers Scottish surnames predominate both in 1622 and 1630, with the exception of Newtown and Lislap in Strabane barony (whose ownership had become English) and Ocarragan in Mountjoy barony (which was adjacent to English settlement in south-east Tyrone and north Armagh). In most English-owned baronies the surnames were predominantly English in 1622. However, in Clogher barony, which was allocated to English undertakers, Scottish settlement was dominant on five estates (only three of which had, by 1622, been purchased by Scots). In 1622 the estates owned by English generally contained tenants with English surnames. However, the English-owned barony of Clogher had already become an area with a substantial element of Scottish settlement. By 1630 the general pattern of English and Scottish settlement was still the same in Tyrone, but in the west of the county there was an increase in the proportion of Scots not only in the Scottish-owned estates of Strabane barony but also in many of the English-owned estates between Strabane and the Clogher Valley, in Omagh and Clogher baronies.[26]

The credibility of the emergence of distinctly English and Scottish localities in Tyrone in the first half of the seventeenth century is reinforced by contemporary documentation. The 1611 survey provides evidence that some undertakers brought with them followers, presumably from the undertakers' home areas in England or Scotland. Direct plantation of this nature was recorded on the Scottish-owned estates of Strabane, Largie (Cloghogenal), Ballyokeuan and Revelineightra and Revelinowtra. In Clogher barony Sir Thomas Ridgeway of Tor Bay in Devon brought men from London and Devonshire to his estate of Portclare and Ballykirgir. Ridgeway also wrote to the undertaker of an adjacent estate to inquire if some of this undertaker's 'young followers' could be invited to settle on Ridgeway's estate 'upon view of the land & lyking of the rent' when they came over during the summer.[27] Bodley's survey of 1613 records 'English' tenants of the servitors' estates of Ballydonnell and Roe in Dungannon barony, but states that the English-owned estate of Moyenner in Clogher barony contained 'inland Scots'. The 1622 survey confirms the presence of Scots in Largie (Strabane barony) and English in Roe (Dungannon barony). The English-owned servitor's estate of Benburb (Dungannon barony) also contained English colonists, but the undertaker's certificate for the adjacent estate of Dungannon is headed 'The English, Scotch and Wealch inhabitants'. Certainly, as the surname evidence suggests, there was a considerable degree of mixing of English and Scottish tenants. The evidence of Scots settling outside their allocated baronies of Strabane and Mountjoy is supplemented by a statement of Lord Audley's in 1614 when he claimed that his estate of Finagh and Rarone in Omagh barony had as many Scots as English on it.[28]

Although there is a considerable degree of continuity between 1630 and 1666 in the distributional pattern of British settlement, and indeed in the persistence of English and Scottish localities, the actual surnames on most estates did change dramatically. This turnover of personnel cannot be attributed simply to the ravages of the 1641 rebellion, for comparable changes can be observed between 1622 and 1630. A high degree of tenant mobility is a striking characteristic of plantation settlement, despite the continuity of settlement patterns.

While definite documentary evidence exists only for the colonial processes of direct plantation and internal migration, the presence of colonial spread in the early plantation period can be established circumstantially. An *a priori* model of colonisation may be constructed along the following lines. If each undertaker was consistent in the number of tenants he introduced, the distribution of settlers throughout the county would be approximately uniform. The subsequent clustering of settlers in the more economically desirable and secure estates would then occur as the process of internal migration took place. However, superimposed on this simplified model must be the influx of colonists which occurred from points of entry and adjacent areas of high colonial population density. It would be expected that all three processes would operate simultaneously, but that their relationship and relative importance would change with time. Unrestricted colonial spread would be expected to predominate in the later stages of the plantation and direct plantation in the early stages.

In the historical context it would normally be impossible to examine these processes without detailed documentation. However, the Ulster plantation consisted of a simultaneous colonisation by two distinct and identifiable national groups:

the English and the Scots. Because of this it is possible to examine each plantation estate individually for the proportion of Scottish settlers and to compare this with *(a)* the accessibility of the most convenient port of entry for Scottish settlers, and *(b)* whether the estate was owned by an English or a Scottish undertaker. In 1622 the percentage of Scots on any Tyrone estate was closely related to whether or not the estate was Scottish-owned, and only marginally related to the physical distance from Londonderry as the natural entry point for Scottish settlers. However, by 1630 the gap between the statistical significance of these two factors had narrowed, and by 1666 it was the distance from Londonderry which was most significant.[29] This supports the model of colonisation outlined above, whereby the process of direct plantation, with subsequent internal migration, operated simultaneously with that of colonial spread. Furthermore, the contention that colonial spread became relatively more important than direct plantation with time is also supported.

5.6 *Direct plantation or colonial spread?*

If direct plantation was as important in 1622 as the relationship between landownership and settlement suggests, this should be especially true of English settlers. There is little reason to suppose a large-scale introduction of English settlers by the process of colonial spread into Tyrone at this early stage. Consequently English tenants, who were mostly settled on English-owned estates, should display other characteristics indicative of direct plantation. The surnames on several English-owned estates can be compared with contemporary surnames of districts in England from which the undertakers and servitors came. There are three localities in England from which landowners came to Tyrone: Devonshire, Staffordshire and Hampshire. Where plantation estates had been continuously owned up to 1622 by landowners from any one of these English counties, it might be expected that the English tenants on these estates would have surnames from the same county.

Sir Thomas Ridgeway of Tor Bay in Devon held the estate of Portclare and Ballykirgir in Clogher barony and the adjacent servitor's proportion of Largie in Dungannon barony up to 1622. His brother George held the estate of Ballymackell in Clogher barony, and Sir Arthur Chichester, who had obtained the servitor's proportion of Dungannon, also came from Devonshire. Thus in 1622 there were four estates in south-east Tyrone owned by Devon men which were mostly settled with English tenants. In Omagh barony a family group headed by Lord Audley had obtained the estates of Finagh and Rarone, Edergoole and Carnbracken, Brad, and Fentonagh. Like Ridgeway and Chichester, Lord Audley had resided in Ireland before the plantation, but his roots were at Audley in Staffordshire. These four estates in Omagh barony which were owned by men from Staffordshire were again mostly settled with English tenants. The plantation estate of Benburb in south-east Tyrone was the only other estate in Tyrone for which it could be established that the owner originated from and had owned land in a particular area of England. This estate was owned by Lord Wingfield, the son of Lewis Wingfield of Southampton. On the estates owned by Devonshire landowners in Tyrone there were 156 settlers in 1622. On those owned by Staffordshire men there were 76, and on that of Benburb (owned by the son of a Hampshire landowner) there were 36.

In order that the surnames of these settlers could be compared with names from Devon, Staffordshire and Hampshire, seventeenth-century parish registers for the appropriate areas were consulted. For each area considered, a list of 2,000 surnames was compiled from parish baptismal registers of the period 1590-1630. Similar lists were also compiled from parish registers in London and Chester (the major English ports of trade with Ireland) for comparative purposes, as these two centres may represent principal source areas of English colonists not directly introduced by the above landowners. Of the surnames on the Tyrone estates owned by Devonshire men in 1622, only 32 per cent could be found in the list of Devonshire surnames. However, 36 per cent of the names on the same plantation estates were found in the list for London, and 36 per cent in the list for Chester. Similarly, while only 21 per cent of the names found in the estates owned by Staffordshire men were contained in the list of Staffordshire surnames, 37 per cent were found in each of the lists relating to London and Chester. In the plantation estate of Benburb, owned by Lord Wingfield of Southampton, 42 per cent were found in the Hampshire list, 33 per cent in the London list, and 31 per cent in the Chester list.

Thus only on the estate of Benburb were more surnames found to be contained in the list pertaining to the home area of the landowner than in the surname lists of London or Chester. Although English-owned estates in Tyrone had predominantly English settlement, a close examination of all the English surnames in the county suggests that they were of mixed origins within England, but perhaps predominantly from London or Chester.

The documentary evidence of direct plantation indicates that Ridgeway (of Devon) introduced men to Tyrone from both London and Devonshire,[30] while Chichester (also from Devon) introduced to Carrickfergus men from Devonshire, Lancashire and Cheshire.[31] In view of the fact that many of the English landowners in Tyrone were resident in Ireland before the plantation, and that many did not own any land in England, the predominance of English tenants on their plantation estates is problematic. If English landowners were introducing tenants, not only from their own lands in England but also from the hinterlands of major ports in England such as Chester, this would provide one explanation of the constant reference to Lancashire and Cheshire men on the English-owned land of mid and east Ulster, and of the association of the present Anglo-Ulster dialect of mid-Ulster with that of the north-west midlands of England in the seventeenth century.

5.7 *A model of colonisation*

A modification of the concept of direct plantation to include the introduction of settlers from areas other than the landowners' own home territories is necessary to help explain the pattern of English and Scottish settlement. However, it should be remembered that there is little historical evidence to suggest that undertakers or their agents actively canvassed for colonists in, for example, Lancashire and Cheshire after taking up residence on their estates. In 1613 one English undertaker in Lifford barony in County Donegal was 'in England to draw over others', while another in Cavan had 'now gone into England to bring over with him more inhabitants'.[32] The attempts by the London companies to 'levy' or 'presse' artificers from London to be planted in Londonderry and Coleraine appear to have been ineffective. A high correlation between the nationality of the tenants and that of the landowners, in the absence of massive direct plantation, may alternatively be explained by a modification of the concept of colonial spread. Scottish settlers colonising Tyrone from an entry point such as Londonderry would have spread according to their perception of the surrounding environment. Estates owned by English landowners, especially if without previous Scottish settlement, may well have been avoided in preference to estates where familiar customs could be expected. In County Cavan the 1622 surveyors recorded that on one estate the English tenants had complained of 'hard usage' by the Scottish undertaker and his agent.[33]

The distinction between the two concepts of colonial spread and direct plantation becomes less clear where they are modified to incorporate the perceived environment and the introduction of tenants by the landowners from source areas other than the landowners' own point of origin. Furthermore, the expected distributional pattern of English and Scottish settlement would be similar if either modified process was prevalent. Direct plantation and colonial spread may be more suitably regarded as two extremes of a continuum. Figure 5 illustrates diagramatically a revised model of colonisation which includes the notion of a continuum between colonial spread and direct plantation. At the colonial-spread end of this spectrum, distance from entry point, the physical environment and economic factors provide a causal explanation of the settlement pattern, while at the direct-plantation end the influence of the landowner in bringing or attracting tenants is predominant. As internal migration is associated with the establishment of a state of equilibrium between the colonist and the environment, it may be regarded either as a distinct process subsequent to direct plantation, or otherwise as a corporate part of the colonial-spread process.

It is not possible to establish even an approximate point along the colonial process continuum which would best represent the relative explanatory powers of the extremes of colonial spread and direct plantation. Any such point would fluctuate between the two under the influence of several factors. With time the colonial process continuum became increasingly orientated towards colonial spread, but the effect of a colonial-spread type of colonisation also decreased spatially with distance from the

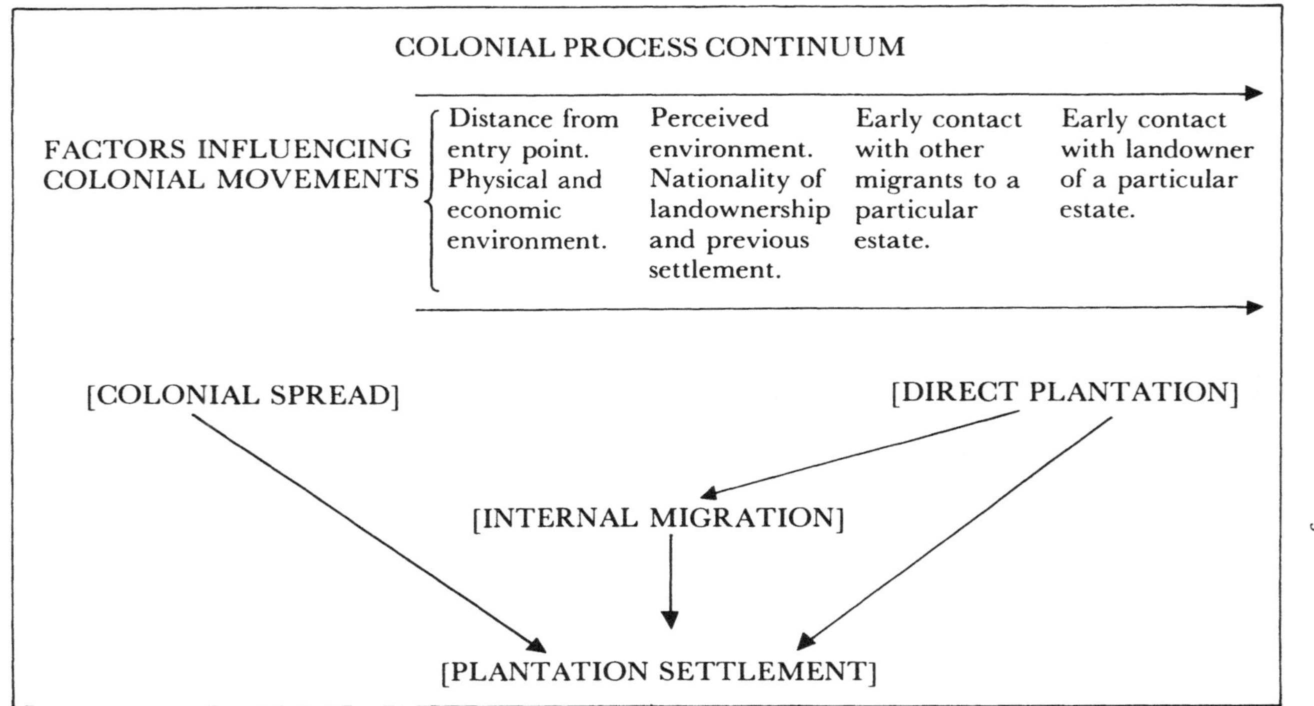

Figure 5: *A model of colonial processes operating in seventeenth-century Ulster*

entry point at any given time. Also in Tyrone colonial spread was more evident among Scottish settlers than English, and among cottagers and undertenants than freeholders and leaseholders (25 per cent of the tenants' surnames on the estates owned by men from Devonshire in 1622 were apparently Scottish, compared with 66 per cent of the cottagers' surnames).

6

The Plantation Building Programme

The purpose of the plantation surveys was to investigate all the undertakings of the plantation grantees, not simply to enumerate British settlers on the estates. All undertakers, servitors and even the larger Irish grantees were required to build bawns, and all those who obtained larger estates had also to build stone or brick houses and castles. The progress of the building programme was duly recorded in each of the plantation surveys. The early surveys of 1611 and 1613 were preoccupied with the buildings and their preparations, perhaps because there was little else favourable to report. By the time of the 1619 and 1622 surveys most of the building programme had been completed. Pynnar reported in 1619 that there had been built '107 castles with bawns, 19 castles without bawns, 42 bawns without castles or houses, 1,897 dwelling houses of stone and timber, after the English manner'.[1] The surviving plantation castles and bawns are the most dramatic and symbolic structures in Ulster dating from this period, but the building innovations which were to prove most enduring and significant were at vernacular level. Of course, stone-built tower houses and bawns, such as the fifteenth-century bawn at Audley's castle in County Down, existed in medieval Ulster long before the plantation. Indeed, just as British settlement was not confined to the escheated counties, neither was the construction of bawns and castles during the plantation period.

6.1 *Plantation buildings: bawns*

Although the word 'bawn' is used freely in the plantation documents, it was really an anglicisation of the Irish *badhún* (cattle fort). What was intended, however, was something more substantial than an earthen bank enclosure strengthened by a hedge or timber palisade. The conditions of the plantation required every owner of an estate of 1,000 acres or more to build a strong court or bawn, but the precise form or building materials were not specified. It was not until after the 1622 survey that the construction of earth or sod bawns and the use of clay mortar in stone-walled bawns were severely censured as 'defects' of the servitors and undertakers.[2] The ideal bawn was a defensible courtyard with strong walls and perhaps small bulwarks or flankers at the corners. Such an enclosure should have a gate to close the entrance, and would be suitable for protecting livestock and even resisting minor attacks. Bawns were intended to be the focal points of each estate, and the tenants were to be drawn to build their houses 'not scattering, but together, neere the principall house, or bawne, as well as for their mutuall defence'.[3] Some bawns constructed in Cavan had more than a local importance, being 'well situated for defence... being upon the border of severall counties'.[4] While the early surveys of 1611 and 1613 reported that a great number of bawns were still being constructed at this time, the later surveys contain descriptions of the optimum number of completed bawns. In 1619 Pynnar noted the presence of 149 bawns, and the 1622 survey found 152. Only twenty-five estates which should have had bawns were found to be lacking.

The actual shape, size and construction of the bawns varied enormously. Mostly they were square or rectangular in plan, and the greatest number measured between sixty and a hundred feet in length and breadth. The walls were usually from eight to fourteen feet high. Corner-flankers were built on a great number of the larger bawns, two or four flankers being most common. Occasionally these flankers were open defensive bulwarks, but on other sites they were roofed and used as stores or even as dwellings. The flankers themselves could be either round or square in plan.

The constructional materials were recorded for all but five of the bawns. It is clear that by far the greatest number (115) were built of stone, either using lime or clay as mortar. Where clay mortar was used the walls were often rendered with lime. Only one bawn with dry-stone walls was recorded, and only one with 'clay and straw' walls. Four bawns were constructed of brick. A significant number of bawns were, however, not built of brick, stone or clay. These were the earth or 'sodd' bawns, which numbered about twenty and to which must be added a further six bawns built of timber and earth. Many of the earth bawns were built by Irish grantees, but by no means exclusively so. Some of these earth bawns were circular in plan. In all, four earth bawns were recorded as being 'round', as were another four built of stone and lime. The other sod bawns of many Irish grantees were not described in detail, nor were any dimensions given. It is tempting to suggest some continuity in rath construction into the early seventeenth century, but this clearly was not the case. However, there was some reuse of raths as bawns. Sir John Fishe in Cavan had built a round bawn of lime and stone 'upon a rath', as had Thomas Flowerdew in Fermanagh.[5] Both these sites were described as raths in 1622 and 'Danish forts' in 1613. Captain Reilly in Cavan, Robert Stewart in Tyrone, and Walter McSweeney in Donegal had also all built in round 'Danes' forts'. The contemporary observation that these raths had been built by the Vikings was, of course, erroneous, and it shows that there had been no continuity of rath construction from the Early Christian period.

Some of the earth bawns were built by settlers, and most of these were square. A group of about six in north Armagh could even be described as 'timber' bawns, for they ranged from timber palisades on earth banks to walls of 'cleft wood' banked inside with earth. Such a bawn built in Armagh by James Matchett was described in 1613 as 'a square bawn of timber clefts of good thickness 10 feet in height rampiered within with earth and sods to the height of 6 feet having 2 whole flanks, each side of the bawn containing 40 yards'.[6]

6.2 *Plantation buildings: castles and manor-houses*

Every plantation grantee of 2,000 acres or more was required to build a castle within the bawn; those of 1,500 acres were to build a stone or brick house and bawn; while those of 1,000 acres were to build a bawn at least. Despite the fact that bawns of some sort were built on the great majority of plantation estates, the more precise building requirements on the larger estates frequently remained unfulfilled. Some estate owners whose grants were only of 1,000 acres built castles, while some who obtained grants of 2,000 acres only built small, vernacular houses. In practice the dwellings of the landowners ranged from castles (in the sense of large fortified stone dwellings) to unfortified manor-houses within bawns. In the latter examples the bawns were presumably intended to be sufficiently secure to defend the dwellings. Apart from the grantees who did not build at all, many only built small, single-storey thatched houses. In some estates where the buildings were more sophisticated even the tenants lived in more substantial dwellings than the undertakers of other estates. Pynnar claimed to have found in 1619 '107 castles with bawns, 19 castles without bawns', making 126 plantation castles in all. The detailed descriptions of these buildings in the 1619 and 1622 surveys reveal that there certainly were not 126 castles, but rather a total of some 126 castles and undertakers' houses of all types: fortified and unfortified, large and small, designed and vernacular.

Of the 164 plantation estates surveyed, 38 had no principal dwelling, 43 had structures described as 'castles', 54 had 'stone houses', and 29 had houses of other types. On the largest estates of 2,000 acres or more, instead of a theoretical total of 50 castles, there were only 20, along with 20 stone houses, four brick houses, two timber houses, and one 'house'. Three had no dwelling constructed at all. The 31 estates of 1,500 acres which were to have 'brick or stone houses' had recorded eight castles, twelve stone houses, one brick house, one 'house', and nine with no dwelling. As might be expected, the 83 estates of 1,000 acres contained a variety of dwelling types for the grantees. Besides six timber houses and one brick house there were 13 small houses variously described as 'poor', 'small', 'mud', 'Irish', or 'old' houses. Twenty-six estates had no principal dwelling recorded, but there were 22 stone houses and 15 castles.

Of the total of 43 castles, seven were not newly built but were reused pre-plantation castles or abbeys. It is, of course, problematic as to how many of the larger stone houses described in the surveys could in fact have also been fortified structures. Most were clearly not anything more than stone manor-houses of contemporary English design. In this sense it is interesting to contrast the dwelling of Andrew Stewart on his 1,000-acre estate of Ballyokeuan in Tyrone with that of Lord Lambert on his 2,000-acre estate of Carrick in Cavan. Stewart's dwelling, known as Roughan Castle, was described in 1622 as 'a handsome Castle, about 20 foot square, with 4 Turretts, being 2 stories and a half high'. Lord Lambert's house, on the other hand, was simply 'a house of stone and lyme 60 foot long, 21 foot broad, 2 stories high'.

As might be expected, the remains of the surviving plantation castles reveal a correspondence between architectural style and the national origin of the undertaker or servitor. The fortified tower house was still current in Scotland and in the English border counties in the early seventeenth century. Consequently the best-developed 'plantation castle' style of building in Ulster has a distinctly Scottish flavour. Many of the more wealthy Scottish undertakers built square tower houses, or castles with an L-shaped or a T-shaped plan. Embellishing a fair number of buildings were architectural details commonly associated with Scottish castles, such as corbelled turrets high on the outer angles, or crow-step gabling.[7]

The English servitors and undertakers had not the same current traditions of defensive domestic buildings to draw on when attempting to comply with the plantation requirements. More often their large stone houses had large stone-mullioned glazed windows at each floor level; these were clearly inappropriate in a dwelling intended to be a defensive structure. Although paradoxically Castle Caulfield in Tyrone, built by Sir Toby Caulfield, was described as a 'castle' in 1622, it was essentially a large Elizabethan-style house with a gate-house at the bawn entrance. The main house had an E-shaped plan and English window and chimney design. Concessions to defence in this structure were nominal rather than dominant, the bawn and gate-house being intended to resist attack. Pynnar described Castle Caulfield in 1619 as the 'fairest building I have seen'. In the 1622 survey a fuller description is given: '. . . formed in three square sides, the front 80 foot longe, and the other two 40 foot long apeece; the comon breadth is 22 foot. It is batlemented round about with freestone. The windows and fonnels of the chymneyes are likewise of freestone; the gutters are substantially leaded, so spatious as men may well use their Armes on them. The height from the foundacon to the top of the Battlemts is 45 foot.'[8]

Other less impressive but nevertheless substantial English houses were built which incorporated English regional characteristics, such as the projecting rear staircase found in vernacular houses of south-west England. Several such houses were recorded in Cavan in 1622: Captain Ridgeway had built at Lough Ramor 'a strong house of stone and lyme slated . . . with a stair case 11 foot square, which goes to the top of the house'; Sir George Mainwaring had a Lisreagh 'a howse of brick and lyme with a round stair case behinde the howse'; Peter Aymes at Tonagh had also built 'a howse of stone and bad lyme . . with a little round on the backside of the howse for a stair case'. In Fermanagh too the same feature was noted on Lord Folliott's house at Drumkeen, 'a strong howse of stone and lyme, 68 foot long, 25 foot broad and 3 stories high, with a large square staire Case on the back of the howse'. Most of the 'stone houses' described in the surveys were less than three storeys high with rectangular ground plans. Few were more than twenty feet from front to back, but in length they were more often from forty to sixty feet. On the other hand, the 'castles' were frequently three or more storeys high and often had approximately square ground plans.

It is not possible to regard all undertakers' houses which cannot be identified as tower houses or 'castles' as having been vernacular buildings. Clearly some were, for they were recorded as small thatched 'Irish' houses, and others were timber-framed houses with distinctive English regional characteristics. However, some of the larger manor-houses were of a more 'formal' design. Some of the best-documented accounts of the building programme relate to the estates granted to the London companies, and in some cases receipts, accounts, contracts, plans, letters and workmen's wage-sheets survive to provide an extremely detailed picture of the construction of these manor-houses. The Drapers' Company considered a number of different designs for their intended house at Moneymore.[9] The original plans for three of these survive, including a unique front elevation, ground plan and first-floor plan titled 'Anthonie Lipsett plott of a howse for the drapers'. Neither this design nor the one which was adopted could be described as representing any English regional house type. Rather these were the personalised designs of individual builders and were unquestionably formal architecture. In the case of Moneymore and on other similar estates 'English' houses in stone, brick or timber-frame were built for the tenants. These were the innovatory vernacular house types which were greatly to influence the development of the traditional house in Ulster in later years.

The stone manor-house built at Moneymore by the Drapers' Company provides a fine example of the unfortified, formal dwelling-house of the plantation period. In place of a wall at the rear of the bawn, the enclosure was completed by a line of buildings consisting of a square corner-flanker, the manor-house and a chapel. The manor-house itself was 71 feet long by 26 feet broad externally and was divided inside into three bays. At ground-floor level the first bay of the house (alongside the chapel) was the parlour. This room was cellared underneath, and a small area between the parlour and the hall in the central bay was partitioned off to form a buttery. The central hall projected out at the front of the house to form an entrance, so that the house had a truncated T-shaped plan. The third bay of the house contained the kitchen at ground-floor level. In all, there were 2½ storeys in the house besides the cellar. Access to the upper floors was provided by three wooden staircases, and the dormers were built in the style of 'Dutch gables'. These were surmounted by ornamental sunburst finials. The gutters were leaded, the roof covered with oak shingles, and bricks were used for the chimneys and to form the openings for the windows and doors. Freestone mullions and iron bars were used in the leaded and glazed windows. Inside the house an oven was constructed in the kitchen chimney, and the internal walls and ceilings were plastered. The lower portion of some walls were wainscotted. Floorboards were well nailed down, and the internal doors were made from cleft oak with one side planed smooth. Such an apparently grand house, however, had its problems, for poor mortar and clay was used in the stone work. This washed out and caused a partial collapse during construction in 1617.[10]

6.3 *'English' houses and other vernacular dwellings of the settlers*

While different house types and numerous local vernacular building features were introduced from various parts of England and Scotland during the plantation, the surveys are an unsatisfactory source of housing information for several reasons. In the first place, the descriptions are generally confined to the dwellings of the undertakers and their principal tenants; and secondly, the house types are often simply described in the surveys as 'English' or 'Irish'. Scottish house types are not referred to; nor is any indication given of what English regional house types were involved. The implication certainly is that the 'English' house was a term loosely applied to houses occupied by settlers that were of a higher standard than those used by the native Irish.[11]

When the plantation surveys are examined specifically to determine which features of the dwelling contributed to its being assessed as 'English' or 'English-like' by the surveyors, the most frequent additional descriptions refer to the nature of the walling material used. Stone houses, with lime or clay mortar, were certainly considered to be English or 'after the manner of the Pale', as indeed were timber-cagework houses. It is interesting to note that only with timber houses were the descriptions worded as being of cagework 'after the English fashion', or houses of 'English' frames, implying that it was the *nature* of the timber-work that was significant. Several references to English houses mention other features known to have been common to Irish houses, such as having thatched roofs or roofs of coupled construction, so that these cannot, in themselves, have been used as diagnostic criteria. It would be misleading, however, to suggest that the occurrence of walls constructed of stone or timber-cagework were the universal criteria on which houses were adjudged to be 'English'. According to the 1611 survey, Thomas Blenerhasset had in County Fermanagh 'a fair large Irish house built with windows and roomes after the English manner', while again in Fermanagh the same survey notes that both Thomas Flowerdew and Lord Burley had built Irish houses 'contrived into rooms' and had added wattled chimneys. In addition to these instances which suggest that chimneys and the internal subdivision of the house into rooms were English characteristics, the 1622 survey records that at Kilcloghan in Cavan there were two 'fair English like houses of stone and clay thatched with stone chimneys' and at Drumcrow in Fermanagh 'two large English like howses . . . one of stone . . . one storie & a garrett high, the other of like length of cagework, 2 stories and a half high', while the 1613 survey records that Sir Patrick McKee in Donegal had built a stone house, though with 'an Irish roof of birchen wood, as yet uncovered'.

Besides castles and bawns, Pynnar claimed to have recorded

'1,897 dwelling houses of stone and timber, after the English manner in Townreeds, besides very many such houses in several parts which I saw not'.[12] It is, however, clear that only a fraction of the plantation settlers dwelt in 'English' houses. Throughout all the surveys only about 500 houses are described in terms of their walling material. In almost all the individual estates where the buildings of stone or English cagework were enumerated these were not sufficient for the numbers of British families recorded. While many British settlers were known to have occupied 'Irish' houses, the extent to which the surveyors could have distinguished these from Scottish vernacular buildings is open to question. Rather than being representative of settler house types, the surveys only indicate the nature of the most sophisticated dwellings, especially those of the grantees and their principal tenants. Where the nature of the walling material is indicated in the surveys, this information has been abstracted and mapped (Map 11). It can be seen that the use of stone (either

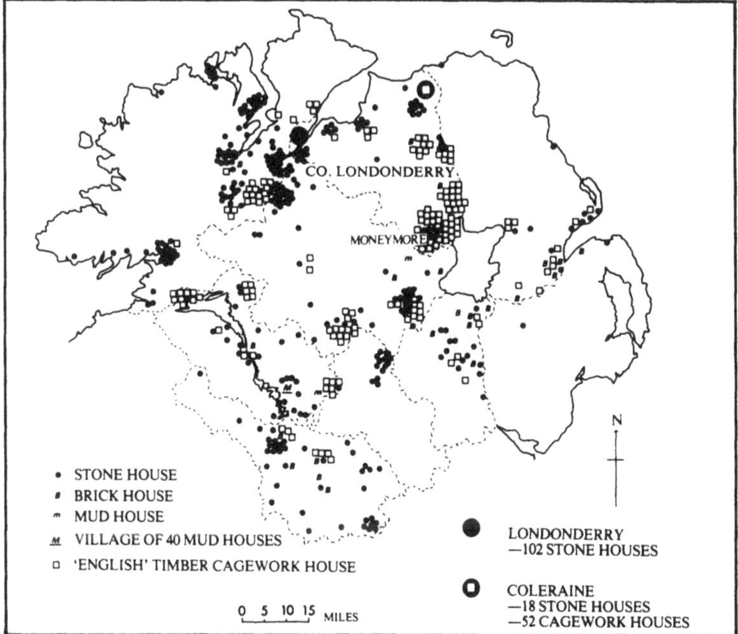

Map 11: *House-walling materials recorded in the plantation surveys*
The 1611 survey also describes some buildings outside the official plantation area, in counties Monaghan, Antrim and Down.

with lime or clay mortar) was ubiquitous throughout the planted areas and was the most common walling material recorded. A large number of timber-cagework houses had also been built, and there was an apparent tendency for these to be concentrated in the areas around Lough Neagh and Lough Erne, which were heavily wooded and in the hands of English rather than Scottish undertakers.

The use of coursed stone with lime or clay mortar in the construction of domestic buildings was undoubtedly one of the most enduring characteristics of plantation settlement. Houses or castles of three and four storeys are described in the surveys, but the great majority were of one or two storeys. Most of these houses were between 18 and 25 feet from front to back, and the most frequently occurring lengths were 20 to 24 feet, 40 feet, 50 feet and 60 feet. The recorded sizes of most of these stone houses are consistent with surviving vernacular dwellings containing two or three rooms arranged in a rectangular plan. There are frequent references in all the surveys to both lime and clay being used as mortar. Although most of the stonework was in random rubble, freestone was occasionally used for quoins and door and window surrounds. English masons were employed in building many of the larger manor-houses, and also dwellings in towns such as Londonderry, Dungannon, Lurgan and Coleraine.

The introduction of large numbers of masons and carpenters into Ulster during the early years of the plantation to cope with the massive building programme was an influence which declined in relative importance as the seventeenth century progressed. This was perhaps most obvious in terms of the construction of elaborate timber-framed houses. Map 11 indicates the extent to which these timber-cagework houses existed in the early seventeenth century, but they have not survived either as relic buildings or as part of the vernacular building tradition.[13] Few timber-framed houses survived the 1641 rebellion. Their destruction was recorded in the Civil Survey of 1654, and only a few survived down to the nineteenth century. The Ordnance Survey Memoirs (1835-39) record some late survivals of oak-framed houses at Coleraine, Antrim and Carrickfergus. In the town of Antrim

> One little old house . . . has a gable elevated on its front and

> there are still four houses constructed exclusively of wood — in two of these the upper storey projects beyond the lower one. . . . The floors, walls and door are all of oak. The spaces between the timbers are filled up with mud or mortar plastered over and roughcast. They are now thatched but it is said they were formerly roofed with shingles.[14]

The demise of timber-framing in Ulster was probably caused as much by the disappearance of suitable woodlands as by the ephemeral presence of the English carpenters in the early seventeenth century. It is clear that the distribution of timber-framed houses as shown in Map 11 coincides with the distribution of contemporary woodland. The woods of Glenconkeyne and Killetra received special attention from the Londoners when they were assessing the potential of their lands, describing 'great stores of goodly oak, fit for all manner of buildings, ash also, with elm of great bigness'. Not only was this timber thought to be enough to supply the county of Londonderry, but the Londoners agreed to allow the settlers in Donegal and Tyrone 'timber for their buildings if they have not enough of their own'.[15] The timber resources in Glenconkeyne were quickly exploited in the early years of the plantation for building purposes. There were numerous saw-pits in the woods, with twenty Irish cabins for workmen. Both English and Irish were engaged in felling and preparing timber. There were vast quantities in various stages of treatment: squared timber, lathes, scaffold poles, and frames of houses. The River Bann was used to transport frames and sawn timber to Coleraine, but distribution from here increased the cost substantially, so that in north-west Londonderry the lack of convenient oak encouraged the use of stone for building. Some house frames were shipwrecked *en route* for Londonderry from Coleraine. By 1700 there was probably not enough suitable oak surviving to sustain a timber-framed house-building tradition on any scale. The Ordnance Survey Memoirs for Ballyscullion parish, situated where formerly had been the extensive woods of Glenconkeyne, are unique in recording for the nineteenth century that 'The houses in this Parish were until a comparatively few years ago constructed of wood — and there circumstances must have tended mainly to the consumption of the timber.' (This parish is where the frames for the timber houses at Antrim were reputed to have been made.)[16]

Picture-maps of the Londonderry settlements in 1622 drawn by the city's surveyor, Thomas Raven, provide vivid representations of the seventeenth-century timber-framed houses. Some fifty such houses are depicted in these maps, each with a chimney-stack in a central position, two dormer windows in the front of the house, and almost all with shingled or tiled roofs. There are no timber-framed buildings shown with cruck construction, but they were all apparently box-framed. The arrangement of diagonal braces and horizontal ties on individual houses is not consistent between two contempory versions of the maps (both of which are in the hand of Thomas Raven).[17] Detailed descriptions of the arrangement of the timbers on some of these buildings suggest that a number were in fact 'half-timbered', that is with the spacing between the timber uprights equal to the thickness of the timber itself. On the Ironmongers' estate one house was built of 'timber, squared to five or six inches square and five inches space between each piece, and between those nogged as we called it with short pieces of cleft oak driven hard between and plastered, so it is very strong and thought equal to stone building'.[18] A contract for the building of timber houses at Moneymore in 1615 required them

> To be all halfe tymbered seven ynches studd and six ynches space and 5 ynches thick: The Grounsell to be seven and nyne the wall plott seven and eight the beames eleven and nyne the Joyce three and halfe and eight or fowre & seaven the Rafters fowre & a halfe and three and a halfe to be made all of sawen tymber and to be strongly made and halfe timbered and the bracs all other work to be mortised and framed in the stayres to be made and one floore with good sawen bords to be shott and layed by the said James and two stoole wyndows of six foote long above and two below with cleare story wyndows in the sydes.[19]

Other contracts for work carried out on the tenants' houses at Moneymore reveal in great detail the form of these timber-framed houses. Masons were contracted separately to build in these houses 'one stacke of good & sufficient chymneyes contayning fowre chymneys two ground chymneis and two Chamber'.[20] A plan even survives of one of these houses confirming the centrally positioned chimney-stack which divides the house into two rooms on each floor.[21] On each floor there were two hearths 'back-to-back', and the stairs were positioned at the rear of the house at the opposite side of the chimney-stack to the front door.

On almost all of the Raven drawings of 'English' houses on the picture-maps of 1622 a single, central chimney-stack is shown regardless of whether the houses were of stone or timber-framed. Here the accuracy of Raven's drawings must be challenged. Masons' contracts for the building of the *stone* houses at Moneymore clearly state that there were to be two chimney-stacks, one at each gable: 'fowre good and sufficient chymneys to be made to cast their smoke well to be brought upp above the house topps at the gable ends at either end two'.[22] Despite the evidence of the Raven drawings (which is remarkably reliable in other respects), the plantation stone houses of the English settlers in Londonderry were 'gable-hearth' houses. Only the timber-framed houses can be confidently described as 'central-hearth' or 'hearth-lobby' houses.

There are few references in the plantation surveys or other contemporary documents to houses constructed of mud or clay. Pynnar's survey of 1619 records a village consisting of '40 houses of Timber Work, and Mud-Wall' at Lisnaskea in Fermanagh, while the 1622 survey notes in the neighbouring estate of Latgir 'a most poor round Bawne of Soddes and as poor a mud wall thatched house in it'. In Tyrone Alexander Richardson's estate of Creigballe had in 1622 'a little dwelling-house of timber, the walls of clay, and covered with thatch'. Unfortunately the surveys give little indication of the types of houses occupied by the lesser tenants and cottagers of British origin. In many cases these were probably not stone-built or of English timber-cagework, for such buildings were normally listed and described. In view of the widespread survival of mud-walled dwellings in Ulster, it is unfortunate that it is still not possible to determine whether the undercurrent of plantation building at the poorest level was in 'Irish' timber-framed construction or in mud walls of mass construction.

The use of fired-clay products, such as bricks and roof tiles, for domestic structures is referred to in the plantation accounts more frequently than the use of unbaked mud. Brick houses were built (Map 11) primarily in the lowland clay areas, especially along the Lagan valley, through north Armagh, in the Erne basin and central Cavan, and also to the west and north of Lough Neagh. These houses are described almost without exception in favourable terms by the plantation surveyors, and in several instances indications are given that the bricks were manufactured locally. In County Armagh James Matchett had in 1613 'about 40,000 of bricks ready for the kiln', and William Powell had '100,000 bricks ready burnt, and as many more ready for burning'. At Enniskillen in Fermanagh Captain Cole had provided 'at his own charge clay and wood for the making and burning of 300 thousand bricks and tile proportionable', and in north Donegal Sir Ralph Bingley 'hath his clay already cast, and his workmen ready to make 20,000 of brick'.

Thatch as a roof covering was, of course, ubiquitous throughout Ireland, England and Scotland, but some of the more sophisticated roof coverings also found in England were tentatively being adopted in Ireland in the seventeenth century. In 1652 Gerard Boate noted that

> In sundry parts of Ireland slate is found in great abundance. ... Nevertheless some years since in places near the sea, especially at Dublin, that kind of Holland Tiles, which by them are called *Pannen* begun to be used generally, the Merchants causing them to be brought in from thence in great abundance. ... Besides these there was another kind of covering in use, both for Churches and Houses, to wit, a certain sort of woodden tiles, vulgarly called Shingles which are thight enough at first, but do not many years continue so.[23]

While all the houses shown on the Barthelet maps of Ulster *circa* 1600 with hipped roofs were thatched, many of the houses with gabled roofs within the forts are shown covered with red tiles.[24] The plantation surveys, however, only refer to clay-tile roofs on a very few occasions, such as the ten cagework houses at the Vintners' settlement in County Londonderry which were 'covered with tiles', and the references to the production of both bricks and tiles at Enniskillen, Coleraine, and Sir Nicholas Lusshe's estate in Cavan. All these references appear to refer to flat clay 'plain' tiles rather than curved pantiles.

The most common types of roof covering described in the surveys are thatch and slates. The use of slate was often associated with stone houses, but with the availability of suitable local slate being restricted to north-west Londonderry, north Donegal and east Down, it was only in these areas that slated roofs became common. The coarse local slates were each hung on the lath by means of a single oak peg. In County Londonderry the best slate quarries were found on the Goldsmiths' proportion, and the agent had occasion to complain that the quarry holes left after the digging of slate for the roofs of the houses in Londonderry city were a constant danger to cattle. In return the company accused the agent of profiteering by exporting slates from these quarries to London.[25]

Wooden shingle roofs are also frequently referred to in the surveys. In County Londonderry shingled roofs were recorded on the Ironmongers', Mercers', Vintners', Salters' and Drapers' estates, in County Fermanagh at Castle Balfour, and on timber-framed houses at Dungannon. While the plantation surveys do not record shingled roofs in the English-settled areas of the Lagan valley and north Armagh, it is clear from later references that shingles were frequently used there to cover buildings of mass construction as well as timber-framed houses.[26] In general, however, slated roofs were associated with stone houses, and shingles with timber-cagework houses. The shingled roofs at Moneymore were applied by Richard Par, a joiner of Dungannon. He was required to make the oak shingles at least two feet long, one inch thick and five inches broad, so that 1,000 would cover twenty square feet. Having covenanted to lay the shingles and find pins for fixing them, the next year (when they had shrunk) he was to remove and re-lay them.[27]

The use of clay tiles and shingles as roofing materials were features of English vernacular building practice which, although introduced into Ulster during the seventeenth century, were never in fact fully absorbed into the Irish vernacular repertoire. As such they belong in the same class as other features introduced but not adopted, such as timber-framing in the 'English' cagework style, the provision of a projecting staircase at the rear of the house, or indeed the provision of built-in bread-making ovens. Several survivals of built-in ovens have been recorded in Ulster,[28] and houses with ovens were certainly built in Fermanagh and throughout Londonderry. These features, however, survive as exceptions rather than portraying any regional survival of plantation building traditions. On the other hand, the use of slated roofs, mass walling in stone or brick and lime, gabled roofs, and probably the provision of internal divisions between rooms, chimneys and lofting are accepted features of vernacular construction in Ulster which were first widely used for domestic buildings by plantation settlers. Coupled roofs, thatch, and probably cruck trusses were constructional features known to the vernacular building traditions of both England and Ulster before the plantation, while the most important casualty of the plantation was the Irish timber-framed and wattled house with hipped roof and sub-rectangular plan.

6.4 *Churches, mills and other buildings*

At Dungannon in County Tyrone Sir Arthur Chichester had built at his own cost 'one Church and steeple of lyme and stone; the body of the same church containeing in length 60 foot and in breadth within the walls, 25 foot. The Steeple is twentie foot square and fortie foot high to the Batlement.'[29] At Tandragee in Armagh Lord Grandison had also built 'a handsome Church, 60 foot in length, and 24 in breadth, well furnished with Seates, Comunion Table, Capp, Font & a good Bell'.[30] Fewer than twenty such new churches were built by the undertakers and servitors, for their provision was not a plantation requirement. Most of the new churches were erected in towns where a need had arisen and where no old structure was available. In Tyrone new churches were built at Strabane, Dungannon and Benburb; in Londonderry at Ballykelly, Muff (Eglinton), Bellaghy and Moneymore; in Donegal at Killybegs, St Johnstown, Castledoe and Ramelton; in Fermanagh at Lisnaskea and Ederny; and in Armagh at Tandragee. At Belturbet in Cavan Sir Stephen Butler had land set aside towards the cost of a church, but by 1622 there was still ' a great store of Protestants in and about the towne and there should be a church builded there'. In most cases the new churches in the towns were built at the undertakers' own charge, but at Lisnaskea Lord Balfour had received the

'Recusants' Fines' of Cavan and Fermanagh towards the building of the church and free school.[31] In other cases of town development the urban centres grew around old church or abbey sites. Both Londonderry and Coleraine were established by the Irish Society on ecclesiastical sites, so that by 1622 Londonderry had an 'old church repaired', as had Coleraine, except that in the latter case a new steeple had been added. On the country estates of the London companies other old churches were reused at Kilrea (Mercers), Macosquin (Merchant Taylors) and Agivey (Ironmongers). Pre-plantation churches, many of them well built in stone and lime but in a ruinous condition, were taken over by the Established Church throughout Ulster. Roof coverings of the stone churches varied, being usually of slate, tiles or shingles on both new and re-edified churches.

The official ecclesiastical reformation in Ireland had in a sense been completed before the plantation, for Protestant bishops had been appointed to all the dioceses in Ulster. However, in practice individual churches and parishes were only anglicised as Protestant settlement progressed. Only in a few instances were Irish tenants recorded as 'going to [the Protestant] church'. Although there had been a suggestion that each plantation estate should become a parish, and that each undertaker would build a church on his proportion, these proposals were not adopted. The old pre-plantation parishes and their churches persisted as a general framework for the reformed church in Ireland.

As with churches, there was no requirement under the plantation conditions for the grantees to build corn mills. However, unlike churches, there was profit to be made in their operation and control. Almost all of the sixty corn mills recorded in the plantation surveys were built by undertakers or servitors. Leases to tenants on the plantation estates frequently bound farmers to use the undertaker's mill. Only on two estates did the surveys suggest that the corn mills were owned or built by tenants. The plantation surveyors found thirty-six water-powered corn mills, six windmills and one 'horse-mill', but these were clearly an underestimate of the number actually built. For instance, the undertakers' certificates prepared for the 1622 survey record another four water-mills in Tyrone not mentioned in the final survey. In fact a total of nine water-powered corn mills are recorded for Tyrone in the surveys and 1622 certificates, and yet the Civil Survey for the same county records nineteen in 1654 (most of which had been destroyed in 1641).

There are no recorded examples of pre-plantation mills being reused or rebuilt. This was because the type of corn mill built during the plantation was a technological innovation. These new water-mills had vertical water-wheels and were of a type known as trundle mills. Unlike the pre-plantation 'Danish' water-mills with horizontal wheels and a direct drive to the millstones, the trundle mill had a large internal wooden trundle wheel driven by the water-wheel in a vertical plane. By means of wooden pegs and cogs this motion was transferred to a vertical 'spindle' or shaft which turned the millstones.[32] These modifications provided a more efficient and flexible use of water power for grinding corn. However, as a rule the trundle mill had still only one pair of stones. In a few examples two pairs of millstones were recorded: at Bellaghy the Vintners had 'a good mill house and 2 mills therein', and at Tandragee there were 'two watermills under one Roofe'. The mill building itself could be either timber-framed or stone-built, reflecting the building materials of adjacent houses.

A detailed picture of such a plantation trundle mill can be obtained from the records of the Drapers' Company. A contract to build the Moneymore mill was made in 1615 with Elijah Heatley, millwright and carpenter. It was to be half-timbered, one and a half storeys high, and 34 feet long, with sufficient stairs and windows. The wooden water-wheel was to be 14 or 15 feet high and 'breast-shot'. The millwright was also to be responsible for providing all the 'tackle and going gears', for bedding and laying the stones, and for all other carpentry work. A separate contract was given for shingling the roof of the mill. In making the mill sluices and 'flood-gates', 1,230 feet of boards, planks and quarters were used. English labourers dug the spring and the trenches for the backwater and scoured and 'sodded' the mill-race. Many other fittings for the mill were provided by the smith at Moneymore. These included three iron pins, forty 'great' nails and a band of iron for the trundle head in the mill; four iron pins for the cog-wheel; one iron brace, two iron plates and a hundred nails for the mill; and twelve mill-picks for dressing the millstones. The smith had also frequently to repair the gudgins (bearings) and was required to shorten the 'spindle and Reame'. This spindle shaft was the only major component of the mill which was not made of wood. It weighed eighty-two pounds and was manufactured at Coleraine. Other components for the mill imported from London included a 'great beam and scales' with an assorted selection of weights. The first set of millstones installed were quarried locally, but when these were being replaced in 1619 the company observed that the miller should be responsible for maintaining the mill and therefore pay for any new millstones himself.[33]

In addition to the numerous water-powered corn mills built, there were a number of corn mills powered by other means. One 'horse-mill' recorded in Cavan in 1613 was probably not intended to be a permanent feature, or else it was found to be insufficient, for the owner was 'in hand with a wind mill'.[34] Besides various windmills shown on seventeenth-century maps, the plantation surveys found two in Cavan, three in Armagh, and one in Fermanagh. Unfortunately no details survive of these mills, but the remains of later examples are all of the tower type. The tower mill was a fixed building of stone or brick with a revolving cap which turned the sails into the wind. There is little evidence of the other type of windmill once common in Britain — the post mill, where the entire timber-framed housing for the mill rotated on a central post. Nevertheless, on John Brownlow's estate in north Armagh his windmill in 1613 was 'ready framed and presently to be reared'.[35]

There were other water-powered mills built besides corn mills, particularly 'tuck' mills for the fulling of woollen cloth. Tuck mills were to be found in almost every plantation county, but as with corn mills there were more on the ground than were recorded in the plantation surveys. A whole range of industrial structures were provided by settlers, including malt-houses and kilns, saw-mills, glass-houses (for the manufacture of glass) and smithies. Agricultural out-buildings were rarely described in the surveys, although substantial stables were built by many grantees. At Castle Caulfield in Tyrone there was a stable of '80 foot long and 18 foot broad of lyme and stone, with a loft over it to hold corne'. Most of the other plantation buildings described were not found in rural settings at all, but were associated with urban development.

Many market towns in Ulster have as their focal point a single building with a dual function. The market- and court-house symbolised the local importance of the town as a commercial centre and as a centre of judicial administration. Such a combined market- and 'session'-house was built by Sir Arthur Chichester at Dungannon:

> one Session house builded of Timber of strong and curiouse Cage Worke, containeing in length 70 foot and in breadth 40 foot, framed with a double Roofe, under wch is a large Markett house with a Ranck of turned Pillars through the same, over wch there is a large hall for the Judges to sitt, with 2 close roomes for the Juries and Country to attend. There are to this house 8 large Windowes, sufficiently glazed; the roof thereof shingled, and the gutters leaded.[36]

Sir Gerard Lowther had built a market-house at Necarn in Fermanagh, and in Strabane in Tyrone the Earl of Abercorn had built 'a Sessions house and a Markett Cross of stone & lyme, with a strong Roome under it to keep Prisoners in untill they can be conveniently conducted to his ma^ties^ goale at Dungannon'.[37] The Dungannon jail was built at the charge of the inhabitants of County Tyrone and was 'of lyme and stone, the walls thereof are 4 foot thick and 24 foot high to the Batlement, 40 foot in length and 20 in breadth, two strong Vaults plancked round about within with Oaken Plankes 3 inches thick, and underneath with Oaken timber, and hath other Roomes above, with 2 stone Chymneys'.[38]

Only a select few of the plantation towns could boast a school-house. A 'free' or 'royal' school was intended to be built in each escheated county, but by 1622 no such school had been erected in Cavan. In 1619 the Fermanagh school was sited at Lisnaskea and was two storeys high of good stone, 64 feet long and 20 feet broad, with the roof framed and ready to be set up. By 1622 the roof was 'up and shingles ready to be put on it'. Although the Earl of Abercorn had built a stone school-house in Strabane, the 'royal' or 'free' school for Tyrone was built in Dungannon. Some confusion surrounded lands reserved for a school in Londonderry, the charge for which had fallen on the Irish Society and one of its commissioners, Matthias Springham of London:

Near to the said church, is a Fair Free Schoole of lyme and stone, slated, with a base court of lyme, and stone, about it, built at the charges of Mathias Springham of London Merchant deceased; and towards the maintenance of the scholemaister thereof the citty of London allowes 20 Markes stipend yearly: And for the lands which his Matie gratiously intended for the maintenance of A schoole there (upon the first survey of the Escheated lands in Ulster) we cannot learne what is become thereof.[39]

7

Towns, Villages and Dispersed Rural Settlement

The concept of urban living was central to plantation theory. As early as 1567 Sir Francis Knollys had suggested the planting of artisans in settlements at Strangford, Lough Foyle and the Bann, 'that after they may growe to be haven Townes'.[1] When the official scheme for the Ulster plantation was in the process of evolution the importance of the settlers living in towns and villages was frequently stressed. Thomas Blenerhasset, later to become an undertaker in Fermanagh, wanted many strong corporations created to ensure the safety of the settlers.[2] Sir Francis Bacon was more specific. He wanted each castle or principal house to draw the farms about it into villages, hamlets or 'endships', and these villages to be supplemented by four corporate towns for artificers and tradesmen.[3] His reasons for advocating that the 'building be altogether in towns' were for ease of settlers procuring all their requirements, for the assistance of trade, and for the increased security of the settlers. The sites of the villages and towns were to be central within the areas assigned to them, so that men would not be drawn too far from their land, 'for in the champion countries of England, where the habitation useth to be in towns, and not dispersed, it is no new thing to go two miles off to plough part of their grounds; and two miles compass will take up a good deal of country'.[4] Of more particular significance was Chichester's agreement on this subject. In fact Chichester even wanted the native Irish 'to settle themselves in Townes and villadges, where they must be inforced to build houses like those of the palle, and not Cabbyns after their wonted manner, the townes and Villadges to be placed as neere as we maie upon passadges and places of best advantage for service or defence'.[5] Understandably the finalised plantation scheme envisaged a colonisation consisting of nucleated settlements in the form of new towns and villages. On the plantation estates agricultural villages in the mode of England were to be the norm: 'Every of the said Undertakers shall draw their tenants to build houses for themselves and their families, not scattering, but together, neere the principall house or bawne, as well as for their mutuall defence and strength, as for the making of Villages and Towneships.'[6] A limited number of corporate towns were also to be established at selected sites.

It is important to distinguish between villages and towns. The village was essentially an agricultural settlement consisting of a small nucleation of farmers and their labourers (cottagers) adjacent to the bawn or castle in each estate. The town, even when not incorporated, was a larger nucleated settlement which provided service facilities, such as a church, school, inn or 'tap-house', and in particular a weekly market. Such towns usually served a more extensive area than a plantation estate, and townsmen were primarily tradesmen and artificers rather than farmers. The largest of the towns also had administrative functions.

7.1 *Proposed corporate towns*

According to the project of the plantation, there were to be corporate towns erected throughout the escheated counties. Most of the baronies were each to have one, and several hundred acres of corporation or 'town' land were reserved for this purpose. The site of each corporate town was to be determined by the plantation commissioners. In 1608 Chichester had suggested that the towns of Cavan and Lifford be incorporated and that Belturbet in County Cavan was a fit place to be strengthened by a ward or other residence of 'Civill people and well affected subiectes'.[7] Because of the possibility of water transport between Belturbet and Cloghoughter in Cavan and Belleek in Fermanagh, these were also suggested as places to be strengthened with lands allocated to them. In similar terms Enniskillen and Lisgoole in Fermanagh and Ballyshannon in Donegal were advocated as places of strategic importance 'fitt to be continued'.

The first list of proposed corporate towns was drawn up in 1609 in association with the project for the plantation.[8] It named twenty-five sites as follows. In Tyrone towns were to be built at Dungannon, Clogher, Omagh and Mountjoy and in the barony of Loughinsholin; in Coleraine county at Limavady and Dungiven; in Donegal at Derry, Lifford, Ballyshannon, Killybegs, Donegal, Raphoe, Rathmullan and Doagh; in Fermanagh at Lisgoole, Lisnaskea, and one midway between Lisgoole and Ballyshannon; in Cavan at Cavan, Belturbet, and one midway between Kells and Cavan; and in Armagh at Armagh, Mountnorris, Charlemont and Tandragee.

While the responsibility for the development of this network of corporate towns was eventually to rest with the most important servitors and undertakers, individual wealth would clearly be insufficient to finance the development of the largest urban centres. This was true even though lands were allocated to help finance their building. At least one major port was necessary to centralise the export of plantation profits and to disperse the influx of colonists and their commodities. Derry was an obvious choice for such a city-port, while Sir Thomas Phillips's town at Coleraine could also play a similar but secondary role. Here the involvement of the London companies became crucial, as their money could ensure substantial private development. In 1609 the small settlement at Derry was still contained in County Donegal. Coleraine was considered to be in County Antrim, and the barony of Loughinsholin was in County Tyrone. When these areas were annexed to County Coleraine to form the new county of Londonderry the subsequent urban development of this area was not typical of the escheated counties. Corporate towns were not planned for each barony as was the case in Tyrone, but the London companies acting together were to develop Coleraine and Londonderry. The estates of the individual companies in the county each contained a plantation village, but because these estates were much larger than the norm for undertakers elsewhere many of these village settlements grew into market towns. However, none of these were to be incorporated. In fact the only town in County Londonderry to achieve borough status (other than Londonderry and Coleraine) was Limavady on the site allocated to Sir Thomas Phillips. This was granted to him as a servitor in compensation for the loss of his earlier investment at Coleraine. In 1609 another corporate town was proposed at Dungiven, but at that time the fort at Dungiven was in the wardship of Captain Edward Doddington. When the ownership of Dungiven passed into the hands of the Skinners' Company

any idea of establishing a corporate town there was dropped.

The intended importance of all the corporate towns was revealed in the plantation project of 1609. They were to have markets and fairs, and other reasonable liberties, and power to send burgesses to parliament.[9] In 1610 the commissioners were given a broader responsibility for the boroughs.[10] They were not only to select the sites but also to plan them. This meant deciding how many buildings were to be erected, ensuring an adequate water supply, and reserving lands for commons, churches and, where appropriate, schools. The political motivation for incorporation was certainly strong, for the new boroughs could be used to ensure a Protestant majority in the Dublin parliament. Indeed, the twenty-five corporate towns suggested in 1609 were more than would be necessary to achieve this political end. In 1611 Chichester considered that in addition to the ancient boroughs of Carrickfergus and Downpatrick, and the recently incorporated towns of Cavan and Derry, a number of new boroughs should be erected.[11] This amounted to a revision of the list of proposed corporate towns, and it was clearly conceived of in political terms. The burgesses from these new boroughs would help provide an estimated total of 123 Protestant voices in a total parliament of 218. In County Fermanagh only Enniskillen was proposed, and the other suggestions made in 1609 for the incorporation of Dungiven, Clogher, Killybegs, Raphoe, Doagh, Tandragee and the proposed town in Loughinsholin were all dropped. The new list of 1611 consisted of the following towns: Limavady, Donegal, Lifford, Ballyshannon, Rathmullan, Dungannon, Mountjoy, Omagh, Strabane, Armagh, Charlemont, Mountnorris, Belturbet, Lough Ramor (later Virginia in County Cavan), Enniskillen and Coleraine. These sixteen new boroughs were to supplement Cavan and Derry which had already been incorporated, but there were also to be other new boroughs outside the escheated countries. Besides the ancient boroughs of Carrickfergus and Downpatrick, the towns of Newry, Newtownards, Belfast and Monaghan were to be included in a new total of twenty-four boroughs throughout Ulster.

7.2 *The borough towns*

In legal terms borough or corporate towns could be distinguished by their form of town government. This was by means of a corporation consisting of a fixed number of burgesses (usually thirteen) which had been established by royal charter. The town corporation could return two members of parliament as well as being responsible for the provision of town by-laws, the clerkship of markets and fairs, and the holding of local courts. On occasion the corporation had town officers known as bailiffs or portreeves, but there always was a principal officer. This leader of the corporation was not always known as the mayor, although this was the case in Londonderry and Carrickfergus. In Dungannon, Strabane and Killybegs he was known as the provost, in Cavan as the sovereign portreeve, and in Ballyshannon and Donegal simply as the portreeve. Elections were not held for the corporation, but the corporate body was formed from nominees among the group of townsmen who held burgage plots in the town. Most boroughs had between twenty and forty burgesses, but usually only about thirteen of these were nominated to the corporation. In Augher the burgesses were categorised into ten 'superior' or 'principal' burgesses and eleven 'inferior' burgesses.[12] The lands allocated as burgage plots to the superior burgesses were of two acres (added 'to their houses'), while the 'inferior' burgesses had only one acre each.

Ideally each borough had an allocation of plantation land ranging from 200 to 1,000 acres. In 1610 the commissioners advised that this corporation land was not to be enclosed until the town was sufficiently peopled. This meant initially that the required number of burgesses had been reached and a total of forty houses built. One-third of the corporate land was to be common meadow, and once land had been set out for house and garden plots, burgages, a church and churchyard, school, streets and a market-place, the remainder was to act as common for cattle.[13] In practice, however, many towns were denied lands for their use. Because the planned boroughs were not to be incorporated until they had actually achieved a stipulated number of houses and burgesses, initial control of the building programme, the corporate lands and the market profits was to be in the hands of a supervisory undertaker or servitor.[14] Although by 1622 Sir Stephen Butler had built thirty-four houses at Belturbet and had a grant of 484 acres for the town, the inhabitants complained that they wanted the portion of land due to them. Some of the townsmen of Cavan also complained that the corporate land was 'disposed to particular uses and not to the best behoof of the towne'.[15] At Strabane no land at all had been reserved, and the inhabitants petitioned the crown that though 'they are made a corporacon, yet they have no land for supportacon of their Ordinarie charge nor Comon belonging thereunto'.[16] In some cases there was confusion between 'fort' land and 'town' land. This frequently occurred where a corporate town was to be erected on the site of a military garrison. The land assumed to be available for such towns had often already been granted to the custodians of the forts. Some of these servitors did proceed with a town-building programme, but clearly their lands would only be reluctantly transferred to corporate ownership.

Londonderry and Coleraine were unique. Their lands were not set out in common, but surrounding each of these towns several thousand acres known as the Liberties were granted to the Irish Society. Many freeholders of these towns also held freehold farms in the Liberties, but much of the land was let independently. On other sites, however, the allocation of land was more in accord with the commissioners' advice. At Dungannon Sir Arthur Chichester was

> to set apart a convenient place of the said 500ᵃ for the site of the town, to be built streetways, another part for a market place; and another for a church and church-yard, the said borough to consist of 20 burgesses, besides cottagers and other inferior inhabitants, for whom he is to build houses and assign proportions of land; and to set apart 60ᵃ of the said last 500ᵃ for the common of the said town; with 2ᵃ more, viz ½ᵃ for the site of a public school, and 1½ᵃ for the exercise of the scholars.[17]

When the authority to allocate freeholds of corporate land was granted to the corporations, it was hardly surprising that the burgesses themselves obtained large tracts. In Carrickfergus this could be seen most clearly when great divisions of Carrickfergus 'county' were parcelled out to freemen of the town as strips called 'alderman's shares'.

When Elizabeth I died in 1603 there were only two parliamentry boroughs in Ulster: Carrickfergus and Downpatrick. By the end of James I's reign in 1625 a total of twenty-four towns had been incorporated (Appendix 11).[18] Only a handful were to follow in the seventeenth century, such as Clogher (1629), Lisburn (1662), Hillsborough (1662), Antrim (1665) and Randalstown (1683). Six of the boroughs erected during James's reign were outside the escheated counties: at Bangor, Belfast, Killyleagh, Newry, Newtownards and Monaghan, and two boroughs emerging inside the plantation area had not been proposed either in 1609 or 1611. By 1670 there were twenty-eight corporate towns in Ulster, only half of which were part of the original planned network of corporate plantation towns.

Of course, corporate towns were not the only ones to emerge and develop within Ulster during the seventeenth century. They did, however, include all the largest and most important urban centres in the province. The census of 1659 provides the best means for comparing the relative sizes of Ulster towns in the seventeenth century.[19] Unfortunately, however, the census is incomplete, and no returns are available for Counties Cavan and Tyrone. In addition, the population totals of several other towns cannot be separated from parish totals. Nevertheless, almost a hundred towns had developed throughout Ulster by 1659. The census records twenty-six of these with a population in excess of 100 adults, so it is possible to examine the relationship between town size and town incorporation. Only four towns had an adult population of over 500. These were the ports of Londonderry (1,052), Carrickfergus (962), Coleraine (633) and Belfast (589). Coleraine was surrounded by an earthen rampart, but each of the other three ports was contained within defensive walls. Another five towns were recorded in the census with an adult population of over 200 — Armagh (409), Lisburn (357), Downpatrick (308) and Enniskillen (210). To these nine largest cities and towns must certainly be added Strabane in Tyrone, which had more than 200 British adult males in 1622. Strabane was also a port, and the hearth-money rolls of 1666 reveal it to have been easily the largest town in Tyrone, a position it had held continuously from the earliest days of the plantation. Of all the other large towns, only Larne in County Antrim did not become a borough in the seventeenth century. More than half of the middle-sized towns with a 1659 population of between 100 and 200 adults had also been incorporated. In fact there were only two boroughs with substantially fewer than 100 adults: St Johnstown and Killybegs in Donegal, with only 37 and 31 adults respectively. Clearly the largest and most successful of the Ulster towns which emerged during the plantation period were incorporated.

Boroughs had many functions other than their political role as the basis for parliamentary representation. They were administrative centres with an enviable degree of local autonomy. They contained buildings with centralised functions, such as churches, schools, market-houses, court- or session-houses and jails, and they even had a strategic and military significance. Many towns had been military forts before the plantation, and their garrisons continued. It was not only the largest towns which were fortified for defence. Even Cavan had a 'town ditch',[20] and the corporate towns were also to be mustering-points for the British men of each barony as and when such assessments were made.

Besides accommodating the weekly courts held by the corporations for by-law infringements, many corporate towns were centres for the broader legal administration. County jails were located in Enniskillen, Dungannon, Armagh and Londonderry — an inevitable consequence of the assizes and quarter-session courts held at 'session-houses' in many of the boroughs. These courts required juries drawn from the freeholders of the county, and these were difficult to form in some parts because of the reluctance of undertakers to grant freeholds. In turn the burden of jury service caused great inconvenience to the restricted number of freeholders expected to attend.

Boroughs may have been political, military, legal and administrative centres, but of particular importance was their economic function. This role was much broader than that of the smaller market towns, especially when trade was concentrated in a seaport. Here the range of services could be very extensive, with merchants and craftsmen of every conceivable type resident, particularly in Londonderry city. Sir Henry Docwra's small settlement at Derry was intended to become the exemplar of a fortified colonial city-port. In this respect its destiny was rapidly fulfilled, for in the space of one generation Londonderry grew to become the largest and most important urban settlement in Ulster and one of the foremost cities in Ireland.

Merchants, tradesmen and artisans were the intended

populace for the boroughs. In 1613 Augher was to have within four years '20 English or Scots, chiefly tradesmen and artificers, to be burgesses'.[21] The 1609 plantation project had even suggested a 'Levie or Prest of Tradesmen and Artificers out of England to People those towns', but there is little evidence that such a levy took place. Several of the London companies did discuss sending over 'unto derry, one Artizan sufficiently furnished with tolles and necesaries there to inhabit'. However, the only such persons actually known to have arrived were 'those children wch were sent latelie over for servants and apprentices out of the hospitalls in London, to be employed in bothe the Townes'.[22] In fact by the second half of the seventeenth century most of the inhabitants of Londonderry and Coleraine were Scots.

7.3 *Dispersed rural settlement*

Although the articles of plantation required settlers to live in towns or villages, more than two-thirds of the plantation estates contained neither. Even where villages were built, many other British tenants lived elsewhere on the same estate. In fact the great majority of plantation colonists did not live in nucleated settlements of any sort, but were scattered among the townlands they leased and farmed. One of the 'defects' of the undertakers noted by the commissioners in 1622 was that few had planted their tenants in villages or towns but 'lett them live scattered and dispersed'. In 1619 Pynnar found that on the estate of Finagh/Rarone in Tyrone 'All these Tenants do dwell dispersedly upon their own Land, and cannot dwell together in a village because they are bound every one to dwell upon his own Land, which if they do not the Lease is void.'[23] He also noted in Cavan '12 families of 15 men who dwell dispersedly', and on another estate he found that the 'tenants dwell dispersedly'. In County Donegal John Murray had '40 men of British birth, but dwell dispersedly'. In Armagh Sir Oliver St John had built five houses near a bawn, with the 'rest dispersedly, 3 or 4 families together', and Michael Obbins's estate of Ballyworran had in 1622 'about 30 scattered English families'.

This tendency for dispersal of the rural population was most obvious in the later seventeenth century. The hearth-money rolls of the 1660s unquestionably display a pattern of dispersed rural British-owned hearths at townland level, as do the 1622 undertakers' certificates in the restricted areas for which they provide detailed information. Where villages were recorded, the number of British families on each plantation estate still exceeded the number of houses recorded in the village, and many of the same villages disappeared shortly after 1619. If villages were being deserted when plantation settlement on the same estates was increasing, their existence must have been artificial and transient.

7.4 *Desertion of the plantation villages*

Pynnar's survey found about fifty villages on undertakers' estates. Most of these contained between five and twelve houses, and frequently there were many more British tenants on the estate than they could have accommodated. Indeed, alongside some villages it was recorded that the 'rest of the tenants doe live dispersed upon the lands'. When nucleated settlements alongside the bawns were larger than about twelve houses they were frequently described as towns. Some of these small towns obtained charters to hold weekly markets, and their occupants were recorded as tradesmen rather than tenants or cottagers. A substantial proportion of the plantation villages had grown into market towns by the mid-seventeenth century, but where this did not occur, agricultural village settlements were deserted in favour of dispersed rural settlement. The progress of the following four villages can be traced through the seventeenth century, and their desertion illustrates how this process took effect well before the 1641 rebellion.

(a) Gortaville, Mountjoy barony

On this estate in 1619 there were 'about the Bawne twelve Houses inhabited by British tenants'. Each of the tenants had a house and garden plot, with commons for their cattle. In 1622, however, the undertaker's certificate describes each townland as let to only one or two tenants, who in turn had sublet to their own British subtenants or cottagers. No market licence was granted to this estate, and the Civil and Down Surveys make no mention of nucleated settlement there. The hearth-money rolls show that no townland on this estate contained more than two or three houses with fixed hearths in 1666.

(b) Aghintain in Ballyconnolly/Ballyranill, Clogher barony
According to Pynnar, Sir William Stewart had built a village of nine houses, with more under construction, by 1619. A further note indicates that eight cottagers each had a house and garden plot, with some commons for their cattle. However, the undertaker's certificate for the 1622 survey reveals that the townland of Aghintain which contained Stewart's castle was 'incloosed in great faire parkes' and had no more subtenants resident than on the other townlands of the estate. No market was established at Aghintain, and there is no subsequent record of nucleated settlement at this site.

(c) Ballyclough, Clogher barony
In 1619 there were fifteen families on this estate, 'most of them dwelling in a village consisting of nine houses'. However, the undertaker's certificate for the 1622 survey reveals that only four British settlers occupied the three townlands of demesne around the castle, while the remainder of the settlers were resident in other townlands in the estate. No further evidence of the survival of this village has been recorded.

(d) Ocarragan, Mountjoy barony
The location of this village or bawn has not been established within the estate. However, Pynnar found that 'near adjoining to the Bawn there are ten little Houses standing together inhabited with Brittish Families'. Again the 1622 certificate shows that tenants and undertenants were dispersed throughout the estate; no further record of this nucleated settlement exists.

The desertion of these plantation villages cannot be explained by depopulation, for if anything the numbers of British were still increasing on these estates between 1619 and 1622. It was almost certainly due to the preference for dispersed settlement among the plantation tenants and subtenants. Dispersed rural settlement was an understandable and practical response to a pastoral economy, but another important factor was the nature of plantation tenancies. The undertakers granted holdings, normally by townlands, to British freeholders and leaseholders, who in turn sublet their holdings or employed British cottagers to help them work the land. Obviously nucleated settlement within plantation estates would be inefficient when farmers held land in consolidated holdings, perhaps several miles from the bawn or castle. On the other hand, the estates were not large enough or sufficiently well peopled for each to support its own market centre.

7.5 *Growth of the market towns*

Although the boroughs were intended to fulfil the centralised requirements of plantation settlement, they were not sufficiently numerous or widespread to provide all the necessary marketing and specialised services for a widely dispersed rural population. There were more than a hundred towns in Ulster by the middle of the seventeenth century. Three-quarters of these were not boroughs and so had none of the benefits which followed incorporation. Instead they were simply small nucleated settlements with perhaps no more than thirty to a hundred adults resident, most of whom were tradesmen and artisans.

It was the acquisition and jealous defence of grants to hold weekly markets in these towns which indicated their primary economic role. The markets formed the basis of an urban network essential to the plantation economy and yet unplanned in the context of the plantation scheme. By 1670 an equilibrium between nucleated and dispersed settlement had been achieved. Towns were related spatially to each other and to the dispersed rural population. Market towns, for instance, were rarely more than eight miles apart and were centrally situated in areas of dispersed plantation population (Map 12). The greater the density of rural British, the closer were the markets. This urban/rural balance was not a late seventeenth-century achievement, for these market towns had all been established by patent well before the 1641 rebellion. Some of the intended boroughs which did not achieve incorporation did develop into important contemporary market towns. Omagh, Lisnaskea, Tandragee, Virginia, Rathmullan and Raphoe were all examples of this. However, most market towns either emerged independently of the plantation scheme or grew from plantation villages.

Although most plantation estates did not have any nucleated settlements at all, where villages were built and were recorded in the surveys, many were embryo market towns. A great number of the plantation villages recorded in the surveys obtained market charters and developed quickly into small towns. In fact some were already being described in the surveys as towns rather than villages. In 1619 the tenants of Sir Stephen Butler on the estate of Leitrim in Fermanagh dwelt mostly in a 'town' adjoining the bawn (Newtownbutler). As a general rule, when the nucleations contained more than about twelve houses the settlements were described by Pynnar as towns rather than as villages. The village of fourteen houses at Lisnarick in Fermanagh had a market recorded in the 1622 survey, and another Fermanagh plantation village of ten houses also had a market-house in 1619. The latter embryo town, which was to become Irvinestown, was on the estate of Sir Gerard Lowther, and by 1622 had several English families recently arrived to set up clothworking. Besides these small plantation towns in Fermanagh, the surveys record the growth of many other towns from plantation villages. Villages on the estates of Sir Robert Newcomen, Lord Burley, Lord Ochiltree, Lord Wingfield and Sir Toby Caulfield in Tyrone had become the towns of Newtownstewart, Fivemiletown, Stewartstown, Benburb and Castle Caulfield. The settlement of Ballynelurgan (Fivemiletown) in Clogher barony was only a village of four houses in 1619, each with a garden plot. In 1622 the townland of Ballynelurgan had a market in it, and several tenements were let to British inhabitants, one a weaver. The market licence was renewed in 1629 with permission to build a tan-house, and it was described as a market town in the Civil Survey of 1654.

Throughout the escheated counties market towns were emerging within the plantation estates, but the rural population of an individual estate was rarely sufficient in itself to support such an urban centre. Only in County Londonderry, where the grants obtained by each of the London companies were in excess of 3,000 acres, could a market town be expected to emerge on almost every estate. Moneymore flourished on the Drapers' estate, Magherafelt on the Salters', and Bellaghy on the Vintners' proportions. Markets were also established at Articlave, Agivey and Artikelly on the proportions of the Clothworkers, the Ironmongers and the Haberdashers.[24] These villages contained very good houses built at the companies' expense and intended for their principal tenants. But rather than remaining simply as plantation villages, markets and industries were established in them, and the settlements rapidly acquired the functions of small towns. The Raven picture-maps which accompanied the 1622 survey for County Londonderry illustrate a market cross, stocks, a church and a mill at Bellaghy, and a smithy, chapel, stocks and a market-pole at Moneymore.

In some respects it is difficult to determine when these incipient towns had developed to the point at which they could no longer be described as villages. This problem is apparent in County Tyrone, for although Benburb in many respects had the characteristics of a small town, it was unusual in not obtaining a grant of a market. However, Benburb was an important bridging-point of the River Blackwater, and in 1622 the nucleated settlement there was occupied by craftsmen and artificers rather than farmers. The undertakers' certificates list six husbandmen, two turners, a tanner, a shoemaker, a cloth-worker, a miller, a tailor, a point-maker, a cooper and a mason all resident. There were two mills at Benburb, a corn mill and a tuck or woollen-fulling mill, and the town persisted as a nucleated settlement throughout the seventeenth century. A similar situation existed at the nearby plantation settlement of Castle Caulfield, where Pynnar had recorded a 'Town, in which there are fifteen English families'. In 1622 a 'village' of twenty houses of English fashion inhabited by British was recorded, 'whereof most are Artificers and handycraftsmen'. Apparently this was also the embryo of a plantation town, but no market charter was obtained as the settlement was less than four miles from Dungannon and no trading was allowed within that limit. In 1629 a market licence was granted to Stewartstown in east Tyrone,[25] and the occupations of the town's inhabitants were also listed in the 1622 undertaker's certificate. They included eight tradesmen, three butchers, three tailors, two weavers, two carpenters, two quarriers, a ditcher, a shoemaker, a maltster, a smith, a schoolmaster and a yeoman.

In north Donegal patents to hold weekly markets were granted to the plantation villages of Convoy, Ballybofey, Castlefin, Manorcunningham and Newtowncunningham.[26] Many other market towns were developing in Ulster at the same time which did not originate as villages on plantation estates. The Mercers wrote to their agent in 1623 that they did not consider Movanagher a fit place for the market and that it was to be moved to Kilrea.[27] Even within the escheated counties market towns were built on church land, such as Cookstown in

Tyrone and Maghera in County Londonderry.[28] In 1628 Allen Cooke obtained a licence to hold a weekly market on the settlement he had constructed on land leased from the Archbishop of Armagh. The Civil Survey described Cookstown as a small market town in 1654, as it did with Kinaird in south-east Tyrone. Kinaird (or Caledon) was allocated to an Irish grantee (Catherine Ny Neill) in 1614 along with a licence to hold a weekly market.[29] Despite its Irish ownership, Kinaird had British settlers before the 1641 rebellion, and the hearth-money rolls of 1666 record six British hearth-owners in the town. Some market towns emerged on the plantation estates later than elsewhere, and where the plantation surveys had not indicated any nucleated settlement. These late towns, such as Aughnacloy, whose market licence was granted in the 1630s,[30] may have been a response to local needs brought about by later colonisation. Of course, outside the escheated counties there was a parallel growth of an urban network. The largest unincorporated town in 1659 was Larne in County Antrim with 211 adults, but other smaller towns had been built at Glenarm and Ballymoney. In County Down sizeable towns had developed at Strangford, Portaferry, Dromore, Comber and Donaghadee, and in Monaghan at Carrickmacross and Glaslough. Lurgan in north Armagh was also an important contemporary town, but the 1659 census does not provide any breakdown between town and country for the relevant parish of Shankill.

7.6 *Relationship between urban and rural settlement*

The British settlement pattern of north-west Ulster in the 1660s (Map 12) represents a state of urban/rural balance which had already been achieved by the 1630s. Almost all the patents for markets shown had been granted by 1635, and the distributional pattern of the rural British settlement indicated in Map 12 had also been established in the first few decades of the seventeenth century. This pattern of dispersed plantation settlement occupying the best agricultural land, the deserted plantation villages, and the emergence of a network of plantation market and service centres may be regarded as evidence of a developing economy in a fluid colonial situation. In this the settlement pattern had to adjust and change in order to achieve a balance within the economic and physical environment.

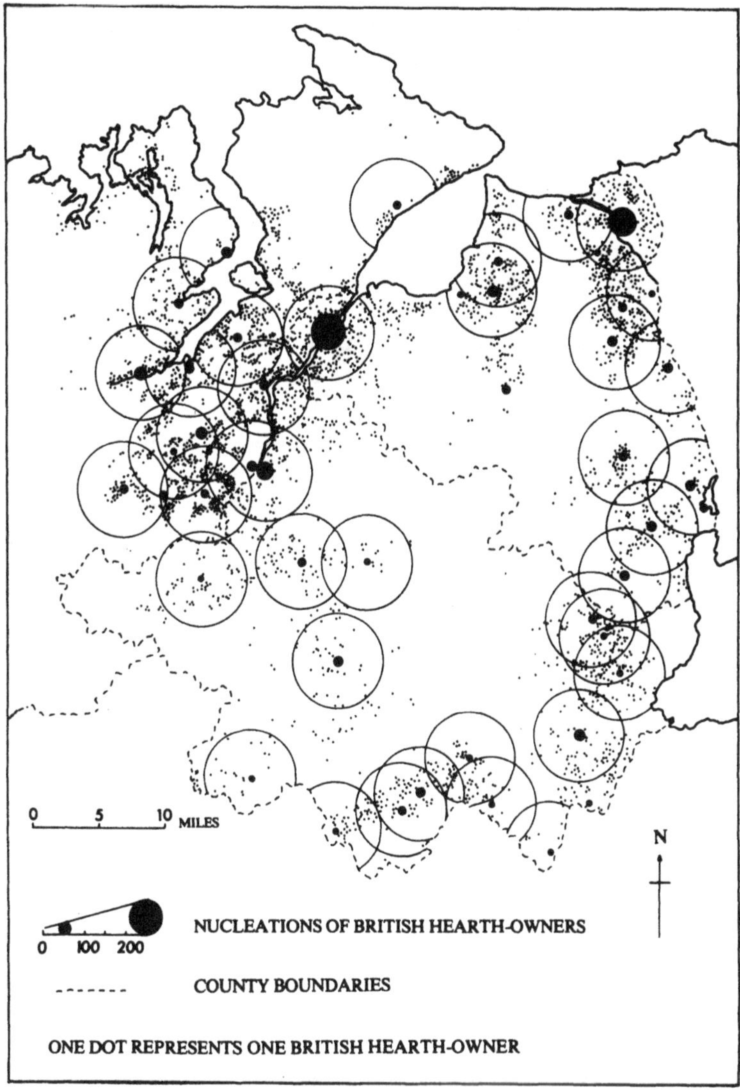

Map 12: *Nucleated and dispersed British settlement in north-west Ulster, c. 1659-1667*
The hearth-money rolls used to construct this map do not provide data at townland level for several parishes in Londonderry and Donegal. Here the parish totals of British-owned hearths have been distributed according to a townland pattern suggested by the census of *circa* 1659. Circles indicating a four-mile radius are shown around each town known to have had a contemporary patent to hold a weekly market.

The pre-plantation settlement pattern and the power centres of the Irish chiefs were important in encouraging favourable locations for several plantation towns. However, the plantation town arose primarily in response to one of the major innovations of the plantation: a market-orientated economy. The competitive nature of the market centres was illustrated in the 1612 grant of market rights to Dungannon which included 'a prohibition from selling goods by retail, within 4 miles of the castle of Dungannon to all except the inhabitants or those planted there by Sir Arthur'.[31] The effective range of the market centre was thus recognised in this grant as four miles, a distance related to the difficulty of travelling more than eight miles per day to and from the weekly market, rather than to the relative merit of the market centre itself. Indeed, four- and five-mile radii have been adopted in studies of towns and markets in medieval and post-medieval England as the effective range of the market.[32] When circles of four-mile radius are drawn around each of the market towns of north-west Ulster in the 1660s (Map 12) it is apparent that the overwhelming majority of the dispersed plantation settlement lay within four miles of the nearest market. Furthermore, where the rural British settlement was sparser these circles had only a minimum overlap. Higher densities of rural population resulted in a greater density of market towns, with a considerable overlap in their effective ranges. Figure 6 illustrates the numbers of dispersed British hearth-owners found at different distances from the nearest market. Most British-owned farms were within three miles of a market, and 90 per cent were within a five-mile radius. Irish-owned hearths, on the other hand, were not so closely distributed in relation to the market centres. Occupying marginal lands, substantial numbers of Irish farms were outside the effective ranges of the markets. Two urban centres had a greater control of the surrounding market potential than the others. These were the Irish Society's settlements at Londonderry and Coleraine. For both there was a prohibition on others trading within *seven* miles written into their charters. While Londonderry managed to ensure this rigid restriction on competition, markets at Agivey and Articlave were tolerated within seven miles of Coleraine. Nevertheless, both Coleraine and Londonderry could depend on their markets drawing on substantially more surrounding farms than other centres. It has already been suggested that the size of plantation towns was related to their range of functions and services, but a positive relationship may also be found when town size is plotted against the numbers of dispersed farms having that particular town nearest (Figure 7). The size of a plantation town was related to the total number of farms using that town as a market centre.

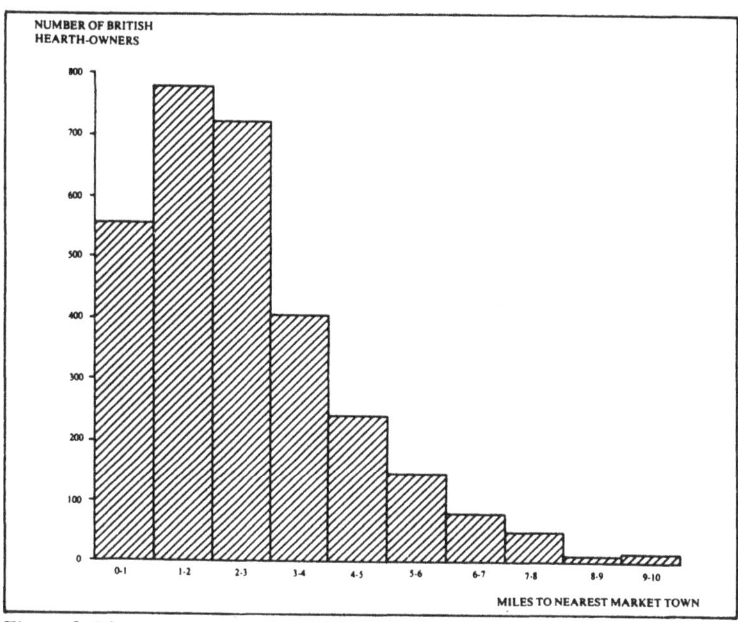

Figure 6: *Distances to market of rural British hearth-owners in north-west Ulster, c. 1659-1667*

These relationships between the plantation towns and the dispersed plantation population illustrate the state of equilibrium which plantation settlement had achieved. It must be assumed that the success or failure of any early plantation village depended on the economic requirements of the surrounding colonial population.

7.7 *Town planning: siting and layout*

The network of planned corporate towns which had formed part of the plantation scheme bore little resemblance to the spatial pattern of urban development which actually emerged in seven-

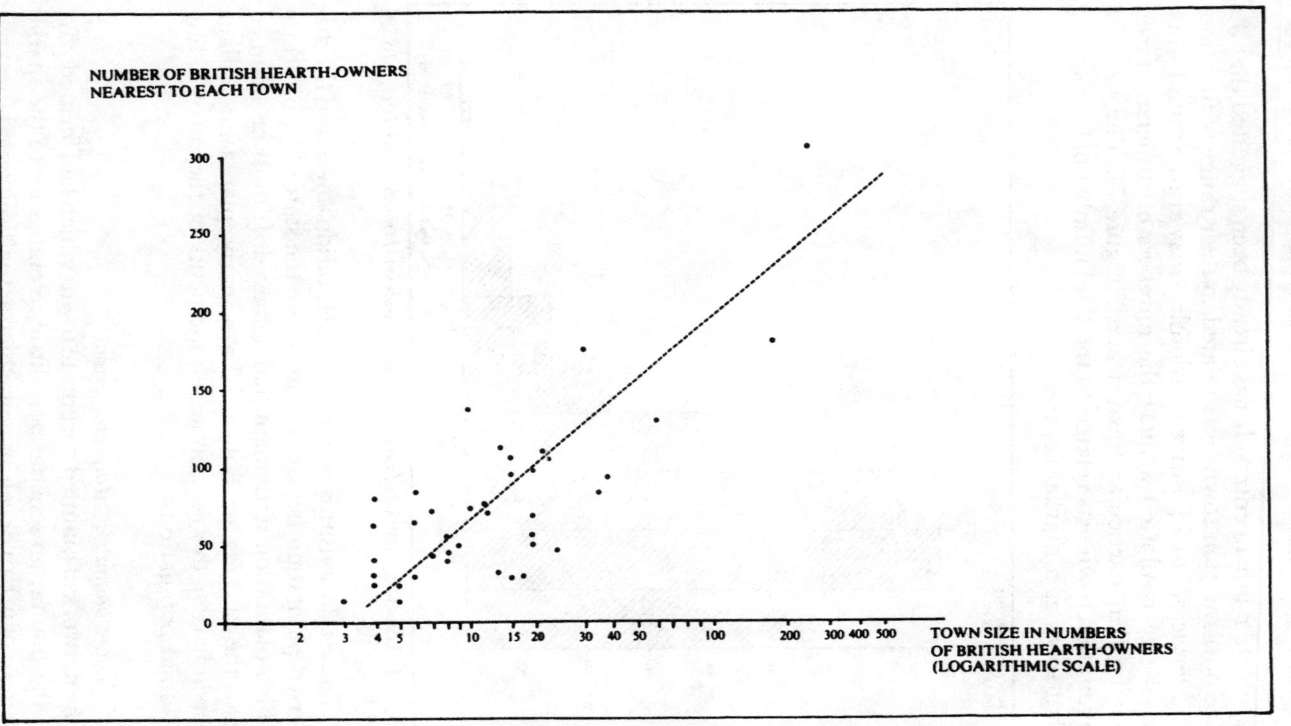

Figure 7: *The relationship between town size and the density of adjacent rural settlement*

teenth-century Ulster. Although the plantation commissioners were to be responsible for the selection of town sites on the ground, the most influential factor governing their decisions was continuity with pre-plantation centres of Irish power, with Elizabethan military forts, with major ecclesiastical sites, and, of course, with the handful of towns already present in Ulster before 1610. Sites were not chosen for strategic consideration alone, but rather it was the continued presence of military garrisons established during the Elizabethan war which became obvious sites for proposed corporate towns. Many of these forts had previously been the strongholds of Gaelic chiefs or the sites of abbeys or priories. Both Enniskillen and Derry were such pre-plantation centres which had been garrisoned during the Elizabethan war and were developed subsequently into important towns. In contrast, the fort at Mountjoy in east Tyrone which had been established to assist military communication across Lough Neagh had not superseded any earlier centre. When Mountjoy was proposed as the site for a corporate town in 1609 and 1611 the commissioners were clearly unaware that the locality had no past or present requirement for such a town, and consequently none was built. Where plantation towns flourished their sites had generally been focal points for the surrounding areas in pre-plantation times. The pre-plantation towns of Cavan and Dungannon had been granted market charters in 1480 and 1587 respectively.[33] The pattern of the developing urban network was influenced more clearly by the physical and economic environment than by any deliberate regional plan. Similarly, the presence of proto-urban centres was a factor in the selection of individual town sites.

The conscious hand of the plantation town planner can best be seen in the morphology of layout of individual towns rather than in the pattern of the urban network. Plantation commissioners were to be responsible for the layout of the corporate towns and for selecting sites for the various town functions. One universal rule was that the focal point of each town, regardless of size, was the market-place. The contemporary term for this was the 'diamond'. As a surviving place-name in Ulster, many 'diamonds' can be found at rural crossroads, but market-places still known as 'diamonds' occur in the towns of Newtownsaville, Belturbet, Clones, Coleraine, Donegal, Enniskillen, Kilrea,

Londonderry, Magherafelt, Monaghan, Pomeroy and Raphoe.[34] Whatever the original meaning of this seventeenth-century term (for it is now virtually unknown elsewhere in the British Isles), it does not refer to the shape of the market-place. Diamonds can follow almost any plan, although they all occur at road intersections.

The characteristic feature of the plantation town market-place was the market cross. Stone crosses which were cruciform in shape can be seen on contemporary picture-maps of Carrickfergus, Limavady, Omagh, Bellaghy and Comber, but the only surviving seventeenth-century market cross (that at Newtownards) is a massive stone octagonal structure which is not surmounted by a cruciform finial. At Coleraine the first market cross was not built in the diamond, but was outside the town on the other side of the Bann. It had been built there by the City of London's agent John Rowley, who had the initials J.R. inscribed on the top. In 1613 this market was transferred to the town centre.[35] Elsewhere temporary markers consisted of tall wooden poles with pendants on top. Representations of such wooden market-poles appear on contemporary maps of Holywood, Bangor, Moneymore and Limavady. From these positions proclamations could be made; and with the site of the market so established, the town could be designed and developed.

The towns with the most obviously planned layouts were Londonderry and Coleraine. In 1619 Londonderry had a stone wall built to surround and fortify the oblong town site. One portion ran alongside the River Foyle where a wooden quay had been built. Along the walls were eight projecting bulwarks and four diametrically opposed gates. The renaissance-style plan was completed by a gridiron street pattern within the walls, based on a central diamond at the intersection of the two main streets which crossed the city from gate to gate. Remnants of the old town were retained within the walls to the north and west, but by 1622 there was still a considerable area of open land reserved for a further six streets and 300 houses. By the mid-seventeenth century this urban development had spilled beyond the walls into the Bogside and across the Foyle to the Waterside.[36] Similar ribbon development outside the gates could be seen at Carrickfergus, where the Scotch Quarter extended to the east and the Irish Quarter to the west of the town.

Coleraine, the other town built by the Londoners, was a less symmetrically planned town, but one whose form bore many close parallels to Londonderry. In place of a town wall, the fortifications were of earth and timber. However, the plan of these town ramparts was similar to Londonderry's walls, with a portion running alongside the River Bann. A central diamond and a gridiron street pattern with open spaces for future development also characterised Coleraine.

Besides Londonderry and Coleraine, few plantation towns could boast much symmetry or obvious conscious planning in their layout. Several, such as Limavady, Moneymore and Holywood, did have a cruciform plan with a market-place at the intersection of two main streets, but elsewhere little formality of design existed. At the other extreme several towns had no distinguishable form in their plans other than a fairly central market-place with random streets leading into it. Such towns often had plans determined by pre-plantation urban development, as, for example, at Armagh, Carrickfergus, Newry, Enniskillen, Cavan, Strabane and Downpatrick. The great majority of plantation towns, however, had the simplest of layouts which consisted broadly of a one-street plan with a market space somewhere along its length. Most of these did follow a pattern of a Y- or T- shaped plan where the main street widened into a market-place at one end. Often a principal building such as market-house, church or manor-house was positioned so that it effectively closed the end of the main street beyond the market, causing the street to bifurcate. Lisburn, Lurgan, Newtownards, Belfast and Magherafelt could all be categorised in this way, although a few contemporary towns such as Bellaghy contained only a wide main street along which the market was spread.

Conscious town planning can only be assumed to have taken place in a few of the largest corporate towns. As the market-place was the focus of each town, the relationship of the market to the street pattern must be used to identify plantation town-plan types. Yet the only identifiable town plans which were common were those with a main-street market, with a cruciform plan, or, especially, with a T-shaped plan. Here the innovative hand of the planner is not as apparent as the less conscious influence of the tradition and precedent of contemporary English and Scottish town morphology.

8

Economic and Social Change

8.1 *Internal communications*

The coastal ports were linked to the principal towns (and the market towns with each other) by a network of inland roads and waterways. Through these the surplus produce of the countryside could be channelled for export, and in turn imported goods could be distributed. A dendritic pattern of minor laneways extended beyond these routes to provide access to each townland and to each dispersed farm site. This has produced a characteristic rural road pattern which today is probably among the densest in Europe, and a landscape which is correspondingly devoid of public footpaths. At first the roads had been important strategically, and some new passages had to be created to enable the transport of building materials to the plantation estates. But because of the continuity of many town sites with earlier pre-plantation centres, there was inevitably a similar continuity in routes and roadways. These were, of course, greatly influenced by the physical environment, avoiding mountainous and boggy tracts where possible, and converging at river fords. The plantation reinforced this road network, upgrading many roads to enable easier passage of wheeled vehicles, along with the creation of many new routes or 'cashes' over bogs. The records of the London companies contain frequent references to the payment of Irish labourers for constructing 'cashes' or causeways by cutting and laying timber faggots horizontally across the bogs. In 1613 Sir Francis Roe had made near Pomeroy in Tyrone 'many causeys (cashes) or highways forced over the bogs, of substantial workmanship, whereof one containeth above four score pole in length'.[1] On drier ground the roads were 'beaten tracks', with the task of construction being little greater than that provided by the constant wear of traffic.

Many plantation castles were built on such unfenced 'thoroughfares', 'highways' or 'places of continual passage'. Sir James Hamilton's castle in Cavan stood upon a 'meeting of five beaten ways', while Lisnaskea in Fermanagh was sited on the 'only thoroughfare in the country'.[2] The constant threat of attack by the outlawed Irish kerne meant that trees and scrub were cleared back from the open-sided major roads to reduce the likelihood of surprise.

The comfort and convenience of the traveller was provided for in addition to his security. Inns could be found along the most important routes as well as at the ports. One at Limavady is represented on the 1622 Raven maps by a building with a hanging sign on the outside wall. Inns were also recorded at Armagh, Omagh, Belturbet and Virginia.[3] At Lifford in Donegal the tenants were 'able to give entertainment to passengers'.[4] Even small villages could provide hospitality: two small settlements established by John Fishe in Cavan had 'two good innholders for they stand upon a roadway'.[5]

Most references in the plantation records to the form of internal transport are in the context of the conveyance of building materials. London companies hired Irish horsemen by the day to transport timber, water, stone and lime, using both carts and pack-horses.[6] Late survival of solid-wheel carts and horse-drawn slipes or sledges in Ulster points to their probable pre-plantation form,[7] but technological innovation could also be found. In the woods of north Down timber was being cut for 'spoakes for carts', and in 1611 four English wheelwrights were employed in Coleraine.[8] Sir Anthony Cope in Armagh had two 'English' carts (with teams of horses and oxen) drawing materials in 1611. In Cavan John Fishe had two teams of English horses with English carts, and in Armagh Francis Sacheverell had 'brought over' four horses and a cart.[9] Almost universally horses were used for drawing materials, but besides mention of oxen in Armagh, there were oxen also used in 1611 around Coleraine. Most of these were employed in drawing timber from the woods.

Rivers and lakes could act either as obstacles to the transport system, or they could be used to supplement it. Certainly many plantation castles were sited on roads at or near river crossing-points. In Donegal Sir Ralph Bingley was building on the River

Finn, 'where is a ford, and the only passage into the country'. Similarly in Cavan John Taylor's buildings were near a 'common passage or ford of the river of Owenmore', Stephen Butler's were 'near the ford of the river of Beltirbet', and Captain Culme's 'near a special ford or passage'.[10] In some circumstances ferries were necessary, but bridges were constructed at the important and most difficult crossings such as at Coleraine, Enniskillen, and across the Roe on the road between Londonderry and Coleraine.

Where inland waterways were navigable, use was made of them. These waters had been the medium for primitive but effective flat-bottomed dug-outs called 'cotts'. Such means of transport continued in Lough Erne and on the lower Bann, where timbers were being transported in great quantities between the woods of Glenconkeyne and Coleraine. In 1611 there were nine cottmen bringing timber from the woods to the Leap, the rest of the journey to Coleraine being completed by 'floaters of timber'. Although twelve boatmen and bargemen were also recorded, the four shipwrights at Coleraine were engaged in building and repairing seafaring vessels.[11] Large planked vessels were also being built by the planters for use on the inland waters. On Lough Erne in Fermanagh Lord Burley had made a boat of '8 ton burden', while in Cavan Captain Ridgeway had contracted for a boat to be built at Belturbet. It was for use on Lough Ramor near Virginia, but Belturbet on the upper Erne system appears to have been quite a centre for plantation boat-building. Sir Hugh Wirrall and Stephen Butler had five boats built there between them. The largest could carry twelve or fourteen tons, and three of the others were 'of 10 ton, 8 and 4'. Again near Belturbet there were another two boats, 'the one of ten ton and the other of 6', on the estate of John Fishe.[12]

8.2 *The ports and external trade*

Coastal ports were the focuses for the surplus provided by the rural economy. Besides providing this outlet facility, the ports also served as entry points for colonists, and so the communications network also functioned as a framework for their dispersal. The ports attracted town-dwelling merchants and traders, while the conditions of the plantation provided a unique attraction for British farmers to settle and exploit the hinterland. For seven years from 1610 the produce of the undertakers' estates could be exported free from tariff, while for five years household goods and a limited quantity of livestock could be similarly imported.[13] This provided a massive incentive for the export trade in grain, butter, cattle and hides from Ulster, particularly to Scotland.[14] When heavy duties were imposed on all grain being imported into Scotland in 1618, the trade pattern had become so firmly entrenched that many Scottish entrepreneurs did not return home, but continued to export and import illegally by avoiding payment of duty. A report on the customs in the Ulster ports in 1637 by the Surveyor-General, Charles Moncke, indicates how this was done.[15] Ports which acted as centres for the collection of customs duty were Carlingford, Strangford, Donaghadee, Bangor, Carrickfergus, Coleraine and Londonderry. Each had numerous landing-points or 'creeks' under their loose supervision. Carlingford, for example, was an unsatisfactory centre for trade in and out of Carlingford Lough, for most of the merchants lived in Newry, and the control by customs officers over Greencastle and adjoining creeks was 'uncertain'. Creeks between Portaferry and Donaghadee on the east coast of County Down were those out of which 'a great part of the corn was stolen and transported in the time of prohibition'. On the Antrim coast 'pedlars out of Scotland take advantage of such creeks unguarded and swarm about the country in great numbers and sell all manner of wares, which they may afford at easier rates than poor shopkeepers that live in corporations'. At Coleraine the merchants also complained of the Scottish pedlars and other Scots who were 'desiring to load and discharge at petty creeks where they may have advantage to steal'. Londonderry was the customs centre for many Donegal creeks, including those of Lough Swilly, where 'many new plantations do border with Scots who have several market towns at Rathmullin, Shiphaven and others, out of which much corn and cattle goes'. The 'time of prohibition' referred to in this report was probably the period between 1618 and 1622 when duty had been imposed on the importation of grain to Scotland at a crippling rate of 1s 8d for each bushel of oats. This was doubled in 1619 to 3s 4d per bushel, but after 1622 the rates were relaxed considerably.[16] By 1637 duty payable on oats being exported from Ulster was 10d per bushel or 3s 4d per barrel. Other contemporary duties were 1s for every pack of linen yarn, 2s 6d per dicker of hides, and 3d for every cow or horse.[17]

Increasingly the trade from the Ulster ports was with southern Scotland, but larger vessels continued to trade from London, Bristol and Chester into Londonderry, Coleraine, Carrickfergus and Belfast. If the amount of customs duty collected at each Ulster port in 1637 was indicative of the relative importance of the ports in that year, then Londonderry, Carrickfergus and Bangor were outstanding, for they each collected in the region of £1,000. Donaghadee and Strangford collected over £600 and £400 respectively, but Carlingford and Coleraine were only responsible for a few hundred pounds duty each. It should be remembered, however, that the duty collected at Londonderry represented not only that from trade through the port itself but also that from Killybegs, Sheephaven and the other 'creeks' of the Donegal coast, including the port of Strabane further upriver from Londonderry in County Tyrone.

In 1616 a commission reported on the best place to establish a ferry between Scotland and the north of Ireland.[18] They concluded that Donaghadee to Portpatrick would be the best route, for Donaghadee was 'the fittest place for that purpose between the river of Strangford and the river of Carrickfergus, both for the safety of boats, the good and easy outgoing, the ability of the town for entertainment of passengers and, what is more, that Sir Hugh Montgomery will erect a pier'. The increasing importance of Donaghadee as the main link between County Down and Scotland came just as Carrickfergus was declining as the major port of east Ulster. At Bangor Sir James Hamilton had been granted rent of the customs for north Down in 1616 which had been surrendered by Carrickfergus. In 1637 Belfast obtained the right to one-third of the remaining rent of the Carrickfergus customs.[19] From this date Sir Arthur Chichester's Belfast began to eclipse the ancient town of Carrickfergus as the main coastal link between the English-settled mid-Ulster plains and the British mainland. As Carrickfergus declined, some merchants transferred to Belfast, and by 1688 Belfast was described as the 'second town in Ireland, well-built, full of people, and of great trade. ... The quantities of Butter and Beef which is sends into Foreign Parts is almost incredible.'[20]

Although great quantities of oats were being grown in the countryside of north Down in 1637, the ports of Donaghadee and Bangor were exporting cattle as the most important commodity. Throughout the seventeenth century most of the exports from Ulster were of agricultural surplus. Cattle, beef, hides, horses, sheepskins, tallow, butter and cheese were shipped out along with oats, oatmeal, barley, malt, linen yarn, fish, timber and some iron-ore.[21]

The types of goods being imported, on the other hand, were mostly household articles: clothing, tools, foodstuffs, ironmongery, and other hardware. In terms of quantity, coal and salt (for butter-making) were among the most important cargoes, but the markets were flooded with an amazing range of English, Scottish and European goods. The overwhelming effect this trade must have had on the local material culture can be judged from the range of goods recorded in the port books of Londonderry and Coleraine, the customs report of 1637, and the various references to goods imported by undertakers and London company agents. In the textile and costume line, imports included sackcloth, grey cloth, blue cloth, linen cloth, woollen clothes, Spanish silk, bone lace, blue starch, needles, cut apparel, stockings, gloves, hats, purses, shoes, rings, sheets and pillows. Kitchen goods included apples, onions, vinegar, pepper, spices, sugar, marmalade, herrings, prunes, wine, whisky and tobacco, brass pots, iron pots, frying-pans, griddles, soap, cups, glasses, bottles, tables and seating-forms. There were tools and hardware, mostly associated with the building programme or farming: hatchets, pick-axes, broad-axes, bits, files, chisels, braces, crowbars, hammers, hand-saws, frame-saws, whip-saws, augers, spades, shovels, scythes, smiths' bellows, anvils, vices, sickles, nails, hinges and locks, iron, glass, lead and solder, nets and ropes. Other important imports included weapons of every sort from the latest French pistols to bows and arrows, gunpowder, church bells, service-books and Bibles, harnessing for horses, copper brewing-kettles, vats and funnels, and beams, scales and weights.[22]

8.3 *The plantation economy*

The types of goods which passed through the Ulster ports indicate the general nature of the plantation economy. Agricultural exports such as beef, cattle, hides, butter, oats, oatmeal and barley were the mainstay of the rural economy. In contrast, the vast range of imported articles suggest an agrarian economy with few craftsmen and a paucity of local industry. This was not, however, the complete story, for substantial numbers of the colonial population were not directly involved in agriculture. Besides the rural weavers, millers, smiths, coopers and other craftsmen who could be found throughout the planted areas, approximately 20 per cent of the entire plantation population were in fact town-dwellers. The occupations of the inhabitants of several towns are known, and these belie any notion that the colonial society was exclusively agricultural. Nevertheless, more than three-quarters of the planters were tenant farmers or farm labourers, and many of the remainder were involved in the trade or processing of farm produce.

Changes in agrarian practices were introduced which had a radical effect on the economy. Increased profit and trade for the planters required an increased surplus of farm produce. This in turn required a greater productivity which involved a shift in emphasis from dairy to beef cattle and arable farming. Such 'good tillage and husbandry after the English manner' meant better tools, techniques and livestock breeds and more efficient processing industries. Although English farmers obtained some of the best land in mid-Ulster, it was the Scottish settlers who were more effective in the early decades. Pynnar noted in the summary of his 1619 survey that

> Many English do not yet plough nor use husbandry, being fearful to stock themselves with cattle or servants for those labours. Neither do the Irish use tillage, for they are also undertain of their stay. . . . Were it not for the Scottish, who plough in many places, the rest of the country might starve.[23]

This enthusiastic tillage by Scots was motivated by the opportunities afforded by the grain trade with Scotland during the early years of the plantation. The north Down area and north Donegal were noted for the quantity of oats grown there in the 1630s, and in north Down there was a tradition that

> The harvests 1606 and 1607 had stocked the people with grain, for the lands were never naturally so productive

> since that time . . . to that degree that they had to spare and to sell to the succeeding new coming planters, who came over the more in number and the faster, because they might sell their own grain at a great price in Scotland, and be freed of trouble to bring it with them, and could have it cheaper here. This conference gave occasion to Sir Hugh's Lady to build watermills in all the parishes. . . . The millers also prevented the necessity of bringing meal from Scotland, and grinding with quairn stones (as the Irish did to make their graddon). . . . Her Ladyship . . . easily got men for plough and barn, for many came over who had not stocks to plant and take leases of land, but had brought a cow or two and a few sheep, for which she gave them grass.[24]

Scottish settlers in east Antrim were growing both oats and barley in the 1640s, although on their small single-tenancy farms the emphasis was on oats. Most of these farms were less than thirty acres in size and kept some cattle, sheep and one or two horses.[25] In west Ulster the plantation surveys reveal that on Irish-owned estates some Irish farmers were still 'ploughing by the tail' despite the outlawing of this practice. Many plantation estates, particularly those in the hands of Scottish undertakers, had 'plows of garrons and some tillage' even in 1611. Lord Burley in Fermanagh had '60 barrels of barley and oats sown and reaped last harvest', and in an adjacent estate Sir John Wishart had 'set up two ploughs sowing wheat'. In the same county Robert Calvert had 'a plough of garrons and three English horses, and in Tyrone Sir Robert Hepburne had 'sowed oats and barley the last year upon his land, and reaped this harvest 40 hogshead of corn'.

The introduction of improved ploughs harnessed to stronger breeds of horses helped to extend the cultivated areas. Spade cultivation and 'ploughing by the tail' were still practised, but these methods would not produce the required surplus of cash crops. Even though scythes rather than sickles had probably been used in medieval Ireland in the Pale, it was not until the plantation period that they were used extensively in Ulster for mowing. Cultivation of flax, wheat and barley was common, but the 'corn' or common crop was, of course, oats. Even the cottagers were given garden plots for spade cultivation of vegetables. 'Garden seeds' were being imported, and the surveys show that a great number of undertakers had planted orchards. These were usually enclosed with 'quickset' or thorn hedges, but enclosure which occurred in addition to this did not involve regular field systems. Such field systems within farms were to accompany the agrarian improvements of the eighteenth and nineteenth centuries and were designed to aid systematic crop rotation. However, the basis for much of the present enclosure pattern, particularly in the English-settled lowlands, was laid in the seventeenth century. Requirements to erect fences around property boundaries (estate, townland and farm mears) were included in many leases.[26] These replaced clauses in earlier leases requiring tenants to 'perambulate the bounds' annually.[27] Within individual farms, and within Scottish and Irish-held townlands where there were joint-tenancy farms, fences were also erected to separate bog, pasture and 'arable' areas.

Some undertakers had brought over cattle, while others had 'English' cows and bulls among their stock. Unlike the case with the extent of tillage, just as many English as Scottish settlers had introduced stock to their estates. In 1609 it was recommended that 'English sheepe will breede abundantlie in Ireland, the sea coast & the nature of the soyle beinge verie whollsome for them'.[28] However, the whole range of livestock and crop types involved in the plantation agrarian economy were present in pre-plantation Ulster (though perhaps with the decline in woodland cover the quantity of pigs may have decreased), and the most important agrarian changes were those involving new tools and techniques, superior livestock strains, and an intensification of land use.

Improved processing of farm produce meant, for example, that the Irish method of preserving butter by mixing with herbs and burying in bogs was replaced by the use of salt. Barrels of salted butter could be marketed, stored and exported, whereas Irish butter was unpalatable, certainly to English settlers. Butchers were to be found not only in the 'shambles' areas of Londonderry, Coleraine and Downpatrick but also in most of the smaller market towns. In fact throughout Ulster malt-houses, tan-houses, corn mills, tuck mills, along with their dependent weavers and dyers, testify to the existence of processing industries even in the smallest of inland settlements. Not all these activities could be described simply as processes for the preparation of farm produce for export, although some undoubtedly were. Local tailors, shoemakers, glovers and even smiths could draw on either local or imported goods for their materials.

The occupations of the town-dwellers, where known, reveal an interesting array of crafts. Of course, the extensive building programme had meant that the early years of the plantation witnessed an influx of building craftsmen. Coleraine in 1611, for example, could boast some forty-one carpenters, twenty-eight sawyers, eleven bricklayers, twenty brick- and tile-makers, two plasterers, eleven masons, ten slaters, five lime-burners and forty labourers. By 1663 occupations recorded for some sixty-two hearth-owners reveal a very different spectrum. Only five carpenters, three slaters and a glazier are recorded to represent the building crafts, while a great number of merchants (many with large houses of three or four hearths) were present. In addition, there were six blacksmiths, five butchers, three shoemakers, five sailors and mariners, three weavers, three coopers, a chandler, dyer, salter and currier.[29] The dominance of a merchant class can also be documented for the other ports, particularly Carrickfergus, Newry, Londonderry and Strabane, but 'tradesmen' were also to be found in the inland market towns. In 1622 Stewartstown in Tyrone contained eight tradesmen, three tailors, three butchers, two quarriers, two carpenters, two weavers, a schoolmaster, maltster, smith, shoemaker, farmer, ditcher and bailiff. The smaller town of Benburb contained six farmers, two tailors, two turners, a mason, miller, shoemaker, tanner, weaver, point-maker and cooper.[30] In fact the market towns were not only centres for merchandising but tended to be the locations for malt-houses (for brewing), tuck mills (for fulling of the locally woven woollen fabric) and tanneries (for the preparation of hides). Corn mills for grinding meal from wheat and oats were very numerous, but were located in both towns and countryside.

Certain activities were rarely associated with towns. Coal, for example, was being extracted in east Tyrone before 1654.[31] Although turf (peat) remained the universal domestic fuel, substantial cargoes of coal were being imported from Scotland. The contracting areas of woodland, initially the scene of heavy exploitation for building materials, continued to decline as their resources were used in the form of bark for the tanneries, wood for pipe and barrel staves, and most importantly charcoal for ironworks.[32] While much of the iron-ore was imported, the production of iron in seventeenth-century Ulster was centred in the woodlands, where charcoal was convenient and where water power was also available to operate bellows and trip-hammers. Between 1683 and 1695 the ports of Belfast and Coleraine exported over 6,000 cleft boards, 1,000,000,000 barrel staves, 900 tons of timber, and 70,000 feet of planks. While these figures may appear to represent a fair quantity of exploitable timber surviving into the late seventeenth century, they were accompanied by the observation that 'The Woods in Ulster in a few years will not supply cask to export our own commodities as beefe, butter, Salmon, Herrings, Shipping and building. Wittness the great woods in the County of Londonderry and Counties of Downe and Antrim almost destroyed.'[33]

8.4 *The new social structure*

Social status on the plantation estates was really established by the quantity of land held, and the means by which it was held, by individual settlers. Tenancies were not granted by the undertakers strictly along the lines required by the plantation commissioners. Rents from the tenants were a crucial part of the undertakers' income, and so tenancies were granted with potential profit in mind. According to the articles of the plantation, each undertaker was to pay a crown rent of £5 6s 8d per annum for each 1,000 acres. Servitors were to pay the same rent if their lands were planted with British, but a higher rate of £8 per annum for each 1,000 acres of land let to Irish tenants.[34] As the average annual income of prospective English undertakers was between £150 and £300, and about £150 for prospective Scottish undertakers, similar returns from rents and other estate profits would be expected if they were to become resident.[35] To achieve a return of £150 from sixteen townlands (1,000 acres) rents in the order of £10 for each townland per annum would be necessary. In fact only fragmentary information survives concerning the rents charged by undertakers to their tenants.

During the early years rents of about £3 or £4 per townland were charged in various parts of Armagh, Tyrone and Londonderry. When large tracts of church land were leased by the Archbishop of Armagh in 1615 most townlands were obtained by adjacent landowners at a yearly rent of £2 10s.[36] In Strabane barony one townland was let by the Earl of Abercorn to a Scottish merchant in 1615 for £6 per annum, to be paid in money or in wine, pepper, sugar and marmalade.[37]

These relatively low rents may have been necessary to attract British settlers, but the Irish were prepared to pay more to remain. Yearly agreements with Irish tenants willing to outbid prospective settlers encouraged rack-renting and provided a major obstacle to the progress of the plantation. A rental of the Eden/Killeny estate in Strabane barony for 1613-15 shows that Irish tenants there were paying up to £10 annually for each townland, as well as providing the undertaker with goods — usually about four barrels of barley, four sheep, four pigs and sixteen hens, and about twenty days' service.[38] The almost inevitable rack-renting not only affected the British settlers as well, but also reduced their security of tenure. By 1628 rents in Londonderry had risen to between £6 and £10 per annum.[39] In Tyrone Pynnar found that rents had been trebled on the estate of Finagh/Rarone in 1619, much to the displeasure of the British tenants.[40] Rent increases must also have been accelerated in 1628 by the doubling of the crown rents to be paid by the undertakers.[41] One townland in Clogher barony was leased in 1629 to Andrew McCreevy for a yearly rent of £10 6s 8d, two fat muttons and twelve fat hens. In 1652 another townland on the same estate was let to Robert Hull for £9 10s.[42]

The way in which the undertakers' estates were to be sublet had been outlined in the articles of plantation. On an estate of 1,000 acres the undertaker was to retain a demesne of 300 acres. Two freeholders were to be allocated 120 acres each, three leaseholders 100 acres each, and the remaining 160 acres were to be allocated to four or more families of cottagers, husbandmen or artificers. Thus the required number of ten British families would be planted on each 1,000-acre estate. However, with no Irish resident, this division would provide a top-heavy social structure with insufficient undertenants and cottagers to work the land. The ten British families on each 1,000 acres were not permitted to take Irish undertenants, servants, labourers or cottagers, and so leases frequently included clauses requiring the tenants to plant British undertenants. In County Londonderry British leaseholders and freeholders did sublet to Irish, but elsewhere it was more common for Irish to farm separate townlands held directly from the undertakers.

The plantation surveyors were instructed to record the nature of the tenancies on the undertakers' estates as well as the actual numbers of British settlers. This task was particularly difficult during the early years, when properly drafted agreements were the exception rather than the rule. Pynnar's survey of 1619 is clearly inaccurate in this respect, and only the 1622 commissioners were careful and persistent in their examination of lease documents. Having completed the survey, they observed that the undertakers had made few *bona fide* freeholders, and

> Some of those that are made, have so smale quantities of land and pay such deare rents, or steep fines, as they are not able to attend at Assizes and Quarter sessions, and some make their own children Freeholders. Some make their Fee Farmers, not absolute, but condiconall, with Provisoes of Re-entry, and Forfeiture, for non payment of Rents.[43]

In addition, the undertakers had granted freeholds and leases by 'verball promise, or by writeing imperfect, without form of law', and the leaseholders and their undertenants (who 'pay rac't rent') were compelled to appear as jurors for want of freeholders. Most freeholders in 1622 were in possession of no more than sixty acres, although the articles of plantation required the undertakers to make freeholds of 120 acres. Some freeholders were non-resident, some were minors, and some absentee names were used in trust by undertakers and agents. Indeed, the 1622 survey only records a handful of freeholders in each county with 120 acres or more. The reluctance of the undertakers to grant large freeholds of good land, while predictable, meant that when influential farmers did seek land on the estates, they were given large leasehold or copyhold tenancies. Even including these leasehold tenants of larger holdings, only about 5 per cent of the plantation population actually occupied holdings of 120 acres or more. Many leaseholders were not in possession of the required 100 acres, but held only about a townland (sixty acres).

It is particularly difficult to distinguish in the surveys between 'cottagers' (some of whom held small leases of up to ten or twenty acres) and 'undertenants' or indeed 'leaseholders' with holdings of perhaps only forty acres. However, if the cottagers and undertenants are collectively defined as all persons holding leases of less than sixty acres, or no land at all, then this social grouping was clearly the most numerous. In 1622 no less than 70 per cent of the rural plantation population were such cottagers and undertenants. This broad base of English and Scottish labourers and small farmers was the principal reason for the success of the plantation, and it was also what distinguished the Ulster plantation from the other, less successful plantations in Ireland.

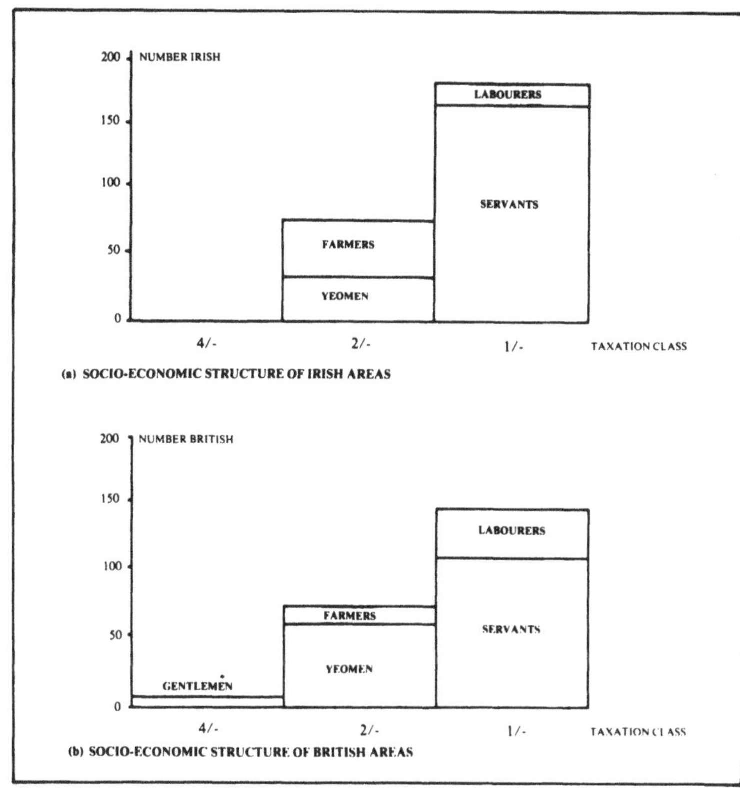

Figure 8: *British and Irish social structure in the parishes of Urney, Donagheady and Termonmagurk, County Tyrone, 1660*[44]

Confirmation of a broad-based British social structure may be had from other sources. The lists of British men mustered on each estate *circa* 1630 appear to distinguish between reasonably well-armed tenants and greater numbers of men with 'no arms'. In Tyrone poll-tax lists survive for the three parishes of Urney, Donagheady and Termonmagurk in 1660. They differentiate between three taxation classes: gentlemen (at 4s); yeomen and farmers (at 2s); and servants and labourers (at 1s). For each townland in these parishes the names of all adult males and their designations (i.e. yeoman, labourer, etc.) are given. British and Irish surnames were clearly segregated by townlands, and when the areas of British and Irish settlement are considered in isolation, the respective British and Irish social structures for 1660 may be obtained (Figure 8). Of all the British names on the Tyrone poll-tax lists below the social level of undertakers, 32 per cent were recorded as yeomen or farmers, and 68 per cent as labourers and servants. This social structure appears to have been very similar to that inferred from the 1622 survey, even if the cottager grouping in 1622 was supplemented by the undertenants and small farmers. The 1622 undertakers' certificates for Tyrone support the notion that British undertenants were the only other occupants on townlands leased to British tenants. A fairly typical entry in the certificate for Ballyloughmaguiffe estate in Clogher barony found the townland of Ballyvaddin 'Let to Robt. Hall gent, in fee farm, his subtenants David Hall, Adam Blackhook, Thomas Pook, Adam Blackyong'.[45]

8.5 *The Irish and the plantation*

The distributional pattern of Irish settlement in Ulster changed substantially during the seventeenth century. Incoming settlers were attracted to areas which hitherto had been favoured by the Irish. But the processes by which the Irish were moved to the marginal areas operated slowly and gradually.[46] Just as British settlers did not restrict themselves to the undertakers' estates, Irish were to be found everywhere, well beyond the limits of the land allocated to church, servitor and Irish grantees. Almost all the undertakers' estates had considerable numbers of Irish resident, and on many poorer estates Irish outnumbered British greatly. It did not make economic sense for the undertakers to remove Irish physically from those townlands for which no British tenants could be found. Because the undertakers used competition for land to increase the rents of both British and Irish tenants, the Irish frequently ended up paying high rents for poor marginal land. By 1622 Irish settlement in the lowlands was interspersed with British settlement. Generally the lowland Irish occupied localised, segregated groups of townlands, but there was an increasing concentration of Irish in the larger, remote areas of marginal land. Many such areas were exclusively Irish and retained a distinctive identity. In mountainous areas fringed with Irish settlement the seasonal migration with cattle to upland summer pastures could continue, although on a much more restricted scale. The economy of the areas of Irish settlement was orientated towards subsistence agriculture. This was exacerbated by distance from market centres and vastly increased population pressure on the resources of the land. However, the market economy was not the sole preserve of the British settler, the difference being rather one of degree.

The continuing presence of Irish on most of the plantation estates raises the question of the extent to which assimilation of Irish by British took place. Assimilation may have occurred in the anglicisation of personal names, in language, in religion, and in the adoption of new cultural practices. In this respect the lowland Irish must be considered separately from those occupying the upland regions. The isolation of the uplands is demonstrated by late survival of the Irish language in those parts. However, in the lowlands some assimilation, albeit on a minor scale, took place. With the Irish involved to a greater extent in the market economy, and Irish artificers permitted in the plantation towns, a greater degree of communication with British settlers was necessary. This inevitably resulted in the adoption of English as the first language. In the town of Dungannon Pynnar recorded in 1619 thirty-six Irish Protestants, and at Tandragee in Armagh nine Irish families who 'come to church', but these were unusual in their implication of religious assimilation. It is interesting to note that the names of the Irish Protestants at Dungannon, given in the 1622 undertakers' certificates, had not been anglicised.[47] Lands within the plantation estates were let in the early seventeenth century to Irish tenants such as 'Phillomy O'Neal' and 'Shane Mule McGerr', and where personal names are recorded in quantity, as in the hearth-money rolls of the 1660s, little anglicisation is apparent. However, in the areas of densest settlement, for example in south Antrim and north Down, where the Irish were greatly outnumbered, there is some evidence that some became Protestant and were totally assimilated into the surrounding culture. Lists of early Presbyterian congregations in these areas of east Ulster indeed display a substantial proportion of local, pre-plantation Irish surnames.[48] When this fact is considered in conjunction with the known historical phases of substantial conversions to the Established Church in Ireland (such as the recorded increase in 'recantations of popery' in the late eighteenth century, and the 'bread-and-butter' reformation of the early nineteenth century), it cannot be assumed that the present-day 'Protestant' areas in Ulster represent populations of exclusively British ethnic origin.[49] Similarly in the predominantly 'Irish' areas of west Ulster it is difficult to establish the extent to which the British surnames of a proportion of Roman Catholics represent hibernicisation of people of plantation origin, or anglicisation of Irish surnames. On balance, however, assimilation processes operated very slowly during the plantation period. Many lowland Irish in Cavan, Fermanagh and Tyrone continued to plough 'after the Irish manner', and some Irish landowners had not made proper leases to their 'tenants' but continued to obtain the old exactions. Attempts to enforce English customs through legislation, such as the wearing of English apparel, conformity in religion, or the prohibition of ploughing by the tail, were often futile.

An unusual situation developed in County Cavan, where a large number of settlers were not of English or Scottish extraction but were recusant 'Palesmen'. Indeed, the broad division of the population into 'British' and 'Irish' is in many ways inappropriate to seventeenth-century Ulster. The attempt to outlaw Irish dress, for example, should be seen against the importation of 'pladdes' and 'skoch cloth' and the wearing of similar Scottish dress by settlers.[50] When the provost-marshal of Donegal attempted to enforce the law regarding Irish dress in 1625 he met with opposition from Scottish undertakers. Having been given authority to destroy any mantles or trews being offered for sale, he 'went into a markett town of Sr. George

Merburies [Letterkenny] and cutt about x^{en} or xii^{lve} mantles, whereof he made a grievous complaint to all the Justices of Peace'.[51]

Even the English undertakers and London company agents whose cultural norms were most distinct from the Ulster Irish considered only the 'rebels' or 'kerne' in the woods to be a threat. Without rents from Irish tenants many undertakers could not have managed the plantation estates successfully, and use of Irish labour indicates co-operation between planters and Irish in the early years. Accounts of the Drapers' Company contain numerous entries for payment of Irish labourers mending 'cashes', cutting wood, making and repairing cabins, and hedging, while Irish 'horsemen' were almost exclusively used for transportation of materials. Some Irish were recommended by the agents to their London companies as suitable persons to be given tenancies, while an intriguing payment in 1615 was given by the Drapers' Company agent to '3 Irishmen that brought word of the kerne in ye woods'. Other payments in the same year were for soldiers to guard workmen, for wood as fuel to maintain a watch in winter time and 'when the rebells move out', and for pikes 'made for us when the rebels threaten us on all sides'.[52]

The distinction made by the planters between Irish generally and 'kerne in the woods' is well illustrated in the following extract from the Ironmongers' Company records in 1615:

> There are yett Irish out in rebellion in thier wooddes and some tymes light upon passengers and Robb them and somtymes light into the houses and doo many villanyes, the last weeke they tooke an Irish man as he was keeping cattell in the woodes upon the Mercers proporcon, and hanged him wth a with in a tree, and tis thought for no other cause but that his Mr being an Irishman had conformed himself and came too the Church.[53]

The Irish rebellion of 1615 was no more than a series of uncoordinated attacks which had little chance of progress even though Irish outnumbered British in most areas. Irish tenants were still hopeful of retaining profitable land, and many had found employment in the new towns or with the building programme. In particular, Irish grantees under the plantation scheme were still inclined to be hopeful that the more absolute powers in English law which they now held over small estates would compensate for the looser control once exerted over larger areas.

By 1641 the mood had changed dramatically. No section of Irish society was gaining from the plantation, while many had suffered considerable loss. Even the Irish grantees who might have had something to lose from a rebellion could feel their influence and status being continuously eroded. Some had failed to manage their estates successfully in comparison with the undertakers and had been forced to sell, lease or mortgage portions of their land. It was involvement of this section of Irish society that ensured general support for the rising planned for 23 October 1641. On the ground in Ulster the revolt was led by Sir Phelim O'Neill, with other leading Ulster Irish landowners such as Philip O'Reilly and Connor, Lord Maguire. Phelim had inherited a large estate around Caledon in south-east Tyrone from his mother, Catherine Ny Neill. The theatre of the rebellion was predictably centred in the pre-plantation heartland of south-east Tyrone. Symbolically, the assaults on Castle Caulfield and Mountjoy were led by leaders of the appropriate pre-plantation septs: O'Donnelly and O'Quinn. Furthermore, it was from Dungannon that Sir Phelim O'Neill issued his proclamation on the second day of the revolt declaring that they were not in rebellion against the king, but were only acting in defence of their liberties, and that no injury would befall anyone who repaired to his own home.[54] However, the undisciplined enthusiasm with which the Irish responded throughout Ulster in the early stages meant that any intention to prevent acts of vengeance or to avoid conflict with the Scottish settlers often went unheeded.[55] Within several days most of mid-Ulster had been cleared of British military strongholds. In this area attacks were concentrated on the most obvious features of plantation settlement: the towns, castles, bawns, mills and ironworks. The settlers themselves suffered mostly through loss of property and dispossession, but accounts of a wholesale massacre were vastly and deliberately exaggerated. Planters in mid-Ulster assembled at the muster-points such as Augher and retreated to Newtownstewart in west Tyrone. When a force of about 600 men returned to Augher they were routed, and the area between Augher and Dungannon was devastated by the returning Irish.

In 1642 Major-General Robert Monro arrived with an advance force of some 2,500 Scottish troops at Carrickfergus, while the nephew of the exiled Earl of Tyrone, Owen Roe O'Neill, arrived to assume leadership of the Ulster Irish forces. All Ireland was by now involved in the conflict. After an attack on Drogheda the Irish converged on Armagh and Tyrone again in 1642, and Turlough O'Neill (formerly of Strabane) led an attack on the strong Laggan (Foyle basin) force under Sir Robert Stewart. However, after the loss of many men and the almost total destruction of plantation structures in mid-Ulster, the efforts of the Laggan force, Monro's army of Scots and various other groups of settlers from Antrim, Down and Armagh brought the war in Ulster to a position of stalemate by 1643. The defeat of Monro's forces at Benburb in 1646 was a major setback for the British, but the period of uncertainty ended in 1649 when Oliver Cromwell arrived with a large English army. After a ruthless and revengeful campaign the rebellion was over by 1653.

The numbers of Protestants killed during the 1641 rebellion are a matter of considerable controversy and depend largely upon the reliability of the depositions taken from witnesses in 1641. Although these depositions mostly relate to Protestants being robbed or driven from their homes, many deaths are also recorded. Estimates of murdered Protestants range from the more plausible figure of about 4,000 (excluding about 8,000 refugees who may have perished in the later stages of the war) to the ridiculous contemporary and subsequent accounts of between 20,000 and 100,000.[56] As British rural settlement was already dispersed by 1641, the most obvious consequence of the war was the temporary removal of British from the most affected areas, despite the widespread destruction of plantation towns and villages. Leases still held good, and when the rebellion was finally over many rural areas appear to have been unaffected; if they were, the settlement distribution rapidly returned to its pre-1641 pattern. Destruction of the towns and villages only served to speed up the rationalisation of the urban network. Only the urban centres necessary to maintain service and marketing facilities were rebuilt.

Following the reconquest, a land survey was carried out between 1654 and 1656. The purpose of this 'Civil Survey' was to quantify and describe the land in each parish, and to establish the 1641 landownership. From the survey and the contemporary mapped 'Down Survey' the Cromwellian authorities were able to distinguish all forfeited land. This meant in practice that most of the land in west Ulster which had been allocated to Irish grantees in the plantation, along with Catholic-owned land in Antrim and Down, was at the Commonwealth's disposal. The original intention was transportation of the dispossessed Irish to Connaught and reallocation of their lands to English 'adventurers' (who had invested money in the reconquest of Ireland in return for pledges of forfeited land) and to Cromwellian soldier settlers as remuneration in lieu of service pay.[57] Transportation never became effective, and few Cromwellian officers settled as landlords in Ulster. Most preferred instead to sell their grants, but nevertheless large estates did transfer from Irish ownership. Although this opened up some more areas for potential British settlement, they were not colonised immediately. During the 1660s much forfeited land was still occupied by Irish, although a major new influx of settlers from England had begun. Large numbers of these were bound for the region west of Belfast: south Antrim, north-west Down and north Armagh. Again, in the last decades of the seventeenth century fresh waves of migrants from Scotland took advantage of the forfeited lands available, particularly in County Antrim, reinforcing the established pattern of English and Scottish settlement in Ulster.

In just over fifty years after the plantation had begun the freehold ownership of land by Catholics in Ulster had been reduced to an insignificant level. The ground rules of the original plantation scheme had long been abandoned, but the process of colonisation continued in spite of the events of the 1640s. With no significant Ulster Irish representation among the upper social strata, erosion of the economic status of Irish tenants in comparison with the English and Scots continued. The official plantation had provided a loose framework for a more general colonisation which was to continue, even accelerate, and perhaps reach its zenith after the late seventeenth century.

8.6 *Conclusion*

Paradoxically, the seventeenth century in Ulster was an era of both change and continuity. Land grants for plantation estates had reused Irish land divisions so that Gaelic place-names and territorial hierarchies became fossilized. A new settlement pattern emerged, but with British settlers in the areas previously favoured by the Irish. New forms of settlement and building types were greatly influenced by pre-plantation precedent and the environment. Indeed, few 'innovations' of the period were genuinely such. English language, improved agricultural techniques and tools, and improvements in wind- and water-power technology were all hallmarks of the plantation, yet they were not totally absent from the pre-plantation landscape. Even the development of an extensive urban network of market towns reflected a change in emphasis rather than a transformation of the rural economy. Gaelic power centres (some of which were already market towns in the sixteenth century) had provided locations for many expanding towns.

Continuity in change was only one of many paradoxes in the Ulster plantation. Another was the fact that more English and Scots came to Ulster outside the years regarded as the official plantation period (1610-25) than were planted during it, and that more had settled outside the official undertakers' estates than on them. English and Scottish settlement areas in Ulster did not necessarily reflect the nationality of the landowner, for many colonists were not 'planted' at all, but came of their own volition.

Finally it may be necessary to correct the impression that the present-day Ulster landscape contains 'pure' Gaelic Irish or British cultural survivals. The concept of cultural purity has no more validity than that of ethnic purity. Certainly some areas contain populations drawn mostly from one or other of these sources, but many perceptions of cultural differences are based on cultural identification rather than on reality. Such perceptions may even have a different significance today than, say, in the late eighteenth century, when English-settled areas gave birth to the Orange Order with its loyalist-conservative philosophy while in many 'Scottish' localities Presbyterians were being caught up in the spirit of French republicanism. With more tangible cultural traits (such as in traditional house types or English dialects) there are clearly elements which can claim ancestry from different source areas. But the end product of cultural contact in Ulster cannot be explained simply in terms of assimilation of one form by another. Cultural fusion, the mutual adoption of traits, interdependent development and subsequent evolution have given rise to patterns of cultural phenomena that are neither 'Irish' and 'Catholic' nor 'British' and 'Protestant' in type. The stimulus for dramatic change in the Ulster landscape has been cultural contact, and in no period can such contact be more clearly identified than during the Ulster plantation.

Appendix 1

Church land in the escheated counties, 1608

County	Termon (acres)	Abbey (acres)	Mensal (acres)	Total church land	
				Acres	% of escheated area
Armagh	11,100	500	2,400	14,000	(18)
Cavan	3,366	480	—	3,846	(9)
Donegal	9,168	8,704	4,560	22,432	(20)
Fermanagh	3,099	1,410	60	4,569	(14)
Tyrone	16,475	5,220	1,800	23,495	(24)
Coleraine	4,950	1,140	420	6,510	(21)
Total	48,158	17,454	9,240	74,852	(16)

Appendix 2

Servitors and their estates, 1610-11

Location	Name of servitor's proportion	Estimated area (acres)	Name of servitor grantee
Orior barony, Co. Armagh	Knockduff	1,000	Sir G. Moore
	Ballymore	1,500	Sir O. St John
	Corinchine	500	Lord Audley
	Mullaghglass	1,000	Sir T. Williams
	Claire	1,000	J. Boucher
	Ballyclare	1,000	F. Cooke
	Curriator	200	C. Poynts
	Ballymacdermot	120	M. Whitechurch
	Mountnorris	300	H. Adderton
Castlerahan barony, Co. Cavan	Kilcronehan	400	Sir J. Elliott
	Lough Ramor	1,000	J. Ridgeway
	Mullagh	1,000	Sir W. Taffe
	Murmode	500	R. Garth
	Mullamore	1,000	Sir E. Fettiplace

Tullygarvey barony, Co. Cavan	Drumshiel	750	Sir T. & J. Ashe
	Tullyvin	1,500	A. & B. Moore
	Iterary	2,000	R. Tirrell
Clanmahon barony, Co. Cavan	Carrick	2,000	Sir O. Lambert
	Tullycullen	1,500	J. Jones
	Drominoh	500	J. Russon
	Aghacapull	1,000	A. Atkinson & Lieut. Russell
Tullyhaw barony, Co. Cavan	Graham	2,000	Sir G. & R. Graham
	Ballyconnell	1,500	H. Culme & W. Talbott
	Largin	1,000	N. Pynnar
	Doughbally	1,200	E. Rutlidge
	Jones	200	T. Jones
Doe & Fanad barony (Kilmacrenan), Co. Donegal	Clonlary	1,000	W. Stewart
	Ballyrehan	1,000	P. Crawford
	Carnagilly	1,000	J. Vaughan
	Kingstown	1,000	J. Kingsmill
	Edencarn	1,000	B. Brooke
	Ramelton	1,000	Sir R. Hansard
	Facker	300	T. Perkins & G. Hilton

continued overleaf

Servitors, 1610-11

Location	Name of servitor's proportion	Estimated area (acres)	Name of servitor grantee
Doe & Fanad barony, (Kilmacrenan), Co. Donegal, *continued*	Radonnell	500	Sir T. Chichester
	Ballynass	1,000	H. Hart
	Rosguill, Castledoe & Carrowreagh	1,100	Sir R. Bingley
	Loughnemuck	400	E. Ellis
	Cranrasse	528	T. Browne
	Moyres	1,000	H. Vaughan
	Legabrack	240	C. Grimsditche
Coole & Tirkennedy barony, Co. Fermanagh	Drumkeen	1,500	Sir H. Folliott
	Coole	1,000	R. Atkinson
	Corrigrade	1,000	W. Cole
	Inishmore	348	P. Gore
Clanawley barony, Co. Fermanagh	Lisgoole	1,500	Sir J. Davies
	Gortin	500	S. Harrison
	Moycrane	246	P. Mostin
Dungannon barony, Co. Tyrone	Dungannon	1,320	Sir A. Chichester
	Largie	2,000	Sir T. Ridgeway
	Benburb	2,000	Sir R. Wingfield

	Ballydonnell	1,000	Sir T. Caulfield
	Roe	1,000	Sir F. Roe
	Altedesert	1,000	Sir W. Parsons
	Clanaghry	480	F. Annesley
Co. Coleraine	Limavady & Toome	3,000	Sir T. Phillips
Total		54,632	

Appendix 3

Major Irish grantees and their estates, 1611-14

Irish grantees with 1,000 acres or more	Size of grant (acres)	Location	
		Barony	County
Sir Turlough McHenry O'Neill	9,900	Fews	Armagh
Connor Roe Maguire	5,980	Magherastephana	Fermanagh
Turlough McArt O'Neill	3,330	Dungannon	Tyrone
Mulmory Óg O'Reilly	3,000	Tullygarvey	Cavan
Catherine Ny Neill	2,620	Dungannon/Tiranny	Tyrone/Armagh

continued overleaf

Major Irish grantees, 1611-14

Irish grantees with 1,000 acres or more	Size of grant (acres)	Location	
		Barony	County
Brian O'Neill	2,380	Dungannon/Tiranny	Tyrone/Armagh
Art McBaron O'Neill	2,000	Orior	Armagh
Donald McSweeney	2,000	Doe & Fanad	Donegal
Sir Mulmory McSweeney	2,000	Doe & Fanad	Donegal
Donnell McSweeney	2,000	Doe & Fanad	Donegal
Turlough O'Boyle	2,000	Doe & Fanad	Donegal
Brian Maguire	2,000	Coole & Tirkennedy	Fermanagh
Mulmory McHugh O'Reilly	2,000	Clanmahon	Cavan
Manus O'Cahan	2,000	Tirkeeran	Londonderry
Henry McShane O'Neill	1,500	Orior	Armagh
Con McShane O'Neill	1,500	Coole & Tirkennedy	Fermanagh
Con Boy O'Neill	1,280	Dungannon/Tiranny	Tyrone/Armagh
Hugh McHugh O'Donnell	1,000	Doe &Fanad	Donegal
Niall O'Neill	1,000	Dungannon/Tiranny	Tyrone/Armagh
Phelim McGauran	1,000	Tullyhaw	Cavan
Mulmory McPhilip O'Reilly	1,000	Tullygarvey	Cavan
Hugh O'Reilly	1,000	Tullygarvey	Cavan
Cowy Ballagh McRichard O'Cahan	1,000	Tirkeeran	Londonderry
Rory O'Cahan	1,000	Keenaght	Londonderry
Manus McCowy O'Cahan	1,000	Coleraine	Londonderry
Brian Crossagh O'Neill	1,000	Dungannon	Tyrone
Total	56,490		

Appendix 4

Grants to Irish clans in the escheated counties, 1611-14

Sept	No. of grants of 1,000 acres or more	Area of grants of 1,000 acres or more	No. of grants less than 1,000 acres	Area of grants less than 1,000 acres	Total	
					No. of grants	Area
O'Neill	10	26,510	30	4,435	40	30,945
O'Reilly	4	7,000	29	6,950	33	13,950
Maguire	2	7,980	32	3,860	34	11,840
McSweeney	3	6,000	8	1,570	11	7,570
O'Cahan	4	5,000	2	120	6	5,120
O'Brady	—	—	7	3,050	7	3,050
O'Boyle	1	2,000	4	667	5	2,667
McDonnell	—	—	12	1,719	12	1,719
McGauran	1	1,000	4	600	5	1,600
O'Donnell	1	1,000	4	472	5	1,472
O'Hanlon	—	—	11	1,340	11	1,340
O'Hagan	—	—	11	980	11	980
McCann	—	—	6	800	6	800
O'Quinn	—	—	7	796	7	796
O'Mellan	—	—	5	780	5	780
O'Donnelly	—	—	5	360	5	360
Others	—	—	77	9,024	77	9,024
Total	26	56,490	254	37,523	280	94,013

Appendix 5

English undertakers and their estates, 1610-11

Location	Name of plantation proportion	Estimated area (acres)	Name of plantation grantee	Origin of grantee
Oneilland barony, Co. Armagh	Teemore	1,000	R. Rollestone	Staffordshire
	Mullalelish & Legacurry	2,000	F. Sacheverell	Leicestershire
	Dowcoron	1,500	J. Brownlow	Nottinghamshire
	Ballynemoney	1,000	W. Brownlow	Nottinghamshire
	Kernan	1,000	J. Matchett	Norfolk
	Ballyworran	2,000	W. Powell	Staffordshire
	Mullaghbane	1,500	J. Dillon	Staffordshire
	Kannagoolan	1,500	W. Stanhowe	Norfolk
	Aghavillan & Brochus	2,000	J. Heron	
	Derrycreevy & Dromully	3,000	Lord Say	Oxfordshire
Loughtee barony, Co. Cavan	Drumhill & Drumemellan	2,000	Sir J. Davies	Servitor
	Dromany	2,000	J. Fishe	Bedfordshire
	Dernglush	2,000	S. Butler	Bedfordshire
	Lisreagh	2,000	Sir J. Davies	Servitor

	Monaghan	1,500	Sir H. Wirrall	Middlesex
	Aghateeduff	1,500	J. Taylor	Cambridgeshire
	Tonagh	1,500	W. Snow	
Lifford barony, Co. Donegal	Stranorlar	1,500	H. Clare	Norfolk
	Aghagalla & Convoy	2,000	W. Wilson	Suffolk
	Acharin	1,500	E. Russell	London
	Monaster	1,500	Sir W. Barnes	
	Killygordon	1,000	R. Mansfield	Servitor
	Corlackey	2,000	Sir T. Cornwall	Shropshire
	Tawnaforis	2,000	Sir R. Remington.	Servitor
	Dromore & Lurga	2,000	Sir M. Barkeley	Somerset
	Lismongan	1,500	Sir T. Coach	Servitor
Clankelly barony, Co. Fermanagh	Ardmagh	1,000	T. Plumstead	
	Cloncarn	1,000	R. Bogas	Suffolk
	Gortganon	1,000	R. Calvert	
	Latgir	1,000	J. Sedborough	
	Lisrisk	1,000	T. Flowerdew	Norfolk
Lurg & Coolemakernan barony, Co. Fermanagh	Rosgwire	1,000	T. Flowerdew	Norfolk
	Edernagh & half Tullynakein	2,000	T. Blenerhasset	Norfolk
	Bannaghmore & half Tullynakein	2,000	Sir E. Blenerhasset	Norfolk

continued overleaf

English undertakers, 1610-11

Location	Name of plantation proportion	Estimated area (acres)	Name of plantation grantee	Origin of grantee
Lurg & Coolemakernan barony, Co. Fermanagh, *continued*	Tullanagh	1,000	J. Archdale	Suffolk
	Necarn	1,000	E. Warde	Suffolk
	Drumunshin	1,000	T. Barton	Norfolk
	Dowross	1,000	H. Hunnings	Suffolk
Clogher barony, Co. Tyrone	Portclare & Ballykirgir	2,000	Sir T. Ridgeway	Servitor
	Fentonagh	2,000	F. Willoughby	
	Ballyloughmaguiffe	1,500	W. & T. Edney	Servitors
	Ballymackell	1,000	G. Ridgeway	Servitor's brother
	Ballyclough	1,000	Sir W. Parsons	Servitor
	Moyenner	1,000	W. Turvin	
	Ballyconnolly & Ballyranill	2,000	E. Kingswell	
	Derrybard & Killany	2,000	W. Clegge	
Omagh barony, Co. Tyrone	Finagh & Rarone	3,000	Lord Audley	Servitor
	Brad	2,000	Sir M. Tuchet	Servitor's son
	Fentonagh	2,000	Sir F. Tuchet	Servitor's son

	Edergoole & Carnbracken	2,000	E. Blunte	Servitor's son-in-law
	Clonaghmore & Gravetagh	2,000	Sir J. Davies	Servitor
Total		81,500		

Appendix 6

Scottish undertakers and their estates. 1610-11

Location	Name of plantation proportion	Estimated area (acres)	Name of plantation grantee	Origin of grantee
Fews barony, Co. Armagh	Clancarney	2,000	Sir J. Douglas	East Lothian
	Coolemalish	1,000	H. Acheson	East Lothian
	Magheryentrim	1,000	Sir J. Craig	
	Kilrudden	1,000	W. Lauder	Midlothian
	Edenavea	1,000	C. Hamilton	East Lothian
Clankee barony, Co. Cavan	Keneth & Cashel	3,000	Lord Aubigny	Stirlingshire
	Tandragee	1,000	W. Baillie	

continued overleaf

Scottish undertakers, 1610-11

Location	Name of plantation proportion	Estimated area (acres)	Name of plantation grantee	Origin of grantee
Clankee barony, Co. Cavan, *continued*	Kilcloghan	1,000	J. Raleston	Renfrewshire
	Drummuck	1,000	W. Dunbar	Ayrshire
Tullyhunco barony Co. Cavan	Clonkine & Carrowtubber	2,000	Sir A. Hamilton	East Lothian
	Cloneen	1,000	Sir C. Hamilton	Dunbartonshire
	Drumheada	1,000	A. Achmutie	East Lothian
	Keylagh	1,000	J. Achmutie	East Lothian
	Carrowdownan	1,000	J. Brown	Midlothian
Boylagh & Banagh barony, Co. Donegal	Rosses	2,000	Sir R. McClelland	Kirkcudbrightshire
	Boylagh-Eightra	1,500	G. Murray	Wigtonshire
	Dunconnolly	1,500	W. Stewart	Kirkcudbrightshire
	Cargie	1,000	Sir P. McKee	Ayrshire
	Mullaghveagh	1,000	J. McCullogh	Wigtonshire
	Kilkerhan	1,000	A. Dunbar	Wigtonshire
	Boylagh-Owtra	1,000	P. Vans	Wigtonshire
	Moynargan	1,000	A. Cunningham	Wigtonshire
Portlough barony, Co. Donegal	Magevelin, Lettergull & Cashel	3,000	Duke of Lennox	Stirlingshire

	Corkagh	1,000	Sir W. Stewart	Lanarkshire
	Ballyneagh	1,000	A. McAulay	Dunbartonshire
	Dunboy	1,000	J. Cunningham	Ayrshire
	Coolelaghy	1,000	W. Stewart	Ayrshire
	Dacastross & Portlough	2,000	Sir J. Cunningham	Ayrshire
	Coolemacitreen	1,000	C. Cunningham	
	Ballyaghan	1,000	J. Cunningham	Ayrshire
	Lismolmoghan	1,000	J. Stewart	
Knockninny barony, Co. Fermanagh	Legan & Carrowshee	3,000	Lord Burley	Kinross-shire
	Kilspinan	1,500	Lord Mountwhany	Fife
	Leitrim	1,500	Sir J. Wishart	Kincardineshire
	Aghalane	1,000	T. Moneypenny	Fife
	Dresternan	1,000	J. Trail	
	Derriany	1,000		
Magheraboy barony, Co. Fermanagh	Ardgort	2,000	Sir J. Home	East Lothian
	Derrynefogher	1,500	R. Hamilton	Lanarkshire
	Drumra	1,000	J. Gibb	
	Drumskeagh	1,000	J. Lindsay	Midlothian
	Moyglass	1,500	W. Fowler	Midlothian
	Drumcoose	1,000	A. Home	
	Drumcrow	1,000	J. Dunbar	

continued overleaf

Scottish undertakers, 1610-11

Location	Name of plantation proportion	Estimated area (acres)	Name of plantation grantee	Origin of grantee
Mountjoy barony, Co. Tyrone	Revelinowtra & Revelineightra	3,000	Lord Ochiltree	Ayrshire
	Ballyokeuan	1,000	R. Stewart	Perthshire
	Ocarragan	1,500	Sir R. Hepburne	East Lothian
	Tullylegan	1,000	G. Crawford	Ayrshire
	Creigballe	1,000	B. Lindsey	East Lothian
	Tullaghogue	1,000	R. Lindsey	East Lothian
	Gortaville	1,000	R. Stewart	
Strabane barony, Co. Tyrone	Strabane & Dunnalong	3,000	Earl of Abercorn	Renfrewshire
	Shean	1,500	Sir T. Boyd	Ayrshire
	Eden & Killeny	2,000	Sir C. Hamilton	
	Newtown & Lislap	2,000	J. Clapham	
	Largie (Cloghogenal)	1,500	Sir G. Hamilton	Renfrewshire
	Derrywoon	1,000	G. Hamilton	Linlithgow
	Ballymagoieth	1,000	Sir J. Drummond	Perthshire
	Tirenemuriertagh	1,500	J. Haig	Berwickshire
Total		81,000		

Appendix 7

Grants to the London companies

Company	Estimated area (acres)	Farmer or undertaker by lease	Location of buildings	
			Site	Barony
Clothworkers	3,210	Sir Robert McClelland	Killowen & Articlave	Coleraine
Drapers	3,210	Sir Thomas Roper	Moneymore	Loughinsholin
Fishmongers	3,210	James Higgins	Artikelly & Ballykelly	Keenaght
Goldsmiths	3,210	John Freeman	New Buildings	Tirkeeran
Grocers	3,210	Edward Rone	Muff	Tirkeeran
Haberdashers	3,210	Sir Robert McClelland	Ballycastle	Keenaght
Ironmongers	3,210	George Canning	Agivey	Coleraine
Mercers	3,210		Movanagher	Coleraine
Merchant Taylors	3,210	Valentine Hartopp	Mocosquin	Coleraine
Salters	3,210	William Finch & partners	Magherafelt & Salterstown	Loughinsholin
Skinners	3,210	Sir Edward Doddington	Dungiven	Keenaght
Vintners	3,210	John Rowley & Baptist Jones	Bellaghy	Loughinsholin
(Total)	38,520			
Irish Society	7,000		Coleraine & Londonderry	

Appendix 8

Corporate towns and associated grants of town and fort land

County	Proposed corporate town	Site of incorporated town	Allocated corporation land (acres)	Proprietor	Allocated fort land (acres)	Servitor
Armagh	Armagh	Armagh		Lord Primate		
	Mountnorris				300	H. Adderton
	Charlemont	Charlemont			300	Sir T. Caulfield
	Tandragee					
Cavan	Virginia		250	J. Ridgeway		
	Belturbet	Belturbet	384	S. Butler		
	Cavan	Cavan	500	W. Brady		
Donegal	Doagh					
	Ballyshannon	Ballyshannon			1,000	Sir H. Folliott
	Rathmullan					
	Donegal	Donegal	300	B. Brooke		
	Killybegs	Killybegs	224	R. Jones		
	Lifford	Lifford	500	Sir R. Hansard		
	Raphoe					
Fermanagh	Lisgoole	Enniskillen	330	W. Cole		
	Lisnaskea					
	Magheraboy					
Tyrone	Strabane	Strabane		Earl of Abercorn		
	Dungannon	Dungannon	500	Sir A. Chichester		

	Omagh	Omagh			330	E. Leigh
	Clogher	Augher	330	Sir T. Ridgeway		
	Mountjoy				300	Sir F. Roe
Coleraine	Londonderry	Derry	4,000	Irish Society		
	Coleraine	Coleraine	3,000	Irish Society		
	Limavady	Limavady				Sir T. Phillips
	Dungiven					
Total			10,318		2,230	

Appendix 9

School lands

Schools in square brackets had not been built during the reign of James I.

County	Barony containing school lands	Area allocated (acres)	Proposed school site	Established school site
Armagh	Orior	720	Armagh	[Armagh]
Cavan	Loughtee	375	Cavan	[Cavan]
Donegal	Tirhugh	200	Donegal	[Raphoe]
Fermanagh	Clanawley	650	Lisgoole	Lisnaskea [then Enniskillen (1643)]
Tyrone	Mountjoy	700	Mountjoy	Dungannon
Londonderry	—	—	Londonderry	Londonderry
Total		2,645		

Appendix 10

British population totals (adult males) on the plantation estates based on the plantation surveys and musters, 1611-c. 1630

1. COUNTY ARMAGH

Plantation estate	Area (acres)	1611	1613	1618	1619	1622	c. 1630
Oneilland barony (English undertakers)							
Teemore	1,000	(24)	(24)	18	24	(41)	34
Mullalelish & Legacurry	2,000	14	[2-12]	48	50	(122)	104
Dowcoron	1,500	(31)	(40)	[40-100]	100	160	42
Ballynemoney	1,000						
Kernan	1,000	(4)	(19)	16	30	(68)	31
Ballyworran	2,000	0	48	16	40	(95)	24
Mullaghbane	1,500	(60)	(67)	12	40	(92)	35
Kannagoolan	1,500	0	0	[0-4]	4	4	16
Aghavillan & Brochus	2,000	0	(36)	[26-36]	26	(90)	45
Derrycreevy & Dromully	3,000	24	0	[0-80]	80	72	155
Fews barony (Scottish undertakers)							
Clancarney	2,000	(27)	(85)	48	173	[173-260]	56
Coolemalish	1,000	9		24	30	(47)	
Magheryentrim	1,000	[2-10]	12	56	30	(119)	113
Edenavea	1,000	(14)	(5)		22		
Kilrudden	1,000	18	(32)	[30-32]	30		

Orior barony (servitors)							
Knockduff	1,000	0	[2-12]	[0-12]	0	(2)	0
Ballymore	1,500	0	0	[0-63]	63	(49)	21
Corinchine	500	0	0	0	0	(2)	0
Mullaghglass	1,000	0	0	0	0	0	0
Claire	1,000	0	0	0	0	0 }	
Ballyclare	1,000	0	0	0	0	0 }	
Curriator	200	0	0	[0-10]	[2-10]	(14)	27
Ballymacdermot	120	0	0	0	0	0	0
Mountnorris	300	0	0	0	0	0	34
Total		227-235	372-392	334-575	744-752	1,150-1,237	747

2. CO. CAVAN

Loughtee barony (English undertakers)							
Drumhill & Drumemellan	2,000	0	50	67	82	71	54
Dromany	2,000	35	(51)	49	60	46	48
Dernglush	2,000	(12)	65	87	139	[82-139]	164
Lisreagh	2,000	0	0	14	48	14	28
Monaghan	1,500	(27)	32	12	26	10	32
Aghateeduff	1,500	[10-22]	(32)	32	54	[58-86]	85
Tonagh	1,500	0	0	16	30	5	9

continued overleaf

British adult males, 1611-c. 1630 (Co. Cavan)

Plantation estate	Area (acres)	1611	1613	1618	1619	1622	c. 1630
Clankee barony (Scottish undertakers)							
Keneth & Cashel	3,000	0	0	61	80	40	16
Tandragee	1,000	0	0	24	28	22	32
Kilcloghan	1,000	0	0	24	40	(16)	54
Drummuck	1,000	0	0	24	30	(13)	5
Tullyhunco barony (Scottish undertakers)							
Clonkine & Carrowtubber	2,000	0	36 }	62	52 }	78	136
Cloneen	1,000	12	0 }		(40) }		
Drumheada	1,000 }	6	(32)	45	100	[38-57]	54
Keylagh	1,000 }						
Carrowdownan	1,000	0	0	24	28	19	20
Castlerahan barony (servitors)							
Kilcronehan	400	0	0	0	0	0	0
Lough Ramor	1,000	(11)	(14)	[14-25]	(25)	(20)	28
Mullagh	1,000	0	0	0	0	0	0
Murmode	500	0	0	0	0	0	0
Mullamore	1,000	0	0	0	0	0	0
Tullygarvey barony (servitors)							
Drumshiel	750	0	0	0	0	0	0
Tullyvin	1,500	0	0	[0-11]	(11)	(8)	0
Iterary	2,000	0	0	0	0	0	0

Clanmahon barony (servitors)							
Carrick	2,000	0	0	[0-11]	(11)	(2)	0
Tullycullen	1,500	0	0	0	0	0	0
Drominoh	500	0	0	0	0	0	0
Aghacapull	1,000	0	0	0	0	0	0
Tullyhaw barony (servitors)							
Graham	2,000	0	0	0	0	(2)	0
Ballyconnell	1,500	0	0	0	0	0	0
Largin	1,000	0	0	0	0	0	0
Doughbally	1,200	0	0	0	0	0	0
Jones	200	0	0	0	0	0	0
Total		113-125	312	555-588	884	544-648	765

3. COUNTY DONEGAL

Lifford barony (English undertakers)							
Stranorlar	1,500	0	(5)	[5-68]	68	33	39
Aghagalla & Convoy	2,000	[2-10]	0	[0-106]	106	87	66
Acharin	1,500	4	[2-10]	[2-36]	36	29 }	45
Monaster	1,500	0	0	[0-46]	46	10 }	
Killygordon	1,000	0	[2-10]	[2-46]	46	18	16
Corlackey	2,000	0	0	[0-60]	54	13	25

continued overleaf

British adult males, 1611-c. 1630 (Co. Donegal)

Plantation estate	Area (acres)	1611	1613	1618	1619	1622	c. 1630
Tawnaforis	2,000	0	0	[0-60]	60	22	
Dromore & Lurga	2,000	0	(19)	[19-64]	64	33	57
Lismongan	1,500	(10)	(12)	[12-56]	56	18	[0-18]
Boylagh & Banagh barony (Scottish undertakers)							
Rosses	2,000	0	0	[0-16]	(16)	0	
Boylagh-Eightra	1,500	4	0	0	0	(2)	
Dunconnolly	1,500	(16)			40	44	
Cargie	1,000	0			40	32	
Kilkerhan	1,000	0	120	[120-162]	[22-32]	7	143
Boylagh-Owtra	1,000	[2-10]			50	27	
Mullaghveagh	1,000	0	4	[2-4]	[2-4]	1	
Moynargan	1,000	0	0	[0-5]	[2-5]	2	
Portlough barony (Scottish undertakers)							
Magevelin, Lettergull & Cashel	3,000	[2-10]	0	[0-122]	[72-122]	[81-122]	166
Corkagh	1,000	0	0	[0-26]	26	25	19
Ballyneagh	1,000	0	24	[24-30]	30	25	13
Dunboy	1,000	(2)	24	[24-40]	50	50	
Ballyaghan	1,000	6	(8)	[8-42]	42	33	124
Coolelaghy	1,000	1	0	[0-40]	40	25	61
Dacastross & Portlough	2,000	(8)	(35)	[35-40]	40		66
Coolemacitreen	1,000	(5)	(24)	[24-80]	80	98	59
Lismolmoghan	1,000	0	0	[0-24]	(24)	134	32

Doe & Fanad barony (Kilmacrenan) (servitors)							
Clonlary	1,000	0	0	[0-20]	20	16	
Ballyrehan	1,000	0	0	[0-50]	50	64	
Carnagilly	1,000	0	0	[0-12]	[3-12]	4	
Kingstown	1,000	0	0	0	0	0	
Edencarn	1,000	0	0	0	1	0	
Ramelton	1,000	0	0	[0-139]	(139)	23	
Facker	300	0	0	0	0	0	
Radonnell	500	0	0	0	0	0	
Ballynass	1,000	0	(7)	[2-7]	(2)	0	[128-144]
Rosguill	500	0	0	0	0	20	
Castledoe	500	0	0	[0-11]	(11)	(13)	
Carrowreagh	100	0	0	0	1	0	
Legabrack	240	0	0	0			
Loughnemuck	400	0	0	0	0	0	
Cranrasse	528						
Moyres	1,000	0	0	[0-10]	10	4	
Total		62-86	286-302	279-1,422	1,349-1,423	993-1,034	1,059-1,093

4. COUNTY FERMANAGH

Clankelly barony (English undertakers)							
Ardmagh	1,000	0	0	6	3	0	19
Cloncarn	1,000	0	0	[0-20]	20	30	44

continued overleaf

British adult males, 1611-c. 1630 (Co. Fermanagh)

Plantation estate	Area (acres)	1611	1613	1618	1619	1622	c. 1630
Gortganon	1,000	6	(18)	13	12	41	22
Latgir	1,000	8	(10)	13	24	12	16
Lisrisk	1,000	6	[2-12]	6	40	(19)	12
Lurg & Coolemakernan barony (English undertakers)							
Rosgwire	1,000	0	0	0	0	0	30
Tullanagh	1,000	0	0	24	42	(54)	
Edernagh & half Tullynakein	2,000	(6)	(14)	[14-26]	26	[2-26]	22
Bannaghmore & half Tullynakein	2,000	6	0	12	40	[26-40]	24
Necarn	1,000	0	0	[0-28]	28	(32)	47
Drumunshin	1,000	0	(5)	[5-16]	(16)	(14)	
Dowross	1,000	0	(16)	[16-38]	(38)	[9-38]	24
Knockninny barony (Scottish undertakers)							
Legan & Carrowshee	3,000	0	18	57	82	(46)	99
Kilspinan	1,500	(22)	(10)	[10-15]	15	(8)	90
Leitrim	1,500	15	(19)	[19-66]	66	(27)	
Dresternan	1,000	4	2	[0-2]	0	0	
Derriany	1,000	0	0	[0-15]	15	(2)	
Aghalane	1,000	0	3	[3-27]	(27)	(24)	6

Magheraboy barony (Scottish undertakers)							
Ardgort	2,000	0	5	[5-30]	30	[18-30]	90
Moyglass	1,500	0	0	[0-30]	30	(29)	
Derrynefogher	1,500	10	(14)	[14-77]	77	55	24
Drumra	1,000	0	0	[0-26]	26	(24)	48
Drumcrow	1,000	(14)	4	[4-60]	60	(31)	
Drumskeagh	1,000	0	(11)	24	34	(95)	68
Drumcoose	1,000	0	2	[2-24]	(24)	(24)	29
Coole & Tirkennedy barony (servitors)							
Drumkeen	1,500	0	0	24	(20)	16	27
Coole	1,000	0	[2-10]		(5)	20	25
Corrigrade	1,000	0	0		18	(7)	13
Inishmore	348	0	0		(22)	(8)	31
Clanawley barony (servitors)							
Lisgoole	1,500	0	0	0	0	1	0
Gortin	500	0	0	0	0	0	15
Moycrane	246	0	0	0	0	0	6
Total		97	155-173	271-679	840	674-753	831

continued overleaf

British adult males, 1611-c. 1630

5. COUNTY TYRONE

Plantation estate	Area (acres)	1611	1613	1618	1619	1622	c. 1630
Clogher barony (English undertakers)							
Portclare & Ballykirgir	2,000	8	(65)	48	56	(77)	138
Ballymackell	1,000	2	(26)	(26)	26	(45)	
Fentonagh	2,000	0	0	22	48	(27)	17
Ballyloughmaguiffe	1,500	0	0	21	60	(68)	47
Ballyclough	1,000	4	(21)	27	38	(63)	59
Moyenner	1,000	0	14	[14-36]	[20-36]	(68)	25
Ballyconnolly & Ballyranill	2,000	0	0	24	64	70	77
Derrybard & Killany	2,000	0	0	0	0	0	28
Omagh barony (English undertakers)							
Finagh & Rarone	3,000	0	0	[0-11]	11	(31)	47
Brad	2,000	0	0				
Fentonagh	2,000	0	0	[0-64]	64	(73)	57
Edergoole & Carnbracken	2,000	1	1				
Clonaghmore & Gravetagh	2,000	0	0	[0-30]	30	(54)	25

Mountjoy barony (Scottish undertakers)							
Revelinowtra & Revelineightra	3,000	33	(31)	31	80	(99)	94
Ballyokeuan	1,000	[2-12]	(12)	16	32	(76)	
Ocarragan	1,500	20	40	23	26	(43)	46
Tullylegan	1,000	0	0	23	36	(81)	36
Creigballe	1,000	0	0	19	39	[33-59]	26
Tullaghogue	1,000	12	(31)	21	30	(58)	65
Gortaville	1,000	[2-10]	0	17	36	(58)	28
Strabane barony (Scottish undertakers)							
Strabane & Dunnalong	3,000	(144)	(240)	[240-386]	286	[280-319]	247
Shean	1,500	0			100	[36-54]	48
Eden & Killeny	2,000	0	0	[0-50]	50	0	43
Newtown & Lislap	2,000	0	[2-24]	43	48	(65)	54
Largie (Cloghogenal)	1,500	[2-10]	[10-50]	[10-50]	50	[36-54]	54
Derrywoon	1,000	0	(21)	21	43	(32)	
Ballymagoieth	1,000	1	(24)	21	30	32	15
Tirenemuriertagh	1,500	0	0	0	(14)	[13-19]	7
Dungannon barony (servitors)							
Dungannon	1,320	[2-10]	0	[0-54]	(54)	(54)	31
Largie	2,000	0	0	[0-5]	(5)	0	30
Benburb	2,000	0	0	[0-30]	30	[38-68]	46
Ballydonnell	1,000	0	[2-10]	[2-20]	20	(36)	12
Roe	1,000	0	(24)	[24-31]	(31)	[23-35]	0

continued overleaf

British adult males, 1611-c. 1630 (Co. Tyrone)

Plantation estate	Area (acres)	1611	1613	1618	1619	1622	c. 1630
Altedesert	1,000	0	0	(0)	0	0	0
Clanaghry	480	0	0	0	0	0	0
Total		233-267	564-634	693-1,170	1,457-1,473	1,669-1,818	1,402

6. COUNTY LONDONDERRY

Plantation estate	Area (acres)	1611	1613	1618	1619	1622	1628	c. 1630
Coleraine	3,000	[89-273]	(151)	100	(158)	124	160	357
Londonderry	4,000	[150-207]	[151-274]	100	[184-245]	171	305 }	599
Goldsmiths	3,210	—	—	49	90	63	104 }	
Clothworkers	3,210	—	—	17		86	106	65
Drapers	3,210	—	—	23	[12-32]	16	34	45
Fishmongers	3,210	—	—	31	40	23	57	42
Grocers	3,210	—	—	42	[14-27]	34	75	57
Haberdashers	3,210	—	—	20	80	123	136	127
Ironmongers	3,210	—	—	56	[14-22]	65	157	123
Mercers	3,210	—	—	17	[14-22]	52	79	87
Merchant Taylors	3,210	—	—	49	40	36	27	48
Salters	3,210	—	—	16	[25-38]	27	76	(76)
Skinners	3,210	—	—	28	80	12	23	(23)
Vintners	3,210	—	—	42	76	80	73	102
Total		239-480	302-425	590	828-951	912	1,412	1,751

British adult males, 1611-c. 1630

7. TOTAL

County	1611	1613	1618	1619	1622	c. 1630
Armagh	227-235	372-392	334-575	744-752	1,150-1,237	747
Cavan	113-125	312	555-588	884	544-648	765
Donegal	62-86	286-302	279-1,422	1,349-1,423	993-1,034	1,059-1,093
Fermanagh	97	155-173	271-679	840	674-753	831
Tyrone	233-267	564-634	693-1,170	1,457-1,473	1,669-1,818	1,402
Londonderry	239-480	302-425	590	828-951	912	1,751
Total	971-1,290	1,991-2,238	2,722-5,024	6,102-6,323	5,942-6,402	6,555-6,589

See overleaf for note on standardisation of data.

Note on the standardisation of the population data in Appendix 10

The tabulated statistics represent the number of adult British males recorded for each estate. Where the surveys or musters do not provide data in this precise form, estimates have been substituted.

For some of the estates surveyed in 1611 and 1613 absolute figures were not given, but rather the presence of 'some' or 'many' British was recorded. Although this ambiguity applied to only a few of the estates in the first two surveys, there is no statistical information whatsoever for many of the estates in the 1618 muster roll. This, it seems, was because Captain Alleyne, who compiled the muster, lacked sufficient authority to summon all the undertakers (or any servitors) to appear. In the cases where ambiguity or omission has resulted in gaps in the statistics, maximum and minimum estimates are presented in square brackets, these being generally calculated from the figures quoted for the same estates in the preceding and succeeding surveys.

The other major difficulty in interpreting the plantation surveys is that in some instances the figures indicate the number of British families rather than the number of British *adult males*. It is apparent that, according to the undertakers' obligations, ten families were regarded as equivalent to twenty-four adult males (2.4 adult males per family). In addition, when the various surveys were examined, numerous estates can be found where the numbers of families (or tenants) and adult males are both given. In these cases there is a difference between the number of adult males per family (averaging 1.8 males per family) and the number of adult males per tenant (averaging 2.7 males per tenant). These differences are apparently due to whether or not British labouring or 'cottager' families were enumerated. Therefore when only the numbers of British families or tenants are provided, appropriate multipliers have been used to provide estimates of British adult males.

Any statistic shown in brackets is an estimate. Where estimates have been achieved using a single conversion factor from families or tenants to adult males, the estimate is shown in round brackets. Where minimum and maximum estimates have been considered more appropriate, these are shown in square brackets.

Appendix 11

Ulster boroughs in the seventeenth century

Corporate towns	Year of proposal to incorporate	Adult population (c. 1659)			Year of incorporation
		English & Scots	Irish	Total	
County Antrim					
Antrim	—	32	28	61 [*sic*]	1665
Belfast	1611	366	223	589	1613
Lisburn	—	217	140	357	1662
Randalstown	—	?	?	?	1683
County Armagh					
Armagh	1609/1611	186	223	409	1613
Charlemont	1609/1611	57	60	117	1613
[Mountnorris]	1609/1611	?	?	?	—
[Tandragee]	1609	72	35	107	—
County Cavan					
Belturbet	1609/1611				1613
Cavan	1608/1609				1610
[Virginia]	1609/1611				—
County Donegal					
Ballyshannon	1609/1611	63	71	134	1613

continued overleaf

Ulster boroughs in the seventeenth century

Corporate towns	Year of proposal to incorporate	Adult population (c. 1659)			Year of incorporation
		English & Scots	Irish	Total	
County Donegal, *continued*					
[Doagh]	1609	?	?	?	—
Donegal	1609/1611	24	71	95	1613
Killybegs	1609	10	21	31	1615
Lifford	1608/1609/1611	44	24	68	1613
[Raphoe]	1609	80	24	104	—
[Rathmullan]	1609/1611	17	6	23	—
St Johnstown	—	19	18	37	1618
County Down					
Bangor	—	62	35	97	1612
Downpatrick	('ancient borough')	146	162	308	medieval charter
Hillsborough	—	96	69	165	1662
Killyleagh	—	126	49	175	1612
Newry	1611	66	108	174	1613
Newtownards	1611	87	59	146	1613
County Fermanagh					
Enniskillen	1611	176	34	210	1613
[Lisgoole]	1609	?	?	?	—
[Lisnaskea]	1609	33	15	48	—
[Midway between Lisgoole and Ballyshannon]	1608/1609	4	2	6	—

County Londonderry					
Coleraine	1611	467	166	633	1613
[Dungiven]	1609	18	21	39	—
Limavady	1609/1611	70	46	116	1613
Londonderry	1609	572	480	1,052	1604 Derry 1613 L'derry
[Loughlinsholin]	1609	?	?	?	—
County Monaghan					
Monaghan	1611	32	101	133	1613
County Tyrone					
Augher	—				1613
Clogher	1609				1629
Dungannon	1609/1611				1612
[Mountjoy]	1609/1611				—
[Omagh]	1609/1611				—
Strabane	1611				1613
County of the Town of Carrickfergus					
Carrickfergus	('ancient borough')	494	468	962	medieval charter

Note: The towns in square brackets were proposed but not incorporated.
The towns in italics were not in the area escheated for the official plantation.

Bibliographical Abbreviations

A.A.A.G.	*Annals of the Association of American Geographers*
Amer. Hist. Soc., Proc.	*Proceedings of the American Philosophical Society*
Anal. Hib.	*Analecta Hibernica*
B.L.	British Library
B.L., Add. MSS	British Library, Additional MSS
B.L., Cott. MSS	British Library, Cottonian MSS
Cal. Carew MSS	*Calendar of the Carew Manuscripts preserved in the Archiepiscopal Library at Lambeth* (London 1867-73)
Cal. Pat. Rolls Ire., Eliz.	J. Morrin, ed., *Calendar of the Patent and Close Rolls of Chancery in Ireland, Elizabeth, 19th year to end of reign* (Dublin 1862)
Cal. Pat. Rolls Ire., Jas I	*Calendar of the Irish Patent Rolls of James I* (Dublin c. 1830)
Cal. Pat. Rolls Ire., Chas I	J. Morrin, ed., *Calendar of the Patent and Close Rolls of Chancery in Ireland, Charles I, years 1 to 8* (Dublin 1864)
Cal. S.P. Ire.	*Calendar of the State Papers relating to Ireland* (London 1860-1911)
Clogher Rec.	*Clogher Record*
E.H.R.	*English Historical Review*
H.M.C.	Historical Manuscripts Commission
I.H.R. Bull.	*Bulletin of the Institute of Historical Research*
I.E.S.H.	*Irish Economic and Social History*
I.H.S.	*Irish Historical Studies*
Inq. Cancell. Hib. Repert.	*Inquisitionum in Officio Notulorum Cancellariae Hiberniae ... Repertorium* (2 vols, Dublin 1826-29)
J.C.H.A.S.	*Journal of the Cork Historical and Archaeological Society*
J.R.S.A.I.	*Journal of the Royal Society of Antiquaries of Ireland*

Louth Arch. Soc. Jn.	*Journal of the County Louth Archaeological Society*
N.H.I., III	T. W. Moody, F. X. Martin and F. J. Byrne, ed., *A New History of Ireland*, Vol. III: *Early Modern Ireland, 1534-1691*, Oxford 1976
N.L.I.	National Library of Ireland
O.S. Mem.	Ordnance Survey Memoirs, Royal Irish Academy Library
P.R.O., London	Public Record Office, London
P.R.O.N.I.	Public Record Office of Northern Ireland
R.I.A. Proc.	*Proceedings of the Royal Irish Academy*
Studia Hib.	*Studia Hibernica*
U.J.A.	*Ulster Journal of Archaeology*

References

Introduction (pp. 1-8)

1. *Cal. S.P. Ire., 1608-10,* 520.
2. A. P. Newton, 'The Beginnings of English Colonisation, 1569-1618' in J. H. Rose, A. P. Newton and E. A. Benian, ed., *The Cambridge History of the British Empire,* I (Cambridge 1929), 55-93.
3. Devon Record Office, Courtenay papers, Articles for the plantation of Munster, 1586.
4. D. B. Quinn, 'The Munster Plantation: Problems and Opportunities', *J.C.H.A.S.,* 71 (1966), 19-40.

Chapter 1: Ulster before the Plantation (pp. 9-42)

1. R. Griffith, ed., *General Valuation of Rateable Property in Ireland* (Dublin 1856-64).
2. P.R.O.N.I., T.1652, Sir Josias Bodley's plantation maps, 1609; J. H. Andrews, 'The Maps of the Escheated Counties of Ulster, 1609-10', *R.I.A. Proc.,* 74, c (1974), 133-70.
3. 'A Booke of the Kings Lands founde upon the Last Generall Survey within the Province of Ulster ... 1608', *Anal. Hib.,* 3 (1931), 151.
4. R. C. Simington, ed., *The Civil Survey,* III (Dublin 1937).
5. E. McCracken, *The Irish Woods since Tudor Times* (Newton Abbot 1971); E. McCracken, 'The Woodlands of Ireland, *circa* 1600', *I.H.S.,* 11 (1959), 271-4.
6. *Cal. Carew MSS, 1603-24,* 308.
7. 1608 Survey, *Anal. Hib.* (1931), 151-218.
8. H. Morley, ed., *Ireland under Elizabeth and James I* (London 1896), 376.
9. *Cal. S.P. Ire., 1608-10,* 61
10. Morley, ed., 363.
11. P.R.O.N.I., T.1365/3, Fragment of a poll-money book, 1660.
12. P.R.O.N.I., T.307, Hearth-money roll. Co. Tyrone, 1666.
13. L. P. Murray, 'The History of the Parish of Creggan in the 17th and 18th Centuries', *Louth Arch. Soc. Jn.,* 8 (1934), 117-28.

14. R. Butler, ed., *Tracts relating to Ireland,* II (Dublin 1863), 27-9.
15. P.R.O.N.I., T.1365/3.
16. *Cal. S.P. Ire., 1600-01,* 93.
17. Cited in R. A. Butlin, 'Land and People, c. 1600' in *N.H.I.*, III, 156.
18. G. A. Hayes-McCoy, ed., *Ulster and other Irish Maps, c. 1600* (Dublin 1964).
19. G. Storey, *Impartial History of the War in Ireland* (London 1693), 16.
20. P. S. Robinson, 'Vernacular Housing in Ulster in the Seventeenth Century', *Ulster Folklife,* 25 (1979), 1-28.
21. Cited in G. Camblin, *The Town in Ulster* (Belfast 1951), 3.
22. G. O'Brien, ed., *Advertisements for Ireland* (Dublin 1923) 33.
23. A. T. Lucas, 'Irish Ploughing Practices', *Tools and Tillage,* 2 (1972-75), 52-62, 67-83, 149-60, 195-210.
24. G. Hill, *An Historical Account of the Plantation in Ulster at the Commencement of the Seventeenth Century, 1608-20* (Belfast 1877), 243.
25. G. Hill, ed., *The Montgomery Manuscripts* (Belfast 1869), 321-2.
26. *Cal. S.P. Ire., 1600-01,* 94.
27. Hill (1877), 242.
28. *Cal. S.P. Ire., 1598-99,* 384-5.
29. Hill (1877), 249.
30. J. Smyth, 'Place Names of the Barony of Monaghan', *Clogher Rec.,* 1 (1954), 19.
31. *Cal. S.P. Ire., 1600-01,* 94.
32. Ibid., 442.
33. Cited in Hill (1877), 57.
34. A. Clarke, 'Pacification, Plantation, and the Catholic Question, 1603-23' in *N.H.I.*, III, 193-6.

Chapter 2: A Scheme for Plantation (pp. 43-65)

1. *An Archaeological Survey of County Down,* Archaeological Survey of Northern Ireland (Belfast 1966), 103-8.
2. G. Hill, *An Historical Account of the MacDonnells of Antrim* (Belfast 1873), 21.
3. *Cal. Pat. Rolls Ire., Eliz.,* 628-9.
4. *Cal. S.P. Ire., 1509-73,* 364; R. Dunlop, 'Sixteenth-Century Schemes for the Plantation of Ulster', *Scottish Historical Review,* 22 (1925), 59.
5. *Cal. S.P. Ire., 1509-73,* 135; *Cal. Carew MSS, 1515-74,* 252-5; Dunlop (1925), 52-5; C. Maxwell, *Irish History from Contemporary Sources, 1509-1610* (London 1923), 254-8.
6. D. B. Quinn, ed., *The Voyages and Colonising Enterprises of Sir Humphrey Gilbert,* I (London 1940), 121; G. Morton, *Elizabethan Ireland* (London 1971), 137-40.
7. *Cal. S.P. Ire., 1603-25,* 523; Dunlop (1925), 117.

8. J.B., *A Letter sent by I. B. Gentleman unto his very Grande Mayster R. C. Esquire, wherein is conteined a large discourse of the peopling and inhabiting the Cuntrie called the Ardes, and other adiacent in the North of Ireland, and taken in hand by Sir Thomas Smith, one of the Queens Maisties privie councel, and Thomas Smith Esquire his sonne* (1572), repr. in Hill (1873), 405-15.
9. *Cal. S.P. Ire., 1509-73,* 485; Dunlop (1925), 119-24: T. K. Lowry, ed., *The Hamilton Manuscripts* (Belfast 1867), 25-8; Hill (1873), 405-15.
10. *Cal. Carew MSS, 1515-74,* 439-50; Dunlop (1925), 124-6, 199-212; Hill (1873), 420.
11. S. M'Skimin, *The History and Antiquities of the County of the Town of Carrickfergus* (Belfast 1909), 296.
12. Ibid., 297-300.
13. M. Perceval-Maxwell, *The Scottish Migration to Ulster in the Reign of James I* (London 1973), 48-9.
14. G. Hill, ed., *The Montgomery Manuscripts* (Belfast 1869), 19-29.
15. Ibid., 30-51; Lowry, ed., 1-12, Appendix i-x.
16. Perceval-Maxwell, 371.
17. R. J. Hunter, ed., 'Carew's Survey of Ulster, 1611: The Voluntary Works', *U.J.A.,* 3rd ser., 38 (1973), 81-2; G. Benn, *A History of the Town of Belfast* (London 1877), 85-8, 674-8.
18. A. P. Newton, 'The Beginnings of English Colonisation, 1569-1618' in J. H. Rose, A. P. Newton and E. A. Benian, ed., *The Cambridge History of the British Empire,* I (Cambridge 1929), 55-93.
19. B.L. Cott. MSS, Titus B, XI, 241, 'Instructions . . . touching the Counties of Leix and Offaly'; R. Dunlop, 'The Plantation of Leix and Offaly', *E.H.R.,* 6 (1891)), 61-96; Maxwell, 227-41.
20. Devon Record Office, Courtenay papers, Articles for the plantation of Munster, 1586.
21. Ibid.; *Cal. S.P. Ire., 1592-6,* 58; *Cal. Carew MSS, 1603-24,* 121-2; R. Dunlop, 'The Plantation of Munster, 1584-1589', *E.H.R.,* 3 (1888), 250-69; D. B. Quinn, 'The Munster Plantation: Problems and Opportunities', *J.C.H.A.S.,* 71 (1966), 19-40; Maxwell, 241-54.
22. Quinn (1966), 39.
23. Ibid., 25; Newton, 58.
24. N. P. Canny, 'The Permissive Frontier: The Problem of Social Control in English Settlements in Ireland and Virginia, 1550-1650' in K. R. Andrews, N. P. Canny and P. E. H. Hair, ed., *The Westward Enterprise* (Liverpool 1978), 18; Morton, 35; Newton, 69-70; D. B. Quinn, 'Sir Thomas Smith (1513-77) and the Beginnings of English Colonial Theory', *Amer. Hist. Soc., Proc.,* 89, 4 (1945), 543-60.

25. G. M. Trevelyan, *English Social History* (London 1944), 193-5.
26. J. Spedding, ed., *Life and Letters of Francis Bacon* (London 1857-74), IV, 116-28, VI, 205-7.
27. C. Carlile, 'Discourse', in R. Hakluyt, ed., *The Principall Navigations, Voyages, Traffiques and Discoveries of the English Nation* (London 1903), VII, 133-50; Newton, 69.
28. Hill (1874), 409.
29. G. Hill, *An Historical Account of the Plantation in Ulster ... 1608-20* (Belfast 1877), 60-70; T. W. Moody, ed., 'Ulster Plantation Papers, 1608-13', *Anal. Hib.*, 8 (1938), 281-6.
30. Hill (1877), 70.
31. Ibid., 70-5.
32. Spedding, ed., IV, 125-8.
33. *Cal. Carew MSS, 1603-24,* 13-22; T. W. Moody, ed., 'The Revised Articles of the Ulster Plantation, 1610', *I.H.R. Bull.*, 12 (1934-35), 178-83; W. Harris, ed., *Hibernica: or Some Ancient Pieces relating to Ireland* (Dublin 1770), 105-30.

Chapter 3: Division and Allocation of the Land (pp. 66-90)

1. S. M'Skimin, *The History and Antiquities of the County of the Town of Carrickfergus* (Belfast 1909), 296-303.
2. 'A Booke of the Kings Lands founde upon the Last Generall Survey within the Province of Ulster ... 1608', *Anal. Hib.*, 3 (1931), 151-218.
3. P.R.O.N.I., T.1652.
4. 1608 Survey, *Anal. Hib.* (1931), 151-218.
5. G. Hill, *An Historical Account of the Plantation in Ulster ... 1608-20* (Belfast 1877), 162, 167-71, 180-1.
6. *The Irish Church Directory and Year Book for 1961* (Dublin 1961), 171-83.
7. R. C. Simington, ed., *The Civil Survey,* III (Dublin 1937).
8. *Cal. Carew MSS, 1603-24,* 39.
9. Armagh Diocesan Archives, A.2.a, New Rent Rolls, 1615-28, Leases 10-13.
10. *Cal. Pat. Rolls Ire., Jas I; Cal. Pat. Rolls Ire., Chas I*; P.R.O.N.I., T.1652; Simington, ed.; Map of the escheated counties of Ulster, c. 1610, attributed to John Norden, reproduced in *Anal. Hib.*, 8 (1938) 298: *Inq. Cancell. Hib.Repert.*, II; Hill (1877), 259-348.
11. T. W. Moody, ed., 'Ulster Plantation Papers, 1608-13', *Anal. Hib.*, 8 (1938), 281-96.
12. P.R.O.N.I., D.1854/1, Books of Survey and Distribution, 1611-80.
13. *Cal. Pat. Rolls Ire., Jas I*; *Cal. Pat. Rolls Ire., Chas I*; Simington ed.; Norden map, 1610, *Anal. Hib.* (1938), 298; *Inq. Cancell. Hib. Repert.*, II; Hill (1877), 259-348; Moody, ed. (1938), 180-297.

14. Ibid.
15. Moody, ed. (1938), 221.
16. *Cal. Pat. Rolls Ire., Jas I*; *Cal. Pat. Rolls Ire., Chas I*; Simington, ed.; P.R.O.N.I., T.1652; Moody, ed. (1938), 180-298; *Inq. Cancell. Hib. Repert.*, II; Hill (1877), 137-49, 259-348.
17. Hill (1877), 137-49.
18. Ibid., 79.
19. *Cal. Pat. Rolls Ire., Jas I*; *Cal. Pat. Rolls Ire., Chas I*; Simington, ed.; Norden map, 1610, *Anal. Hib.* (1938), 298; *Inq. Cancell. Hib. Repert.*, II; Hill (1877), 137-49, 259-348; M. Perceval-Maxwell, *The Scottish Migration to Ulster in the Reign of James I* (London 1973), 317-68.
20. Perceval-Maxwell, 106-13.
21. Ibid., 317-68.
22. *Cal. State Papers, Colonial Series, 1574-1660* (London 1860), 5-22; A. H. Johnson, *The History of the Worshipful Company of the Drapers of London,* IV (Oxford 1922), 51-67; G. D. Ramsey, 'Clothworkers, Merchant Adventurers and Richard Hakluyt', *E.H.R.*, 92 (1977), 504-21.
23. T. W. Moody *The Londonderry Plantation, 1608-41* (Belfast 1939), 81-2.
24. Moody, ed. (1938), 261-3; Moody (1939), 107-8.
25. Moody (1939), 143-58; Goldsmiths' Company Records, B.393, Collection of plantation documents, 1609-19, compiled by Henry Carter, clerk of the company in 1615-16.
26. Drapers' Company Records, Ma.Dr., Book + 793, Survey of the Irish plantation, Sir Thomas Phillips, 1622; 'Schedules of the Lands in Ulster allotted to the London Livery Companies, 1613', *Anal. Hib.*, 8 (1938), 299-311; Simington, ed., 142-246; Moody (1939), frontispiece map, 444-7, 451-6.
27. Moody (1939), 122-42.
28. Moody, ed. (1938), 242-5, 286-96; *Cal. Carew MSS, 1603-24,* 134-6; *Cal. Pat. Rolls Ire., Jas I*; R. J. Hunter, 'Towns in the Ulster Plantation', *Studia Hib.*, 11 (1971), 40-79.
29. Norden map, 1610, *Anal. Hib.* (1938), 298.
30. Moody, ed. (1938), 242-5, 286-96; Hill (1877), 105; Moody (1939), 35, 188-9, 198; W. C. Trimble, *The History of Enniskillen,* III (Enniskillen 1921), 793-800.
31. Moody (1939), 198.
32. *Cal. Pat. Rolls Ire., Chas I*, 132-4.
33. Moody, ed. (1938), 286-96; Hill (1877), 128, 216, 228-9.
34. *Cal. Pat. Rolls Ire., Jas I; Cal. Pat. Rolls Ire., Chas I;* P.R.O.N.I., T.1652; Simington, ed.; Schedules of London companies' lands, 1613, *Anal. Hib.* (1938), 299-311; *Inq. Cancell. Hib. Repert.*, II. The

names of the townlands contained in many of the individual grants have been collated and printed in Hill (1877), 259-353.

35. R. Griffith, ed., *General Valuation of Rateable Property in Ireland* (Dublin 1856-64). These land-valuation categories are the same as those employed in the construction of Map 2.

Chapter 4: British Settlement in Ulster, 1610-70 (pp. 91-108)

1. T. W. Moody, ed., 'The Revised Articles of the Ulster Plantation, 1610', *I.H.R. Bull.,* 12 (1934-35), 178-83.
2. *Cal. S.P. Ire., 1615-25,* 224.
3. Moody, ed. (1934-35), 178-83.
4. *Cal. Carew MSS, 1603-24,* 68-9, 75-9, 220-51.
5. H.M.C., *Hastings MSS,* IV, Sir Josias Bodley's Survey, 1613 (London 1947), 159-92.
6. *Cal. S.P. Ire., 1615-25,* 26.
7. R. Steele, ed., *Tudor and Stuart Proclamations, 1485-1714,* II (Oxford 1910), 22.
8. *Cal. Carew MSS, 1603-24,* 392-423.
9. B.L., Add. MSS, 4756, Entry book of the 1622 commissioners; P.R.O.N.I., T.1576, Commissioners' survey of the plantation in the six escheated counties, 1622. The 1622 survey has been transcribed and printed for each county: Armagh: V. W. Treadwell, ed., *U.J.A.,* 3rd ser., 23 (1960), 126-37; Donegal: V. W. Treadwell, ed., *Donegal Annual,* 2 (1951-54), 511-17, 3 (1954-57), 41-7; Fermanagh: P. Ó Gallachair, ed., *Breifne,* 1 (1958-61), 60-75; Cavan: P. Ó Gallachair, ed., *Clogher Rec.,* 2 (1957-59), 293-310; Tyrone: V. W. Treadwell, ed., *U.J.A.,* 3rd ser., 27 (1964), 140-54; Londonderry: *Cal S.P. Ire., 1615-25,* 364-78.
10. *Cal. S.P. Ire., 1615-25,* 220-8.
11. P.R.O.N.I., D.1759/3c/1-2, Muster rolls for Counties Down, Antrim and Londonderry, 1630-31; T.808/15164, Muster roll for Co. Tyrone, 1631; T.934, Muster rolls for Counties Armagh, Fermanagh, Tyrone and Cavan, 1631; R. J. Hunter, ed., 'The Settler Population of an Ulster Plantation County', *Donegal Annual,* 10 (1971-73), 124-54.
12. P.R.O.N.I., T.283, D/2, Hearth-money roll, Co. Tyrone, 1664; T.307, Hearth-money roll, Co. Tyrone, 1666, Co. Antrim, 1669, Co. Londonderry, 1663, Subsidy roll, Co. Down, 1663; T.307.c, Hearth-money roll, Co. Donegal, 1665; T.604, Hearth-money roll, Co. Armagh, 1664; T.808/15068, Hearth-money roll, Co. Fermanagh, 1665-66.
13. P.R.O.N.I., T.1365/3, Fragment of a poll-money book, 1660; Earl of Belmore, ed., 'A Return of the Parish of Termont McGoork for the Second Pole Money' in *The History of Two Ulster*

Manors (Dublin 1903), 305-9.
14. S. Pender, ed., *A Census of Ireland, circa 1659* (Dublin 1939).
15. P. S. Robinson, 'British Settlement in County Tyrone, 1610-66', *I.E.S.H.*, 5 (1978), 16-25.
16. *Cal. Carew MSS, 1603-24*, 423.
17. P. S. Robinson, 'The Plantation of County Tyrone in the Seventeenth Century' (unpublished Ph.D. thesis, Geography Dept, Queen's University, Belfast, 1974), 338-9.
18. *Cal. S.P. Ire., 1615-25*, 322-3.
19. *Cal. S.P. Ire., 1625-32*, 351.
20. *Inq. Cancell. Hib. Repert.*, II.
21. N.L.I., MSS 8013/folders 1-11, 8014/folders 1-10, Rich papers, Undertakers' certificates, 1622; Northamptonshire Record Office, Kimbolton MSS, 70/35, Undertakers' certificates, 1622.
22. *Cal. Carew MSS, 1603-24*, 422.
23. Ibid.
24. W. Knowler, ed., *The Earl of Strafford's Letters and Dispatches*, II (Dublin 1740), 184-5.
25 M. Perceval-Maxwell, *The Scottish Migration to Ulster in the Reign of James I* (London 1973), 314.
26. Ibid., 313.
27. Sir W. Brereton, *Travels in ... Ireland ... 1634-5*, ed. E. Hawkins (Manchester 1844), 119-20.
28. J. C. Hotten, ed., *The Original Lists of Persons of Quality, Emigrants ... who went from Great Britain to the American Plantations, 1600-1700* (New York 1931).
29. Perceval-Maxwell, 29-33.
30. Library of the Representative Church Body, Dublin, Transcripts of the Parliamentary Religious Returns for 1766.
31. L. M. Cullen, 'Population Trends in Seventeenth-Century Ireland', *Economic and Social Review*, 6 (1975), 152-7; V. Morgan, 'A Case Study of Population Change over Two Centuries: Blaris, Lisburn, 1661-1848', *I.E.S.H.*, 3 (1976), 5-16; W. H. Crawford, 'Landlord/Tenant Relations in Ulster, 1609-1820', *I.E.S.H.*, 2 (1975), 5-21; W. Macafee and V. Morgan, 'Population in Ulster, 1660-1760' in P. Roebuck, ed., *Plantation to Partition* (Belfast 1981), 46-63.

Chapter 5: The Processes of Colonisation and the Development of English and Scottish Localities (pp. 109-128)

1. J. Braidwood, 'Ulster and Elizabethan English' in G. B. Adams, ed., *Ulster Dialects* (Cultra 1964), 5-109; R. J. Gregg, 'The Scotch-Irish Dialect Boundaries in Ulster' in M. F. Wakelin, ed., *Patterns in the Folk Speech of the British Isles* (London 1972), 109-39.

2. Braidwood, 5-109; R. A. Gailey, 'The Scots Element in North Irish Popular Culture', *Ethnologia Europaea,* 8 (1975), 2-21.
3. *List of Electors for the 1971 Register* (Counties Antrim, Armagh, Down, Fermanagh, Londonderry and Tyrone), H.M.S.O. (Belfast 1971); *Register of Dáil Electors, 1963-4* (Counties Cavan, Donegal and Monaghan), Stationery Office (Dublin 1964); *Census of Ireland, 1911*, H.M.S.O. (London 1912); Gregg, 109-39.
4. Gregg, 109-39.
5. G. B. Adams, ed., *Ulster Dialects* (Cultra 1964), 1-4.
6. N.L.I., MSS 8014/8, Undertakers' certificates, 1622.
7. R. C. Simington, ed., *The Civil Survey,* III (Dublin 1937), 23.
8. P.R.O.N.I., T.615/3, Report of the Surveyor-General of Customs in Ireland, 1637.
9. Ibid.
10. D. J. Owen, *A Short History of the Port of Belfast* (Belfast 1917), 11.
11. A. Hume, 'Origin and Characteristics of the Population in the Counties of Down and Antrim', *U.J.A.,* 1st ser., 1 (1853), 252-4; Braidwood, 14, 21.
12. T. Hägerstrand, 'A Monte-Carlo Approach to Diffusion', *Achives Européenes de Sociologie,* 6 (1965), 43-67; G. Olsson, 'Complementary Models: A Study of Colonization Maps', *Geografiska Annaler,* 50 (1968), 115-32; R. L. Morrill, 'The Development of Spatial Distributions of Towns in Sweden: An Historical-Predictive Approach', *A.A.A.G.,* 53 (1963), 1-14; E. Bylund, 'Theoretical Considerations regarding the Distribution of Settlement in Inner North Sweden', *Geografiska Annaler,* 42 (1960), 225-31.
13. Hume, 252.
14. Braidwood, 31.
15. *Cal. Carew MSS, 1603-24,* 77.
16. Ibid., 411.
17. P. Ó Gallachair, ed., in *Breifne,* 1 (1958-61), 61.
18. N.L.I., MSS 8013-4.
19. J. C. Hotten, ed., *The Original Lists of Persons of Quality, Emigrants ... who went from Great Britain to the American Plantations, 1600-1700* (New York 1931).
20. Chester Record Office (Cheshire), Parish registers: Holy Trinity, 1599-1630; St Bridget's, 1600-30; St Mary's, 1601-30; St Michael's, 1590-1624; St John's, 1599-1629; St Martin's, 1612-30; Bebington, 1590-1605.
21. Staffordshire Record Office and William Salt Library, Parish registers: Bettey, 1590-1623; Audley, 1590-1630; Keele, 1590-1627; Wolstanton, 1624-30; Newcastle-under-Lyme, 1593-95.
22. Hampshire Record Office, Parish registers: St Michael's, 1590-

1630; Portchester, 1607-25; Farlington, 1590-1630; St Andrew's, 1590-1601.
23. Devon Record Office, Parish registers: Tor Mohunn, 1612-25; St Mary Church, 1614-28; Paignton, 1599-1630; Marlden, 1620-30; Cockington, 1612-30; Felton, 1599-1612; Barnstaple, 1596-1600.
24. London Record Office, Parish registers: St Clement's, 1590-1600; St Olave's, 1597-1608.
25. *Cal. Pat. Rolls Ire., Jas I,* 306-7.
26. P. S. Robinson, 'The Plantation of County Tyrone in the Seventeenth Century' (unpublished Ph.D. thesis, Geography Dept, Queen's University, Belfast, 1974), 217-26.
27. P.R.O.N.I., MIC 387/1, Plantation papers relating to the Munster and Derry areas, 1611-31.
28. *Cal S.P. Ire., 1611-14,* 539-40.
29. Robinson (1974), 231-45.
30. *Cal. Carew MSS, 1603-24,* 223.
31. Braidwood, 11.
32. H.M.C., *Hastings MSS,* IV, Sir Josias Bodley's Survey, 1613 (London 1947), 164, 171.
33. Ó Gallachair, ed. (1958-61) 74.

Chapter 6: The Plantation Building Programme (pp. 129-149)
1. *Cal. Carew MSS, 1603-24,* 422.
2. P.R.O.N.I., T.1576, Survey of the escheated counties, 1622, 118.
3. T. W. Moody, ed., 'The Revised Articles of the Ulster Plantation, 1610', *I.H.R. Bull.,* 12 (1934-35), 181.
4. P. Ó Gallachair, ed., in *Breifne,* 1 (1958-61), 60, 64, 71, 74.
5. Ibid., 67; P. Ó Gallachair, ed., in *Clogher Rec.,* 2 (1957-59), 197.
6. H.M.C., *Hastings MSS,* IV, Sir Josias Bodley's Survey, 1613 (London 1947), 174.
7. E. M. Jope, 'Scottish Influence in the North of Ireland: Castles with Scottish Features, 1580-1640', *U.J.A.,* 3rd ser., 14 (1951), 31-47.
8. V. W. Treadwell, ed., in *U.J.A.,* 3rd ser., 27 (1964), 150.
9. Drapers' Company Records, Ma.Dr., b.1858, Accounts, rentals, bills of exchange, agreements with workmen for building and repairs, and plans of castles and houses, 1609-29.
10. Ibid.; Drapers' Company Records, Ma.Dr., B.271, Disbursement by William Rowley for the company's work, 1615; B.40, Copies of letters etc. concerning the plantation in Ireland, 1616; B.261, Particulars of workmen's wages etc., 1616; B.176, Letter of Edmund Pyke to Sir Thomas Roper, 1619; Book +383, Irish Letter Book; Book +782, Cash Book, Ireland, 1615-16.
11. P. S. Robinson, 'Vernacular Housing in Ulster in the Seventeenth

Century', *Ulster Folklife,* 25 (1979), 1-28.
12. *Cal. Carew MSS, 1603-24,* 422-3.
13. Robinson (1979), 17-20.
14. O.S. Mem., Co. Antrim, Box 2, 1 (Antrim parish, 1838).
15. Cited in G. Hill, *An Historical Account of the Plantation in Ulster ... 1608-20* (Belfast 1877), 375.
16. O.S. Mem., Co. Londonderry, Box 30, V (Ballyscullion parish, 1836).
17. Drapers' Company Records, Ma.Dr., Book +793, Survey of the Irish plantation, Sir Thomas Phillips, 1622; P.R.O.N.I., MIC 11, Carew MSS, 634, Sir Thomas Phillips's maps of Londonderry, surveyed by Thomas Raven, 1622.
18. Cited in T. W. Moody, *The Londonderry Plantation, 1608-41* (Belfast 1939), 308.
19. Drapers' Company Records, Ma.Dr., b. 1858.
20. Ibid.
21. Ibid.
22. Ibid.
23. G. Boate, 'Ireland's Natural History' in *A Collection of Tracts and Treatises* (Dublin 1861), 122.
24. G. A. Hayes-McCoy, ed., *Ulster and other Irish Maps, c. 1600* (Dublin 1964).
25. Goldsmiths' Company Records, B.393, Collection of plantation documents, 1609-19, compiled by Henry Carter, clerk of the company in 1615-16.
26. P.R.O.N.I., T.970/1, Brownlow Lease Books, 1667.
27. Drapers' Company Records. Ma.Dr., b. 1858.
28. R. A. Gailey, 'A House from Gloverstown, Lismacloskey, County Antrim', *Ulster Folklife,* 20 (1974), 35; B. Lacy, 'Two Seventeenth-Century Houses at Linenhall Street, Londonderry', *Ulster Folklife,* 27 (1981), 57-62.
29. Treadwell, ed. (1964), 149.
30. V. W. Treadwell, ed., in *U.J.A.,* 3rd ser., 23 (1960), 134.
31. Ó Gallachair, ed. (1957-59), 294.
32. W. A. M'Cutcheon, *The Industrial Archaeology of Northern Ireland* (Belfast 1980), 235-6.
33. Drapers' Company Records, Ma.Dr., b.1858, B.261, B271.
34. *Hastings MSS,* IV, 162.
35. Ibid., 174.
36. Treadwell, ed. (1964), 150.
37. Ibid., 141.
38. Ibid., 150.
39. *Cal. S.P. Ire., 1615-25,* 364-8.

Chapter 7: Towns, Villages and Dispersed Rural Settlement (pp. 150-171)

1. D. B. Quinn, ed., *The Voyages and Colonising Enterprises of Sir Humphrey Gilbert,* I (London 1940), 121.
2. J. T. Gilbert, ed., *A Contemporary History of Affairs in Ireland from 1641 to 1652,* I (Dublin 1879), 317-26.
3. C. Maxwell, ed., *Irish History from Contemporary Sources, 1509-1610* (London 1923), 272.
4. Ibid., 273.
5. T. W. Moody, ed., 'Ulster Plantation Papers, 1608-13', *Anal. Hib.,* 8 (1938), 285-6.
6. T. W. Moody, ed., 'The Revised Articles of the Ulster Plantation, 1610', *I.H.R. Bull.,* 12 (1934-35), 181.
7. Moody, ed. (1938), 281.
8. Ibid., 286-96; R. J. Hunter, 'Towns in the Ulster Plantation', *Studia Hib.,* 11 (1971), 40-79.
9. Moody, ed. (1938), 288.
10 *Cal. Carew MSS, 1603-24,* 56-7.
11. Ibid., 134-6.
12. *Cal. Pat. Rolls Ire., Jas I,* 256.
13. *Cal. Carew MSS, 1603-24,* 56.
14. Hunter (1971), 40-79.
15. P. Ó Gallachair, ed., in *Breifne,* 1 (1958-61), 75.
16. V. W. Treadwell, ed., in *U.J.A.,* 3rd ser., 27 (1964), 141.
17. *Cal. Pat. Rolls Ire., Jas I,* 217.
18. *Cal. Pat. Rolls Ire., Jas I; Cal. Pat. Rolls Ire., Chas I: Report on the Fairs and Markets of Ireland* [1674], H.C. 1852-53, XLI, 79; S. Pender, ed., *A Census of Ireland, circa 1659* (Dublin 1939).
19. Pender, ed.
20. Hunter (1971), 73.
21. *Cal. Pat. Rolls Ire., Jas I,* 256.
22. Goldsmiths' Company Records, B.393, Collection of plantation documents, 1609-19, compiled by Henry Carter, clerk of the company in 1615-16.
23. *Cal. Carew MSS, 1603-24,* 410-11.
24. P.R.O.N.I., T.640/5, Clothworkers' Company Records; T.520/1, Haberdashers' Company Records; *Report on the Fairs and Markets of Ireland* [1674], H.C. 1852-53, XLI.
25. *Cal. Pat. Rolls Ire., Chas I,* 533.
26. Ibid.; *Report on the Fairs and Markets of Ireland* [1674]. H.C. 1852-53, XLI.
27. Mercers' Company Records, Acts of Court, 1619-25, 168.
28. P.R.O.N.I., T.1731, Patent for Cookstown market, 1628; *Report on the Fairs and Markets of Ireland* [1674], H.C. 1852-53, XLI.

29. *Cal. Pat. Rolls Ire., Jas I,* 262.
30. *Cal. Pat. Rolls Ire., Chas I,* 605.
31. *Cal. Pat. Rolls Ire., Jas I,* 217.
32. E. M. Jope, 'Models in Medieval Studies' in D. Clarke, ed., *Models in Archaeology* (London 1972), 963-90.
33. D.B. Quinn and K. W. Nicholls, 'Ireland in 1534' in *N.H.I.*, III, 18.
34. G. B. Adams, 'The Diamonds of Ulster and Pennsylvania' in *Ulster Folk and Transport Museum, Year Book 1975/76* (Cultra 1977), 18-20.
35. P.R.O.N.I., D.683/27, Report of Smith and Springham, 1613.
36. P.R.O.N.I., T.307, Hearth-money roll, Co. Tyrone, 1666.

Chapter 8: Economic and Social Change (pp. 172-194)

1. H.M.C., *Hastings MSS,* IV, Sir Josias Bodley's Survey, 1613 (London 1947), 179.
2. *Cal. Carew MSS, 1603-24,* 392, 398.
3. P. Ó Gallachair, ed., in *Breifne,* 1 (1958-61), 64; P.R.O.N.I., T.1668/36, Early seventeenth-century map of Omagh; R. J. Hunter, 'Towns in the Ulster Plantation', *Studia Hib.,* 11 (1971), 65, 75.
4. *Cal. Carew MSS, 1603-24,* 221.
5. Ibid., 395.
6. Drapers' Company Records, Ma.Dr., B.261.
7. G. B. Thompson, 'The Distribution and Form of Primitive Types of Farm Transport in Northern Ireland' (unpublished M.Sc. thesis, Geography Dept, Queen's University, Belfast, 1951).
8. *Inq. Cancell. Hib. Repert.,* II, 105; *Cal. Carew MSS, 1603-24,* 220.
9. *Cal. Carew MSS, 1603-24,* 225, 227.
10. *Hastings MSS,* IV, 161, 163, 165.
11. *Cal. Carew MSS, 1603-24,* 220-1.
12. *Hastings MSS,* IV, 162-3; *Cal. Carew MSS, 1603-24,* 76, 227.
13. T. W. Moody, ed., 'The Revised Articles of the Ulster Plantation, 1610', *I.H.R. Bull.,* 12 (1934-35), 178-83.
14. M. Perceval-Maxwell, *The Scottish Migration to Ulster in the Reign of James I* (London 1973), 290-308.
15. P.R.O.N.I., T.615/3.
16. Perceval-Maxwell, 303-8.
17. P.R.O.N.I., T.615/3.
18. *Cal. S.P. Ire., 1615-25,* 136-7.
19. S. M'Skimin, *The History and Antiquities of the County of the Town of Carrickfergus* (Belfast 1909), 159-60.
20. Cited in G. Benn, *A History of the Town of Belfast* (London 1877), 321-2.

21. P.R.O.N.I., T.615/3.
22. Ibid.; Drapers' Company Records, Ma.Dr., B.40, Copies of letters etc. concerning the plantation in Ireland, 1616; Book +782, Cash Book, Ireland, 1615-16; P.R.O.N.I., MIC 199, Customs due in Londonderry, 1614-15; Leeds City Library, TN/PO7/I/1-4, Sir Arthur Ingram's papers, Customs records of Ulster ports, 1612-15, cited in Perceval-Maxwell, 290-308; P.R.O., London, E190/1332, Port Books, Chester etc., 1614-18; E190/1133-6, Port Books, Bristol etc., 1601-49.
23. *Cal. Carew MSS, 1603-24*, 423.
24. G. Hill, ed., *The Montgomery Manuscripts* (Belfast 1869), 62-4.
25. Scottish Record Office, GD.154/514, Agnew estate survey, c. 1645. The author is indebted to Dr R. Gillespie for this information.
26. P.R.O.N.I., T.970/1, Brownlow Lease Books, 1667; P. S. Robinson, 'The Spread of Hedged Enclosure in Ulster', *Ulster Folklife,* 23 (1977), 57-69.
27. Armagh Diocesan Archives, A.2.a., 79, New Rent Rolls, 1615.
28. Cited in Baron Heath, *Some Account of the Grocers' Company* (London 1869), 568.
29. P.R.O.N.I., T.307, Hearth-money roll, Co. Tyrone, 1666.
30. N.L.I., MSS 8014/8, Undertakers' certificates, 3622.
31. R. C. Simington, ed., *The Civil Survey,* III (Dublin 1937), 265.
32. E. McCracken, *The Irish Woods since Tudor Times* (Newton Abbot 1971), 57-96.
33. P.R.O.N.I., T.552, Account of timber barrel staves etc. . . . in the ports of Belfast and Coleraine, 1683-95, 59.
34. T. W. Moody, ed., 'Ulster Plantation Papers, 1608-13', *Anal. Hib.,* 8 (1938), 221.
35. *Cal. S.P. Ire., 1608-10*, 549-51; *Cal. Carew MSS, 1603-24,* 231-2.
36. Armagh Diocesan Archives, A.2.a., New Rent Rolls, 1615-28.
37. P.R.O.N.I., D.623/6, Indenture between Hugh Hamilton and the Earl of Abercorn, 1615.
38. P.R.O.N.I., D. 623/7, Rental for the proportion of Eden/Killeny, 1613-15.
39. T. W. Moody *The Londonderry Plantation, 1608-41* (Belfast 1939), 332.
40. *Cal. Carew MSS, 1603-24,* 410.
41. *Cal. S.P. Ire., 1625-32,* 350.
42. P.R.O.N.I., T.1089/60, Seventeenth-century leases of townlands at Blessingbourne, Co. Tyrone.
43. P.R.O.N.I., T.1576, Commissioners' survey of the plantation in the six escheated counties, 1622.
44. P.R.O.N.I., T.1365/3, Fragment of a poll-money book, 1660; Earl

of Belmore, ed., 'A Return of the Parish of Termont McGoork for the Second Pole Money' in *The History of Two Ulster Manors* (Dublin 1903), 305-9.

45. N.L.I., MSS 8014/9.
46. T. W. Moody, 'The Treatment of the Native Population under the Scheme for the Plantation in Ulster', *I.H.S.*, 1 (1938), 59-63.
47. N.L.I., MSS 8014/8.
48. W. T. Latimer, 'The Old Session-Book of Templepatrick Presbyterian Church', *J.R.S.A.I.*, 25 (1895), 130-4.
49. D. Bowen, *The Protestant Crusade in Ireland, 1800-70* (Dublin 1978).
50. Perceval-Maxwell, 301.
51. B.L., Add MSS, 3287, ff. 62-3, Robert Cartwright to Falkland, 28 Jan. 1625.
52. Drapers' Company Records, Ma.Dr., b.1858, B.271, B.261.
53. B.L., Add. MSS, 4780, Accounts of expenditure by the agent for the Ironmongers' Company in Ireland.
54. P. J. Corish, 'The Rising of 1641 and the Catholic Confederacy, 1641-5' in *N.H.I.*, III, 291.
55. A. Clarke, 'The Genesis of the Ulster Rising of 1641' in P. Roebuck, ed., *Plantation to Partition* (Belfast 1981), 29-45.
56. W. E. H. Lecky, *History of Ireland in the Eighteenth Century*, I (London 1892), 46-89.
57. R. C. Simington, *The Transplantation to Connacht, 1654-58* (Dublin 1970).

Index

9 781903 688007

CPSIA information can be obtained
at www.ICGtesting.com
Printed in the USA
LVHW021810080622
720759LV00003B/242

9 781903 688007